DOUBLE TAKE

by

Vicky Harper

Advised by Martin Kay

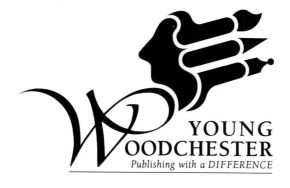

YOUNG
WOODCHESTER
Publishing with a DIFFERENCE

Published by
Young Woodchester
PO Box 26
Stroud
Gloucestershire
GL5 5YF

ISBN 0 9524796 4 8 Hardback
ISBN 0 9524796 5 6 Softback

Cover design and typesetting by
Create Publishing Services, Bath

Printed in Great Britain by
The Bath Press, Somerset

Contents

Acknowledgements

Our Families for their love and support

Cotswold Physiotherapy Centre for all their kindness to us both

The Fire Brigade for their work which often goes unpraised

My Dad and Pat for the Memorial Service Flowers (arranged by Bloomers)

Chris and Rose Harper for the Order of Service card and the Christmas cards

The printers for printing the Christmas card each year

The Forensic Scientists who worked so hard for us to try to find the answers

All those who took the time to attend the Memorial Service

Sir Charles Irving (deceased)

Carlos, Sally, Andy, Peter and all our friends in Spain for their love and kindness

Canon John Harwood and Richard Inglesby

Christ Church Choir

Ken Stephens and the staff of Selim Smith (Undertakers)

All the twins' friends who have remembered them over the last 5 years

My Solicitor and Barrister

GLOSCAT for their Memorial Trophy in memory of Beckie

Broadlands Nursery for their tribute to Emma

Ken and Trish Helps for listening and understanding

Colin Harding (Head—Christ Church School) for his help and the cherry tree

Eric Harper for his paintings—especially Mother Teresa

Chief Inspector Bill Gaskins for his honesty

DS Barbara Harrison

WDC Sarah Morris

All the other Police involved in the case

Hillary Alison, Police Press Officer for her help

Mr John Coopey, Coroner's Officer for his patience

Bourneside School for their tribute to the twins

My Mother for her poetry

The photographers whose pictures appear in this book

Dr Giraldi and Linda Jones from Sixways Surgery for the Harper Clinic

Central News for their sensitive reporting

BBC Radio Gloucestershire for their interest and for finding me a publisher

Anita Syvret and the Gloucestershire Echo for their continued compassionate reporting

Baroness Margaret Thatcher

To all our friends for their help and kindness

All those who came to the trial to offer their support

Peter Nelson at Bristol Crown Court (Witness Support)

Marilyn and Peter Quigley for everything

Pat, my Victim Support volunteer, for the ear bashings she tolerates

Felicity, Victim Support, for taking care of my Mum

Ladies at Tewkesbury Court for looking after us so well

Martin Kay, Publisher, without his courage and help this book would still be a dream

Alison Flowers, Editor, for being piggy in the middle

Gill Croft-Griggs, for marketing me and the book—not an easy task

Huw Harries

Wendy and Dave, for looking after our hair and our home

And to Steve, thanks, to whom life is still possible

Credits

Cover and frontispiece photograph of Emma and Beckie by Jeremy Benyon

Jacket photograph of Vicky and Steve Harper by kind permission of the *Mail on Sunday*

Thank you to the *Gloucestershire Echo* for permission to quote them extensively

Thank you to the *Western Daily Press* for permission to quote them

Thank you to Baroness Thatcher for permission to reproduce her personal letters to Vicky

Thank you to the Gloucestershire Police Force and Fire Service for their contributions

This Book is dedicated to Raymond, Anna, Sarah, David, Anthea, Jamie and Julie, to their parents and families—the walking wounded.

And, of course, to my own Emma and Beckie.
May they all find peace.

VH

Prologue

On Wednesday, 23rd January 1991, Emma and Beckie Harper left their home in Cheltenham, Gloucestershire, to go to a party. Later that evening, something evil and still unknown happened to them. By the early hours of the following morning, some human remains had been discovered in a burnt-out barn at nearby Uckington. More pieces were recovered from the adjacent area where fire-fighters had cleared the site.

Today, more than five years after their deaths, the circumstances of that terrible night have not yet been adequately explained. No-one has been held legally responsible for the deaths despite admissions from Emma and Beckie's companions at the time, that they had caused the fire. And there is no apparent prospect of official action to keep the investigation alive.

For the parents of Emma and Beckie, time and reason stopped on the morning of 24th January. That's what happens when something kills your children.

Vicky:

Being a mother is the most responsible job in the world. I can think of nothing else to compare with it. For the first years of your children's lives, you are completely responsible for them. They are completely dependent on you for existence.

I was responsible for Emma and Beckie. I worried about them, about whether a sneeze meant 'flu and about whether a new bicycle would mean scraped knees or worse. Every time they left the home without me, I worried about car accidents, rape and even death. You do it because they are yours. Because you are responsible for them.

Fortunately for most parents, worries become nightmares that pass. It never happened, they're alright. For us, the nightmare became reality. We are living what could never happen to you. Everyone reads in the newspapers about the deaths of children. It happens to other people. But we are living what could never happen to you.

Let me tell you about reality.

A policeman is the man in blue, sometimes ridiculed, sometimes helpful, but someone you never really get involved with.

A Court is where people go if they misbehave. Once there, they are told off, dealt with. And that's the end of it. A magistrate brings common sense and experience to the Court. A judge is highly trained and deals with bad situations. The truth comes out. The proper things are said and done.

When you die, someone buries you a few days later. People sing at your funeral. You are usually old. It's a fitting end to a full life.

That's what I thought was reality. Simple. Uncomplicated. I believed, like you, that life worked like that.

May you never have a 24th of January in your lives.

CHAPTER ONE

Emma Louise Harper

Vicky:

At 5.30 pm on 3rd April 1973, Emma Louise made her way into the world, bringing with her hope and joy for the years ahead. In time, she acquired family names—silly names like Em Pem, Magic Mushroom, Will o' the Wisp, Nesbitt, which translated meant "we love you". But at that moment on 3rd April 1973, she was Emma Louise, making a reluctant appearance and encouraged with the use of forceps.

You must remember these things. They become more important than you can imagine.

I want to remember more about the birth but I was high from the pethadine and all I can recall are the congratulations of those standing around me. I hear a cry, a lusty, healthy cry. I am pleased. I have done well.

Emma weighed 5lbs 1oz and measured 16 inches. She was delivered by Drs Chattergy, Bashford and Frazer ably assisted by Staff Nurse Vipond. These are the names which remain with me. There were more there, I know, but their faces were just a sea of shapes and colours. So many people touched my children's brief lives, some still remembered, many long forgotten. How I'd love to hear their memories.

During that first night, after the births, I felt quite poorly but it was not until the next day that things began to go wrong. A paediatrician, Dr Candy, came to see me and told me that the twins were very ill. He said that I would have to give them some of my blood and that they were going to be taken by ambulance to Bristol Children's Hospital where there was a specialist who might be able to save them.

He asked me if I had thought of names yet as the twins would have to be christened before going to Bristol.

They put me on a trolley and wheeled me to look at Emma through the glass of the incubator. A tiny thing, wrapped in white clothes and a bonnet ready for her perilous journey. She looks like an Emma Louise. Her life has begun.

Hold them, never miss a chance of holding them. I hadn't held either

1

Vicky with Emma (*left*) and Beckie, aged 6 months.
(*By kind permission of James Kirkwood*)

of them before they left for Bristol—the telegrams and cards of congratulations had been withheld, too. Everyone looked very worried. The Ward Sister brought me daily reports on their progress and told me that Emma had a 50% chance of survival: she was blocked with meconium from having been inside me for too long and was considered very poorly. Sister said that the twins were pretty with lots of dark hair but it was two weeks before I could see for myself. Try to count the good days and to store the precious ones away to pore over time and again. Too often, we count the nothing days.

I had not fed the twins or had anything to do with them since their birth and the doctors were concerned that I try to bond with them at the first opportunity. Would I travel to Bristol the night before they were due to come home and stay with them at the Hospital? I had not really been told what was wrong with them and was uncertain what to expect. Never let anyone tell you an incomplete story. You must know everything. Everything.

We arrived at the Hospital in time for the 4.30 pm feed and were shown into a room where I could rest between feeding times. As they took us down corridors, I glanced into some of the rooms the way that you do when you are near sickness. What would I find? There were all sorts of shapes and sizes in the cots. Deformed babies. Hideous babies. Pathetic tiny, yellow babies. Sad little things covered in so many tubes and bandages that it was hard to believe they were human. And then, at last, they give me my own bundle. Will I please undress Emma and then bathe her before feeding?

She looks awful. Her head has been partly shaven and it looks misshapen. I undress her and put her in the bath but she slips out of my hands and I burst into tears thinking that I have killed this tiny, delicate thing. We cry together, at each other, me not knowing how and her not wanting my inexperience. She refused the bottle I gave her and so the long night continued, inauspiciously. Deprived of my moment of glory by their illness at birth, I had become tired, scared and deeply upset when the time arrived to see the Consultant.

I suppose that, in those days, parents were not credited with as much common sense and intelligence as they are nowadays. I was 18 years old with just my mother to accompany me. I must have looked very inexperienced to Professor Butler whom we met inside a very dark, box-like room. Did he have to be so brief and matter of fact? Or is my recollection at fault? He told us that the twins had Cystic Fibrosis, a diagnosis which could not be confirmed before the age of 3 years. Their life expectancy was very short and the interval before their deaths would be fraught with illness and trauma.

He suggested that we realise from the start that the twins would not be with us for very long. We should continue, even increase, our hobbies so that we would have things to fall back on when they died. Observations like this will cross your mind time and time again.

And that was how I was given back my girls the first time.

Emma cried all the way and seemed never to stop. She was much more fretful than her sister and would frequently wake Beckie up with her wailing before falling asleep herself. Although she continued to gain weight she underwent regular checks at the local Children's Hospital to monitor her condition. To me, the slightest sign of illness meant imminent death—and Emma seemed closer to it in those early years, despite her better start at birth.

Much happened in my own life during the first few months after the twins' birth. Broken relationships, a broken marriage. It led to my nervous breakdown and to their being fostered with a friend for a while. What happened to me is only important for its disruption to my bonding with Emma and Beckie. In fact it proved to be a turning point. I met Steve and began to live again in earnest. The twins were so young that they grew to accept him as their father although we never concealed their parentage from them.

Emma was Daddy's girl. She was a very trusting little thing who loved to be whirled and twirled in the air by any male friend who happened to look her way. With her wispy blond hair and long eyelashes, which she learnt to flutter at a very early age, she was irresistible!

It is only when you have twins that you become aware of oddities that other parents tend not to meet. In school plays, for example, neither of them will be considered for the main part because "it wouldn't be fair" to the other one. This and similar frustrations were to continue until finally, in their teens, one particular Choirmaster risked all and gave Beckie a solo. For Emma, however, it was always drama and very good at it she was too, even though she invariably played the part of the Cat rather than the beautiful Princess. Unsurprisingly, I suppose, she would get very upset by failure to win the school fancy dress contests. On one occasion, they had gone together as 'Mary and her little lamb', with Emma as the lamb. It had taken me hours to stick little cotton wool balls all over her white leotard and leggings which Emma thoroughly enjoyed pulling off when it became clear that the Queen of Hearts had actually stolen the judge's heart that day.

For most of the time, however, Emma was a very good-natured little girl, always with a smile and ready to lend a hand. Her personality was quite placid, too, apart from one short uncharacteristic episode at the age of 6 years when she took to biting the ear of her 'boyfriend'. This revolting habit stopped after a dose of the same treatment from me and the boyfriend was none the worse for the experience. His mother reminded me of it quite recently—

—get people to understand that your children are still with you, to be talked about and to be recalled.

It was at this time that we noticed that Emma had a tiny triangle missing from her ear. 'Pixilated' we called it. Some friends were with us at the time and teased her for being a changeling—armed with which information she alarmed the school the next day by announcing that she was a-changing. On another occasion, however, she heard and recalled some playground remarks rather more clearly and shocked both my mother-in-law and our vicar, John Harwood, by telling them sweetly and innocently to 'fuck off'. It happens to all young children, I know, but you will learn to hold on to that which you would otherwise have long since put out of your mind.

The girls had by now moved from nursery school to Christ Church Primary School. I had taken the Consultant at his word and was working hard—and we had just bought our first home, a garden flat in Lansdown, a lovely flat with a large garden shared with the family from upstairs. It was a happy house in which the children of the two families often played together. We acquired three cats, one for each of us girls. Emma's was a chinchilla called Henrietta, a pretty docile kitten which, when we tried to have it spayed, turned out to be a tom. Re-christened Manuel and swiftly neutered all the same, the kitten seemed to develop something of an identity crisis but he and Emma became great friends.

She loved all animals and was fascinated by nature and by creepy-crawlies. Her desire to help all God's creatures resulted in a strange assortment of casualties being brought into her bedroom until Beckie, who shared the bedroom, and I had to put a collective, metaphorical foot down. The flow of insects reduced but Emma's love of nature remained.

We struggled, too, over toilet training which was something of a disaster. Perhaps trying to potty-train two toddlers at the same time is not a good idea because Emma and Beckie always ended up trying to push each other off the pots with predictable results. Self-discipline at school was no better either. I seemed unable to get through to them, especially to Emma, that in order to go to the toilet one only had to ask. Perhaps somewhere along the line, her request had been refused? Too often it seemed, I would be greeted in the playground with a cheery "Mum, I wet my pants!" And out would come Emma or Beckie—or both—proudly holding a plastic bag containing the offending knickers, the other hand clutching frantically at the outsized pants kept spare for such emergencies. I even donated a few pairs to ensure that the school did not run out and waited for things to improve, which eventually they did.

When they started at Christ Church Primary School, Emma and Beckie were put in the same class. But it didn't work. Emma appeared to think that, provided Beckie was paying attention, she had no need to. Instead, she would contentedly sit there watching the butterflies, one of her favourite pastimes, dreamily thinking goodness knows what—but certainly not paying attention.

In the end, they were separated which was a wise decision, both allowing and obliging Emma to come into her own. Looking back through her school reports, I am reminded that some things never changed over the years. In 1982, her teacher wrote that Emma, then aged 9 years, constantly disregarded the need for capital letters and full stops—when earlier as a small child learning to spell, she had persisted in writing Louise without the 'i' and as 'louse'. Even now I come across things she has signed in this way. But if spelling was difficult for Emma, her talent for art and crafts did show through strongly from an early age. Her drawings and sketches were lovely. Indeed, she was never happier than when she had some paper and crayons or perhaps some sewing to do.

Both girls went through the usual phases, Emma opting for ballet, brownies and gymnastics but initially with mixed success. I remember once going to a display at the Gymnastics Club where I was appalled that, despite endless rehearsals, she could still not remember what she was supposed to do. With remarkable aplomb and captivating all who noticed, she just twirled the ribbon on the end of her stick, smiled and left the stage! But it didn't matter, the audience loved her for it. In later years, both the dancing lessons and the love of gymnastics returned and

Emma did achieve a great many medals and awards in each. As she grew older, she turned to tap dancing, my kitchen floor bearing testimony to her rhythm and beat.

At Primary School, they were encouraged to keep diaries and it was with great anticipation that we looked forward to parents' evenings to see what they had achieved. There were her pictures on the wall and, once, a prize for handwriting—but imagine our dismay at our first such evening when, being shown to Emma's desk and reading her account of the previous six week-ends, we realised that each page said exactly the same: "went to a fête and then to the pub, had a nice time". It made us sound dreadful when the truth was quite different: we had bought a car, a white Mini called Sammy which ran more on strength of character than a sound chassis and four wheels. And in company with two close friends, Eileen and Grant in their Reliant Robin, we would set off in convoy with blankets, toys and picnics in search of fêtes, fairs or anything of interest. We would always finish the day with a cool drink and a packet of crisps at a convenient pub on the way home. They were happy days although we were very poor.

Occasionally, after a day of great excitement, Emma would sleep-walk. We would wake to find her standing over us or would open the sitting room door to find her there. It never seemed to bother her and in the morning it was forgotten. We never mentioned it to her until much later but I don't think she believed us even then.

Emma's best friend at this time was Lisa whose parents ran a hotel just around the corner from our flat. Emma thought it great fun to spend the day in the hotel although I doubt that the kitchen staff felt the same. I knew that she would always be in their way, looking out for a leftover roll or a scoop of ice cream, and people must have wondered if we ever fed her at home. Once she stayed the night at the hotel and Lisa's mother allowed the pair of them to have room service, an unimaginable treat for young children.

Living in a hotel must have been a godsend when it came to birthday parties—I dreaded them but they usually passed successfully with the help of my own Mum who sang and played the piano for the little ones. Luckily, most of their good friends lived close by and they were no strangers, always popping in and out.

Before long, Emma was showing an interest in religion and was always aware that you should try to help others. But this would often end in disasters when trying to grill some toast for us or to make a cup of tea. There is nothing quite like it, at 6 o'clock in the morning, to have tea with cold water and burnt toast with thickly spread marmite. But we ate it just the same. I remember when Emma started cookery at Primary School. Her first attempt was at fairy cakes which we seemed to chew for ages while the chef looked on encouragingly. I couldn't help noticing that she never sampled them herself.

During their first years at Christ Church, the school doctors were always concerned about the girls' weight. Every year it was the same question, "do they eat enough?" I don't think the doctors realised that, as a young child, I had been thin and weedy too. This and the fact of their being twins probably accounted for their puny appearance because their appetites, particularly Emma's, had little to do with it. We even referred to Emma at home as the 'human dustbin' as she was quite capable of eating us out of house and home. Steak was a favourite meal. Sometimes, as a treat when inviting a friend home for a meal, we would give them steak and chips followed by strawberries from Steve's parents' garden. We would even pretend that they were in a restaurant and Steve would wait on them! When you consider that they were only about 7 years old, I really think that they did quite well.

At about this time, Emma and Beckie had friends who were twin boys. Sometimes, their mother and I and both pairs of twins would walk to school together. People approaching us would smile at seeing a little boy and girl walking together—and then do a 'double take' in surprise at seeing an identical boy and girl walking behind. Sadly, only one of the four children remains alive today as one of the boys has died too.

The girls were both used to causing a stir wherever they went, perhaps because twins were something of a novelty. I think Beckie became a little annoyed at people staring at them but Emma loved it. She was possibly the more immediately appealing of the two. She was so sweet and trusting, qualities which remained with her throughout her life and which endeared her particularly to small children whom she loved. Often she would come home with some tiny tot in tow and always send them home with a bag full of 'goodies'. I remember being approached by a mother in the school playground on one occasion who handed me a watch saying that it was very kind of Emma to have given it to her daughter but they could not accept it. It was my watch. When I questioned Emma, she unhesitatingly explained that I never wore the watch and that the other little girl had remarked how pretty it was. There is something disarming about young children's logic, isn't there?

We had many happy times in that flat. It had a huge walk-in fireplace in which it seemed we could fit a great tree trunk. Certainly we would have a roaring fire in winter around which friends readily gathered. One of the cats was always having kittens and, with our friends, we would pass the evening drinking cider or home-made wine watching the twins and kittens at play together. There were always plenty of people around to bath the girls and put them to bed. We may not have had much money but we did have many companions and much love to support us.

Beckie (*left*) and Emma, aged 5.

Steve's parents, Mary and Eric, lived just over the road and sometimes popped in. My own Mum visited us often and brought treats. On Sundays, I always cooked a big joint and we would sit as a family in the huge kitchen at the old pine table and put the world to rights. We tried to include the twins in most of the things we did, indeed they were invariably the centre of attention.

One Christmas, we bought them new bicycles with stabilisers and we left them with Mary and Eric until Christmas morning. This was an essential precaution as Emma particularly would start hunting for hidden presents long before the due day. That Christmas morning, we gave them their stockings and watched them sitting there surrounded by paper and pieces of string. It was quite normal for them to receive gifts from many of our friends which, once the parcels had been unwrapped, we would hide for later in the year as distractions if ever they fell ill. There was rarely a sensation therefore of something else still to come.

As soon as Eric had signalled that the two bicycles were now outside, we invited the twins to go out into the hall—to their understandable annoyance. But when they saw their presents, their faces lit up and Emma cried out with delight. It was very cold and slippery but out we all trooped. Even Beckie's cat, which never left her side for long, came too.

They both suffered from the normal coughs and colds, Emma especially so. She had also developed frequent nose bleeds which we assumed was associated with Cystic Fibrosis. On one occasion when she was noticeably unwell and the normal things didn't seem to touch it, we took her to the doctor, a new man from a different practice whom we had not seen before. To his evident surprise, we explained about the Cystic Fibrosis which he then assured us neither of them had. They each been cleared after sweat-tests at the age of 3 years but no-one had thought to tell us.

Emma steadily recovered from a bout of old-fashioned 'flu but I found great difficulty in coming to terms with the memory of needless worry and heartache: the girls were not going to die young; they were quite safe provided I looked after them. I think that all the love I had held back just surged out and I became very protective and doting. It is so obvious why females with young must be treated with circumspection. Even my mother's continuing insistence that the twins remained at death's door became a source of irritation.

A favourite pastime in winter was to set off very early on cold, crisp mornings to Cranham Woods. There the twins would run about in the snow while we collected any fallen branches. We would race each other, shouting, playing, hiding and seeking. Steve once put Emma up a tree to hide and we forgot that she was there—but at last we recovered the little mite, cold and shivering, waiting to be discovered. Sometimes she would disappear by herself and we would find her conversing with nature. Prince Charles would have been impressed.

She would also find wounded birds which we would then have to bring home to a cage set aside for her waifs and strays. They rarely lived, probably dying from fright and human attention. But although many did not survive, Emma never tired of tending them. One bird she did manage to nurse back to apparent health and, to our amazement, the same bird returned later on the day of release to be gathered back in and cared for once again. It died during the night but, despite her distress, Emma was thrilled that the little creature had come back to her.

Fledglings or full grown, they all received her complete love and attention—and our inevitable involvement. The little 'skinnies' were very sweet but scrabbling around in the garden looking for worms to satisfy their appetites was not my idea of fun. One day, however, Emma excelled herself. She came in from the garden and announced that there was a goldfish on the path. This was too much to believe but she persisted with her story until we went to look—and, sure enough, there was a goldfish on the garden path. Quickly, we put Fred, as we named him, in a pudding basin of water which Emma carried ceremoniously inside. Fred lived for five years until finally expiring from a tumour caused by the claw of the cat which had brought him into the garden. And even in his last hours, Emma insisted that I carry him, still in his aquarium, to the vet in order that he shouldn't suffer unnecessarily. None of our other goldfish arrived so spectacularly—or lived so long.

As the twins grew, we decided eventually and reluctantly to move to a bigger home. Although Steve was working for a Building Society, they were doubtful about giving us a mortgage on the sort of property we wanted and it took some time to find somewhere suitable. Eventually, after many disappointments, we bought a house near Christ Church School. It needed a lot of work and proved a disaster in more ways than one.

The first sad event was that Emma's cat was run over outside the house and dragged itself, minus a leg, into the basement to die. Next, Beckie's cat went back repeatedly to the old flat and was eventually found poisoned, evidently an intolerable nuisance to someone. And then my cat disappeared and never returned.

11

Everything in that house went wrong and caused Steve and me to live apart for a time. In that time, Emma made me realise how much she loved Steve. Not only how much she loved him but how much we all loved him. Thank God we came together again. Emma showed her love for Steve on many occasions but none more so than when she became quite protective towards him. Nothing I did was good enough and she took on chores determined that she could perform them better. She probably did too.

Horse-riding became the next hobby for both Emma and Beckie and we would watch them every Saturday morning trooping off to the riding school. They enjoyed it. It was expensive but we felt there was value in the money we had spent. We recognised, too, that it was time that we all had a good holiday abroad. And so we booked to go to Lindos on Rhodes island—it would be an adventure, a surprise which everyone but the twins would know about in advance.

It was easy concealing the holiday from them. In the same month, there was a church camp and a school trip to France organised by their new secondary school. The twins just assumed that the packing was for one of those two outings. All seemed well until, two days before departure, we received an urgent 'phone call from the secretary at the school saying that Beckie had fallen and broken her leg very badly. There was panic. We rushed to the hospital dreading what we might find there but enormously relieved to learn that it wasn't a break after all. It was merely a twisted ankle. And it wasn't Beckie either. It was Emma who had fallen over.

When we spoke to the teacher who had brought both girls to the hospital, we asked him if he taught them but he said "No". Emma then pointed out that he was actually their Form Master, a second error which caused us to remove the girls forthwith and send them next to Bourneside School.

Meanwhile, the countdown to the surprise holiday was well underway. We had arranged with Steve's father, Eric, that he would 'phone us from Gatwick Airport saying that, on the point of departure for his own holiday, he had discovered that he had forgotten his passport. Would we take it down urgently? And so off we went, the four of us crammed into a yellow soft-top MGB which had earlier replaced the old white Mini. The girls thought it very exciting—we even told them on arrival that a friend had arranged for us to see on board an aeroplane. But our elaborate plan misfired when the flight was delayed for 7 hours. Beckie quickly discovered her name on one of the cases and Emma was soon in tears at being teased so.

In fact, it was a lovely holiday. As usual the twins were the centre of attention for their prettiness and caused quite a stir. Working at the local restaurant was a gorgeous young Greek boy who performed exhibition Greek dancing around the tables. It took him only a short time to spot how much the twins would enhance his routine if they joined in too—and so, every night, we would troop down to the restaurant to sit at a table at the front and watch another eye-catching display of dancing. The girls caused a sensation and were soon well-known in the village. Emma spent her days talking to local frogs and lizards and her evenings dancing with beloved George. What bliss.

We were able to continue our trips abroad, twice a year to Spain, with the girls also enjoying holidays with the Church as well as those from school. Emma had a deep religious belief and would have been well suited to a life helping and working with the less fortunate. They had both joined the Church choir at an early stage and had sung in performances in a number of places. Even in St Paul's Cathedral which was a proud moment.

One of Emma's less endearing habits developed at about the age of 10 years. She started a nervous tic, something which children get from time to time but which drove us to despair. It would start around her nose, hitch up an eyebrow and leave her with a lopsided grin and an un-flattering expression. Most unfortunately, the habit started at about the time of her first appearance on television. The BBC had filmed a Palm Sunday service at the Church in 1984. The cameras roved around the congregation but did at one point settle on Emma in the choir. She had a heavy cold, which didn't help, and looked distinctly disownable with her red, twitching nose and hitched eyebrow.

Her second TV appearance was not much better. She and Beckie had been invited to participate in a documentary about twins. Most of the filming had to be done in a swimming pool and I had to buy them matching costumes and arrange their hair in the same way. This was scarcely popular as they had individual tastes in clothes and as we had never made them dress alike. Neverthless, we did what was asked and set out to make the best impression possible. Off we went to Pebble Mill where we met the producer, a circus elephant and the actor John Thaw. I disgraced myself in the girls' eyes by bumping into Ben E King without realising who he was—apparently, he was a pop singer, high in the charts with a song called 'Stand by me'.

Unfortunately that morning, Emma had started her period and we had to explain discreetly that she would not be able to go in the water. This upset things somewhat and several planned shots had to be altered. Everyone kept asking why my girls were the only ones not swimming and word soon spread that they were the stars of the show and would soon dive off the iron bars in the roof over the water. It got a little out of hand and in the end I had to explain that Emma had verrucas.

She nearly won another TV role. Through my modelling contacts, Emma and Beckie joined the Molly Tanner Agency in London and, within two weeks of my sending off their photographs, the summons came. It seemed that Knorr Soup had sent a talent scout to England to find blonde-haired twin girls aged about 12 years to appear in a soup advertisement. They liked the photographs and off we went to London to find out more. In the train on the way, Emma started a nosebleed and I suppose I became anxious and kept telling them to behave, and so on. It was a mistake. At the audition, the producer wanted the girls to fight and push each other around—but, of course, on pain of dreadful punishments, they were on their best behaviour and their natural boisterousness had deserted them. We lived in hope but it seemed that the girls looked 'too English' for Knorr Soup's tastes and in the end some German twins were chosen. Emma and Beckie did undertake some other modelling assignments with me but, although Emma enjoyed it, it was not until later that I realised how keen she was. Looking at the last photographs of her, I think she would have been a natural.

Both girls had decided that they wanted to be confirmed as soon as possible and they applied themselves to their choral exams with the choir and their classes with the curate. They were never ashamed or secretive about their beliefs, would express them clearly and were proud to be associated with the Church which provided them with much love and a family atmosphere. They had many friends there and Sundays were full of activities separated only by Emma's urgent need for frequent refuelling. Every Sunday, as a matter of routine, she would come out of the Morning Service and ask Steve whether lunch was yet ready. Well rehearsed, he would tell her that lunch would not be on the table until 1 o'clock whereupon she would march into the house and insist that she could not possibly last until then. But even if she won the subsequent battle over whether to have a snack, she always did full justice to the Sunday roast. Just before Evensong, the pattern re-emerged. She would creep upstairs to watch TV well supplied with cheese, a loaf and a jar of pickle.

We had bought them each a colour television and made their rooms as nice as possible in the belief that being together all day was quite enough for each to put up with. They needed time and space to be by themselves in the evening. At mealtimes, however, we were always together and would discuss the latest heartthrob or the best pop group. Emma was rather fickle—one week it would be Bros and the next Wet, Wet, Wet and her bedroom wall suffered from many pinholes as a result. At the time of her death, it was Paul Gascoigne.

At school, Emma scored her highest marks in science although she later failed her science GCSE. Examinations were not her strong point, nor mine either. I had gone to the same school which they were now attending and some of my old teachers were still there. The Maths teacher even observed to me once that, while Emma had achieved 34% in her Maths exam, the most he could recall that I had managed was 3% for writing my name and the date correctly at the top of the page. Gloomily dismissing the mathematical ability of the women in our household, the teacher had to smile when learning from Steve that he was an accountant by profession.

Emma's first venture in the world of teenage employment was an early morning paper round. It lasted one day only when the hard truth of no breakfast until afterwards hit home. Food was simply more important. Next came a part-time Saturday job in a shoe shop. She was a great success selling, on one memorable day, a total of £1,000 of shoes. Obviously her natural kindness and the time she took with each customer was paying off, although unfortunately not in the form of commission as she was only paid by the hour.

She had decided that she wanted to work with children, a logical development it seemed to us who had long since first observed her natural ease with them. Perhaps impetuously, however, Emma decided that she wanted to start work straight away and dispense with further study. I had to agree with her that no amount of exams passed would alter the fact that someone had, or hadn't, a gift with children but we did persuade her to undertake YTS childcare training on leaving school. Having to retake her English and Maths exams was not popular with Emma until we explained to her the importance of guiding pupils in her care with their school work and general development. Once she understood, she applied herself, working hard and using her spare time to devise games and activities for her children.

She worked first in a school where she could help a teacher with whom she got on very well. She went on weekly day release to college and all seemed set fair until something happened that probably affected her more than any of us knew.

At 5.15 pm one bright sunny September evening in 1989, Emma was walking home from a visit to the theatre when she was grabbed from behind and indecently assaulted. I arrived home some 20 minutes later to find Beckie, white-faced, comforting her sister who immediately rushed into my arms. When she told me, I was very shocked. I could not understand how such a thing could happen in broad daylight and just around the corner from our home. Apparently, she had been walking past the entrance to a lane when the man had come up behind her and putting his hand over her mouth had pulled her to the ground. She kicked and shouted and he ran off in one direction while she got up and ran round the corner bumping straight into two men. They asked her if she was alright but she ran past them. Her attacker had not disturbed her clothing which was dirty from the ground but he had fondled her.

I rang Steve and called the police. They sent round a huge policeman, well over 6 feet tall, which was scarcely helpful in the circumstances. He took the best statement possible from Emma who was very upset and, I think, ashamed. I know they say this about victims of rape and sexual attacks. But what do they say, I wonder, about those who die violent deaths?

After this first statement was taken, the incident was handled by a woman police officer from the CID. There was little information to go on but Emma's experience sounded similar to other attacks on women in Cheltenham at the time. The officer brought round a file of photographs, 'mug shots', but Emma could not pick anyone out. All she knew was that the man had blonde hair, oily or newspaper-stained hands and was generally dirty. Several days after the incident, Emma came home from work and said that she had seen the man getting into a van not far from our house. I went out with her and took the registration number and the name on the van. It was owned, we thought, by people living nearby. The police were told and Emma went with them to keep watch but the van, on that day, did not reappear. There were several other attacks in the area after that although no-one was caught and our own incident seemed closed. Emma appeared not seriously affected by her experience but she would not talk about it to the Victim Support lady (who later became my Victim Support volunteer). For a time she was reluctant to go into town on her own and avoided the road with the lane in it. She got on with her life, so we thought, as normal. We could not tell if there had been any long term effect.

Soon, Emma found her first boyfriend, a friendship which endured until shortly before she died. She met Mark on a church camp holiday where he was visiting with a group from America. Emma and Beckie each made friends with them all and we even drove them up to London to see the boys and their group leaders. Mark kept in touch with Emma and once came over and stayed with my Mum. They planned that Emma would pay a return visit in the summer of 1991—and I often wondered if Mark's parents experienced the same shock that Steve did on seeing our telephone bills at the time. Even a few, short, clandestine 'phone calls soon add up.

By now, Oliver's shoe shop had closed and Emma was looking for another part-time job. I thought it a shame as she had been so happy there and I had been so proud to call in sometimes during the holiday and take her to lunch. She always looked so neat and smart and took great care of herself.

In the meantime, Beckie had met a boy called Richard. He was very pleasant and took her out to some nice places. But this was a little disappointing for Emma who had no boyfriend at the time to take her out. Eventually, Beckie generously asked Emma if she would like to accompany Richard and her—a bad mistake for as soon as Richard met Emma he was lost. Beckie gave in gracefully but I know she was hurt. Emma and Richard saw each other for some time but he was a little too old for her. She was not ready for the sexual relationship he sought and she told him so. Nevertheless, this had been a good experience for each of them especially as Richard had always been so very polite and considerate.

The girls went out with their friends a few times but unfortunately Cheltenham did not have many places for their age group. There were certainly some nightclubs which had early evening discos with a non-alcoholic bar but most of the time the young people went over to Gloucester. Emma and Beckie soon met new boyfriends but it lasted no more than a few weeks and before long our dining room had become their normal evening haunt.

Emma (second *left*) and Beckie (*third left*) as Mary and her Little Lamb.

Shortly after the latest boyfriend had moved on, Emma met Chris. I was wrong about Chris whom I felt was not good enough for her. In fact, I know now that Chris was a lovely boy and a credit to his parents. Emma was very fond of him. But, after his sisters had joined the choir, it seemed that all I heard about was Chris and his family. Through jealousy I suppose, I managed to split them up—which I deeply regret. Beckie now had two boys in tow, one of whose mother I had known some years before, and once again Emma appeared to attract the one whom Beckie was keen on. Eventually, I tried to stop the girls going out together whenever there was a boy around but they insisted on doing it their way.

A Chris Harper and companion next came on the scene. They were all just friends together and spent many hours in the house listening to records. Beckie also had a new friend, Nick, who has stayed in touch since their deaths. He and another boy called Dino would often take them out for a drive in a group.

To our concern, Emma came home from her nursery school work one day and announced that she intended becoming a nanny. So much was planned but we were upset that she was not going to finish her YTS course and that she had already applied for, and found, a job. I think we were swayed by her prospective employers who seemed very pleasant and whose three sons appeared to love Emma already. They had discussed wages and Steve and I seemed to have been presented with a *fait accompli* as a contract was quickly signed. Emma left home for her new job one week later.

Initially, she seemed to do well but after a while she was expected to assume steadily more housework responsibilities. This did not suit Emma at all, as I had feared. Next she began going out at night and then being too tired in the morning to get things done. Before long, the stress was manifesting itself in a familiar form of migraine that we once thought might have been meningitis. Finally, she left a deteriorating situation and returned home.

Finding another job was difficult for her without her qualification as a Nursery Nurse. She was also too young for the work that she really wanted to do, which was to devote herself to sick and needy children. Emma seemed thwarted at every step by red tape and her morale soon fell. It was a difficult time for her. While on the YTS course, she had contributed £10 a week to housekeeping but now could not pay anything. She wanted to find her own way in life and was rebelling against the label 'twin'.

Through their friends, Nick and Dino, Emma met a boy she had been at school with and became very close to his sister. They spent more and more time with each other and at his house—a period in which we were doing our best to help her find a job and recover her self esteem. In fact she was turning against us and, when the boy's mother invited Emma to stay with them, she leapt at the chance.

It was a bad situation although the family were kind to her. There were many people in the house and Emma had to sleep on the floor. I imagine that this was when she lost her virginity—while we were fighting desperately to get her back. I felt that this sad state of affairs was all my fault, which it probably was, and may have tried to compensate by giving Beckie more freedom than either of them had been allowed. But this made matters worse: Emma now felt that Beckie was benefiting from her own struggle.

I could do nothing right. However, Emma eventually returned home after some very difficult times. But she had lost interest in herself and in life in general. And she was only 17 years of age.

In the meantime, Beckie had met Chris Harper's brother, David, and had started dating him. David seemed clean and respectable if a little distant—Nick and I had got on very well but David I found hard work.

Before long, Emma found work at another shoe shop and things seemed to look up. But there she was as beautiful as ever, clean and tidy, when the inevitable happened. David fell for Emma and Beckie was unceremoniously dumped. Beckie was very upset indeed and for a time neither would speak to the other.

I felt so sorry for Beckie although I soon began to have misgivings about Emma's new acquaintances. Things seemed fine while Emma had money in her purse but too often, it seemed, she would telephone home, penniless and stranded somewhere. Steve would go and pick her up but on some occasions she still found herself walking home. To us, David's friends appeared not to care that a young girl could be put in such a vulnerable situation. Soon Emma was staying out all night and in circumstances we could not approve of. It seemed, too, that she was being encouraged to drink and, on one occasion, I came home from work unexpectedly and found Emma and David drinking at 3.00 pm in the afternoon. I asked him to leave at once but not before it was made clear that Emma would not be staying out at night in future and that she should always be brought home.

This last promise was not kept and the situation became progressively uneasier. We tried hard to get Emma away from David and had much hope of a new friendship with a local boy who was entering the Army. But it came to nothing despite several telephone calls by Emma and some generous Christmas presents she bought for him.

That last December, she was very excited by the idea of giving presents but we managed to persuade her to save hers to us until Christmas Day. She had spent a lot of money, as well as lending David £60, and to have to postpone the pleasure of giving upset her greatly. However, we insisted and the grey scarf she bought for Steve and the umbrella for me remain among our most treasured possessions.

Things were still very strained between Emma and me. Indeed, I did not understand her until it was too late. But a few days before she died we were reunited and on the day she died she drew me pictures of flowers from a nature book. She was little more than a child at heart—kind, loving, generous, affectionate, impulsive—but a child who wanted to be her own person. Even when she was at loggerheads with me, she was to the world a sweet and pleasant creature with time for young and old alike.

She wrote once on a card to me. *"To Mum, I love you. You'll never realise how much I do."*

I pray that, at the end, Emma realised how much I had always loved her and that our differences were only my trying to protect her from the bad things in life. But when the telephone rang on the 23rd of January, unexpectedly asking her to a party, I couldn't even do that.

CHAPTER TWO

Rebecca Sara Harper

Vicky:

Thirty minutes after her sister had arrived, Rebecca Sara made her appearance—forceps, feet first and desperately ill. She weighed 5lbs 8oz and was 16 inches long, slightly heavier than Emma but so quickly into the incubator. It was not until the twins had reached Bristol, however, that I realised just how critical was her condition. She had jaundice and pneumonia as well as the meconium blockage that afflicted Emma. After the first day, the Sister came to me.

It seems that Beckie has no chance of survival. The odds are stacked too highly against her and it is just a matter of hours. The Sister advises me that it will be better if I can forget that I am the mother of twins and that I must concentrate on Emma.

How could any mother manage this? How can I forget even now, 22 years later, that I am still the mother of two girls who have suddenly been taken away from me?

I became determined that Beckie should live and I focused on her, willing her to survive. It was some days before she was able to take liquid and not until the tenth day was she formally conceded the hope of a future. Not being with them was very difficult, especially not knowing what they looked like. We had been told that their heads had been partly shaved and that drips had been fed into their skulls. The poor things did look dreadful when I was allowed to see them—Beckie looked like a monk, a ring of her hair missing right around her head.

On the way home and once there, the twins cried pitifully. But Beckie responded quickly to routine and became the more placid of the two. She would lie happily in her cot absorbed by the mobile above her head or by the number of toes on her feet. She was a Mummy's girl and resembled me in a number of ways. She was also the twin who reliably achieved things before the other—the first smile, the first words and much more. Perhaps this was because I spent more time with her at the beginning?

You start to wonder like this, you see, when they've gone for ever and brutally so. You pore over everything that was, re-living everything you possibly can, for only then, before the 24th of January, was there some measure of sanity in your life.

Emma would wake and scream between feeds—and Beckie and I would retreat downstairs once peace had been restored above. We were often up at odd times of the night, she and I. And, in those days before 'disposable' became commonplace, I would even find myself boiling towelling nappies at 3 o'clock in the morning. Or putting Beckie in her pram and going for long walks at dawn. It was hard work because, as soon as I had fed, washed and changed one twin, the whole process would start again with the other. But I was lucky to have my Mum to help me. Breast feeding was not possible but bottle feeding too proved difficult and exhausting. The midwives had advised me to take my time over feeding, doing one baby at a time and cuddling them as they fed. But this image of calm maternity was so remote from the howls and hysteria of the twin who was waiting that by an early age they had each learned to hold their own bottles. In truth, they weaned themselves.

When the twins began to crawl, there was bedlam. It was difficult to watch the two of them at the same time and I seemed constantly to be running from one to the other in an attempt to forestall disaster. Neither of them was quick to start walking but the breakthrough came when someone offered Beckie a piece of cake. And as soon as one had led the way, the other quickly followed. There was no stopping them as we nearly found to our cost at a small park near our home. It was a very convenient park, if closer to the traffic than we might have wished.

One frightening day, the twins were happily playing on the grass when each made a run for it—but in opposite directions and towards main roads. Emma made for the High Street exit, where I judged there were more likely to be people to stop her and so dashed after Beckie who ran straight across the other adjacent main road. Thank God nothing was coming. And I thanked Him again on running back carrying Beckie to find Emma laughing and gurgling in the arms of a friend. Miraculously, she had arrived with her own baby son just as Emma was about to hit town. After that, I attached a long lead to their reins. Never letting go, I spent many happy hours in those gardens with that friend and her son.

Taking the girls out in the pram was quite an operation. Someone had kindly given us a huge, coach-built Silver Cross twin pram that was so big that I could hardly push it or see over it when the hood was up to

Emma (*left*) and Beckie aged 6. (*By kind permission of James Kirkwood*) keep out rain. But I did love taking them out in it for walks. Sometimes, I would start the pram gliding along the pavement and would manage to get them off to sleep when some well-meaning person would come up to us loudly exclaiming how sweet Emma and Beckie were and generally cooing in a loud voice. The twins would immediately wake to find a strange face peering at them—and begin bawling as a result. The well-wisher would then disappear and leave me to push the pram another mile before the girls rocked off to sleep again. This would be repeated several times, taking me longer and longer to reach my destination.

Shopping was just as difficult. I dared not leave the pram outside shops but couldn't really carry both girls into the supermarket with me. Beckie once fell through the leg space of a supermarket trolley seat where I had perched them, side by side in the space meant for one. Until they were older, therefore, and could sit securely in the trolleys, I used to ask a friend to come with me and stand guard over the pram. Before long, however, we had progressed to a large twin pushchair which was much more satisfactory and made life much easier.

On cold days, I would tuck them up cosily and take them for long walks. Each would be wrapped in a blanket with a hot water bottle and have plenty to eat and drink on the journey. The toys would come too as we set off for the park or some other place of interest. Only on bus rides was travelling with the twins a nightmare. It was impossible to manage by myself and I would reliably annoy the queue behind as I struggled to hold two wriggling babies while folding up the pushchair. Usually, some kind soul realised that life might progress more quickly with a little help—but no sooner would we be on the bus than it was time to reverse the procedure and get off.

We were poor, like so many young families, and were very grateful for any 'hand downs', especially clothes. I suppose I was quite lucky because my mother was the head of the local infants' school and the parents of girls used to pass things on to us. Clothing became more of a problem, however, when the twins themselves started at school. They were so tiny that it was almost impossible to get any uniform to fit them. Even the smallest blouse was three sizes too big around the neck and gymslips had to be shortened by at least six inches.

Their hair also caused great anguish. Because their heads had been shaved as babies, neither of their scalps showed more than fluff—and what little there was grew on the very top of their heads. They each looked a little like an old-fashioned 'Tressy' doll whose hair shot out of the top of its head as soon as a button was pressed on its tummy. Undoubtedly, Emma and Beckie looked odd, if not comical, setting off to school.

At this time, we lived just over the road from Steve's parents who had a fantastic garden, full of every fruit that could be grown. We had some lovely days there in the sunshine where Steve's sister, Julia, would chase the girls around the garden with a spurting hose. Sometimes, they would sneak off to return later with their mouths and clothes stained with blackberry and strawberry juice. They would never admit to having more than one berry each when the evidence was that they must have crammed the fruit in.

Both girls had difficulty shaping their words, with sometimes curious results. Whenever the doorbell rang, for example, Beckie would shout "Summondebody at the door!" which led, in turn, to a family chorus of "Summon the body, the legs are here!" Wood lice were not easily pronounced either and were known as 'licences' until the day the girls died. Recalling such codes and rituals is a powerful reminder of the happiness and innocence that once prevailed in our secure, little family. As with Emma's nicknames, calling Beckie variously Blondie, Beevie, Fatty Arbuthnot and Beck Beck Boo was no more than telling her that we loved and cherished her too.

Soon the girls had started ballet. Off they went to a local dance school every Saturday, to pirouette and twirl the morning away. Eventually they took part in a display and we were asked to equip them with tutus. Trying to find some that would fit was almost impossible and in the end I had to borrow them, literally sewing up each twin as she stood there in her costume. In the end they looked very sweet and did us proud—even though Beckie had had to be unsewn and then stitched back up again so that she could go to the loo.

Beckie read absorbedly and loved nothing better than to curl up in some corner with a favourite book. She also started learning the recorder which she never seemed completely to master. She would practise for ages, to our unspoken but increasing discomfort, before proudly giving us a 'concert' comprising a tuneless sequence of notes repeated endlessly and screechingly. We did try to encourage her but it was difficult and the neighbours were especially pleased when the phase passed! Like me, she was also a disaster at ball games and, flinching, would look the other way hoping the ball wouldn't hit her. But she did have a keen interest in chess and played regularly at school. She was very good at art and craft, too, and we still have many pieces of her work around the house.

Not everything went so well however. Beckie's maths left a lot to be desired and, I fear, her early behaviour sometimes let her down. On one occasion, she decided that she had been at school for quite long enough and, informing her teacher so, left and came home. It took some reasoning on my part to make her understand that such decisions were not yet hers to make.

Similar additional explanation was necessary at the time of their first periods to which development, characteristically, Beckie had just beaten her sister. I bought them each a bunch of flowers and a present and tried to make the experience as easy as possible. Once over, Emma expressed her satisfaction that all was done—at which it rapidly became apparent that neither had completely grasped that periods were recurring events and not a one-off milestone. They were not best pleased.

The twins were active Brownies and enjoyed working for their various badges. They were keen gymnasts and would also come with me in the evenings when I went swimming with friends. I am not completely convinced, however, that swimming was their cup of tea as Beckie always wanted to get out as soon as she had got in. This was a battle she never won as I always thought it fair to make her wait for the rest of us. I was strict, I think, but even-handed in their upbringing too, although I am still not sure whether they paid much attention to the guidelines I tried to lay down.

Beckie had her illnesses in early childhood with all the usual complaints as well as Scarletina, a mild form of Scarlet Fever. They both had German measles on the day of the Queen's Silver Jubilee and we must have been the only people who did not attend a street party. But apart from that, the twins were very different medically which surprised me.

Beckie's first teeth refused to come out which caused her second teeth to start growing through the roof of her mouth. And so she had to go into the local private hospital for a horrid operation during which she was so brave. First, they removed the obstinate baby teeth and then they cut into the roof of her mouth to allow the next ones room to come through. She was very poorly and for a time could only have liquids through a straw. It took quite a while for her to recover her strength and she had to wear a brace from then on. This was to have been removed on her 18th birthday, a celebration she never saw. She also had Glandular

Fever and necessarily missed a lot of school. However, I suppose we were quite lucky really when I remember that early, dreadful diagnosis of Cystic Fibrosis.

At one stage, as if to match Emma's nervous tic, Beckie developed a bizarre and time-consuming fad. She decided that she had to do everything six times. Whether it was getting out of bed or going down the steps outside the house, it applied to everything. For about two weeks, therefore, our days lengthened as we accommodated this infuriating habit. The bedroom light would have to be switched on six times—a sudden flashing and there would be Beckie on her way to bed. We got through quite a few bulbs, I can tell you! It was also quite difficult if you happened to be following her upstairs. She would suddenly decide that she had not done one stair enough times and would come to an abrupt standstill while I waited for her to go up and down until satisfied. Eventually, of course, the fad departed as quickly as it had arrived and life returned to normal. I wish things could be so simple now.

In stark contrast to her sister, Beckie was an untidy girl. On Saturday mornings, I expected them each to tidy their rooms—which Emma managed spotlessly within half an hour. But Beckie would insist on taking everything off the shelves and out of the room. It would all be dumped on the landing and then she would start trying to rearrange everything. I could see something of myself in her disorganisation but knew that my daughters were firmly individuals in their own right. In fact, they were different in so many ways that it was easy to forget that they were twins.

In looks, however, they would always be alike. When they were young and before they had developed their different dress senses, they were virtually identical. Friends who knew them well did not have too much difficulty in telling them apart but it always took a few minutes and one or two long stares. This worked to the twins' advantage if they wished to play tricks on anyone but it could also prove a frustrating obstacle to winning prizes or auditioning for parts in school plays, for example. Confusion over their identity would also annoy them intensely—and us for that matter—especially if people could not be bothered to look beyond their obvious similarity for the distinguishing features in each. There lay the cause of some grand rows and arguments between them, I can tell you.

However, they were not slow to exploit their singular appearance, especially at school where each wore her name on her cardigan. We were unsurprised to learn that, if one twin did not want to do something or was about to be scolded, they were not averse to sneaking off and exchanging cardigans before the event. For a time, they were genuinely indistinguishable in school uniforms and I used quietly to sympathise with the teachers who could never have been completely confident of which of my girls they were actually talking to.

In a similar vein, I can remember reactions of fellow diners at the restaurant we used in Miami during our American holiday when the girls were 10 years old. All children's menus could be turned into masks once orders had been taken and Emma and Beckie were invariably offered menus bearing the faces of princesses. In keeping with the busy informality of the place, our masked girls would soon be wandering around the restaurant receiving nice compliments from the other tables. But nothing compared with the general looks of astonishment when the girls removed their masks to eat their own meals.

They and I were hopeless gigglers and, try as we might to contain ourselves, such moments would often end in peals of harmless, helpless laughter.

The girls were both very beautiful but in distinctly different ways. Emma was delicate while Beckie's features were much stronger. That's what Steve and I thought anyway and I suppose that we must own up to some bias. Nevertheless, the spotlight would often move their way and perhaps with reason. At the age of 13, they were taken by my mother, as in previous years, to the Ocean Hotel in Brighton, a Butlins hotel with events and activities to match. They made lots of friends and enjoyed themselves tremendously. One evening, they all decided to enter the Junior Miss Ocean Hotel contest in which, the judges being unable to decide, Emma and Beckie came joint first. Only a junior 'beauty' contest but a proud moment all the same.

Sometimes during my various modelling assignments, an opportunity would arise for the twins to take part too. On one occasion my agent rang to say that Kay's Catalogue need a child for some photographs— but only one. In the end I had to toss a coin and Beckie won. To Emma's eventual amusement, however, the modelling requirement was for a picture on the bathroom accessories page which meant that Beckie had to sit in a bath. She was only 9 years old at the time and was not too embarrassed at being photographed—until Emma smuggled the published Catalogue into school to show all their friends!

They each loved dressing up and pretending to be models. Two nights

Emma (*left*) and Beckie, aged 14 at their confirmation at Christ Church.

before they died, they put on an impromptu photographic session and fashion show at home. Poor Steve was more interested in a sports programme on the television and became slightly bored with the constant cry of "What do you think of this, Dad?" But I was quite impressed by their flair and grace. A Tuesday's child, each of them.

As they matured, the difference in their choice of clothes became stronger. Emma was always very neat while Beckie liked a well-worn look which meant that even new clothes had to be adapted in some way or other. Perhaps a collar chopped off here or a few badges pinned on there. When holidays were planned I would allow them to pick some items from a catalogue but those that Beckie chose were either never worn or else rapidly changed beyond recognition. I despaired of her.

Perhaps unreasonably, I sometimes found myself at odds with them on holiday. We went each year to Spain where Steve and I would adore relaxing in the sun and fresh air—whereas the girls, who had made their own friends there, always seemed to prefer being inside with them watching 'Dirty Dancing' or some other popular video for young people. We held their sixteenth birthday in Spain thanks to an old friend, Peter, who ran the local restaurant. Earlier, I had written to ask if he would mind my bringing a cake and presenting it to Emma and Beckie in the bar. But on the day in question, we discovered that he had organised a buffet and champagne for them. Friends and friends of friends were invited and a great party was enjoyed by all.

Understandably, the girls did not spend too much time with us on our Spanish holidays except when a particular acquaintance, Carlos, was around. Carlos would take us to Mini-Hollywood, a local film set used for many of the spaghetti westerns, and the twins loved it there. He knew all the stunt men and the girls would be allowed to dress up and, supervised, ride their horses. This was not actually the most straight-forward of tasks. Once again the girls impressed me (those early riding lessons had evidently paid off) as they managed to stay in the saddles while the specially trained horses did unpredictable things at the slightest touch, tug or command.

Such attention, generosity and kindness was typical of our friends in Spain and we did appreciate it.

Beckie loved to collect things. It began with postcards and our holidays helped to boost her collection significantly. But next it was carrier bags. I was working at the time in the perfumery business where there were some lovely bags and wrappers. At first, it was just these which we collected but soon we began to accumulate the things from everywhere. I calculate that there are still at least three hundred carrier bags of Beckie's in the loft.

She was renowned for more than hoarding things however. Beckie was capable of sleeping all day without a thought for the needs and demands of the outside world. Given half a chance, she would curl up in some corner, far away in her dreams. Time-keeping was definitely low in her priorities if it figured at all. Weddings, buses, trains, school—whatever the event, they could all wait as far as Beckie was concerned. It was even our family joke that Beckie would be late for her own funeral. In fact, she was years too early for it, a sad end to a private joke.

Despite her lack of concern for time, Beckie was just as unselfish and generous as Emma, although more discerning about whom she helped. Furthermore, as they had been brought up strictly, not least because we had been very poor at times, each was well aware of the importance of sharing. I recall, on one occasion, that friends invited me, with the girls, to accompany them to the fair. I only had about £2 in my purse and explained to Emma and Beckie that we would have lunch before we went, that there would be no candy floss or other treats and that I could only afford one ride each. They both knew I had no more money and were not to embarrass me by asking for things they could not have. Off we went after lunch and the girls had their one ride each. I remember one or two sidelong looks at the candy floss stall but there was never a word of complaint from them. Even when one of my friends offered to buy them each a stick of the sugary stuff, they looked at me for permission which of course I gave. I will never forget how they determinedly shared out their candy floss among us all and in the end had very little themselves.

It was the same at our last Christmas together. Beckie had not been working and she had very little money to buy presents. But she made the most of what she could afford to spend and her tiny gifts were every bit as special as Emma's grander ones.

I remember how much she was longing to have her dental brace removed. We all hoped that it could be taken off on her eighteenth birthday and we had long since promised the orthodontist a case of champagne if he could make it happen. Sadly of course, Beckie did not reach her eighteenth birthday and the champagne was neither bought nor celebrated. She suffered a lot wearing that brace. She was teased but, although it clearly upset her, her courage always held. When the orthodontist replaced the first brace with the second much more noticeable metalwork, Beckie was as much in pain as apprehensive about what her friends would say. I advised her not to give any of them the opportunity and to make the first joke herself—and so she walked into class the next day and said "Just call me Jaws!" There wasn't much point in anyone else saying anything after that.

Beckie could seem harder than Emma and yet at times she would touch me with her kindness. When I was in hospital on one occasion, she bought a card and went round to the shops I had worked in, asking all my friends and acquaintances to sign and send me their best wishes. It was a lovely gesture and I still treasure that card.

She was also more patient than Emma and certainly understood Steve's odd sense of humour better. But when it came to her sister and to her borrowing things without asking, Beckie's patience ran out. Part of the problem was Beckie's own habit of sleeping late on a Saturday, an opportunity of stealthily using up that last bit of hairspray or that vital lip-liner which Emma was never slow to take. Beckie would wake up after the event only to discover that an essential item had been plundered—and the sparks would immediately fly. I would have to reassure her, agreeing that Emma had been quite wrong and that I would intervene sternly upon her return. But we all knew that whenever Steve or I went to scold one or other of them, the girls would immediately break off any argument and join forces in self-protection against us. They were, of course, so very close that one would have done everything possible to defend the other. Were they able to help each other at the end, I wonder?

Although they were close, they enjoyed being apart and days out separately were always a great treat. Emma had some nice times with her Nana who, I think, probably favoured her. But Beckie would love going with Steve's father to Weston super Mare—especially if it was raining. If ever there was a thunderstorm or heavy rain, Beckie would be outside, face upturned, absolutely soaked and relishing the elements. Soon she went through a fad of jogging during the early hours. But the passion did not last too long as bed was a much more comfortable place to be.

The real passion of Beckie's life was Marilyn Monroe. There can have been few books or posters about the film star that Beckie didn't possess. The walls of her room were covered with blonde memorabilia and Beckie would read and write articles about her, watch her films and even copy her hairstyle, clothes and appearance. It would have looked stunning on a mature woman but I could not feel completely comfortable with teenage Beckie's portrayal of Hollywood glamour. However, it was pointless trying to resist completely: if Beckie wanted to recreate Marilyn Monroe, she was going to do so regardless of what I thought. It was better to try and control this passion the strength of which I did not grasp until after Beckie's death. Indeed I had not realised either quite how devoted to religion the girls had become until we found so many Christian books and pamphlets on their shelves and Bible quotations in their notebooks.

How much do you think you know your children? Perhaps all you know, or can have confidence in, can be the experiences you help them to assemble as they pass through the years allowed them.

Church holidays meant just as much to Beckie as they did to Emma and, while her sister met Mark from America, so Beckie fell for a young man called Pat. He was one year older than her and they stayed in touch until distance made the friendship falter and fade, much to Beckie's sadness.

She applied to join the Police Cadets and had been put on the waiting list. We had earlier taken them to an Open day at Police Headquarters and Beckie had thoroughly enjoyed talking to the Careers Adviser in attendance. Height might have been a problem but, as it would not have been possible to join the full Police Force for some time, Beckie concentrated first on becoming a Cadet—and on growing a bit taller.

We felt that a different activity, quite separate from Emma, had to be a good thing and we encouraged her. It must be difficult, after all, being a twin shadowed by an ever-present reflection of your own qualities and characteristics. But Emma was now developing ideas and hobbies and we were very pleased that Beckie too wanted to do something by herself. We were proud, furthermore, that she had chosen the Police Cadets. It would at least give her a little more experience of the world and help her to decide whether the full Police could offer her a career. She did carry through her intention of joining the Police Cadets but, while she enjoyed the experience, she found the physical demands too daunting to continue. Eventually, she decided it was not for her.

Beckie was very determined in every thing she did or planned to do. Typically for a teenager I suppose, her clothes reflected her resolve— and sometimes to my embarrassment. When I was working in a big store in Cheltenham, the girls would come in on a Saturday afternoon. It was always during the afternoon because Beckie could never be ready any earlier. At about 3.00 pm, Emma would appear looking very smart and neat followed by a sight that made me groan inwardly. I have to admit that I would try to look as if I had never met this apparition...

The fashions at the time were not conspicuously attractive anyway but Beckie somehow managed to plumb new depths. Thick black tights, cut-off denim shorts, several tee shirts of different lengths and a dreadful black top. What made things worse was that her hair was not always the same colour. She had the most beautiful blonde hair but would insist on experimenting. So one day it would be bright orange and the next day pink. I think Beckie was actually aiming for strawberry blonde but did not know how to achieve it. Her lovely hair would be quite concealed in a construction of hairspray and back-combing to support the currently favoured style—which often looked more like a bird's nest than the beehive which earned her nickname 'Beevie'.

Eye-liner was another of Beckie's trade marks. And so was red lipstick. She succeeded in looking like a weird combination of Marilyn Monroe and Madonna. She could even sing like Madonna although she earned more lasting acclaim in the Church Choir where, incongruously with her odd appearance, she was soon performing solo. Perhaps her taste for striking make-up was more an aspect of her strong flair for art and design? We have many of her pictures up on the study wall still.

Beckie had taken over Emma's paper round and worked at the job for a year. Soon she progressed to Saturday employment in W H Smiths. It seemed to be hard work, standing all day especially over the Christmas period, and she was undoubtedly very tired. But at least it gave her some money, except during the exam period when she would give up her part-time work and concentrate on school. She also worked as a waitress, which she enjoyed for the tips and free meals, but before long found herself involved in an old people's home.

Beckie had first discovered her gift with the elderly while doing work experience at school. Against all advice, she had insisted on going to Coney Hill psychiatric hospital in Gloucester. She arranged the opportunity herself and thrived on an experience which the school had thought unsuitable for a fifteen year old. I think it important to encourage young people to plan things and carry them through, to achieve things: Beckie would keep us entertained for hours telling us about the patients and their ways and about the staff and hospital life. Her superior said she was a natural with the patients and that they loved her in return. She would have liked to have spent time with the younger people but this was felt to be too disturbing. Neverthless, Beckie had found what she wanted to do. When she left school she went to Technical College to start work on the necessary preparation courses leading to a nursing career.

As her love of singing suggests, music was a strong, persistent part of Beckie's life. Disco dancing was a specially favoured form of expression and she would practise for hours—to our discomfort in the kitchen below. Nevertheless, the herd of elephants she kept up there earned a bronze medal and were also Highly Commended. Clearly they and she were doing quite well. Perhaps the volume and combination of sounds had something to do with it, too? Church music would give way to heavy metal first thing in the morning—and Iron Maiden in Beckie's room competing with Elvis Presley in Emma's was awesome.

Before long, Beckie admitted to smoking cigarettes—and I doubt that Emma was far behind her. In truth, Beckie's admission was the result of being caught outside school and reported, as seems to happen frequently to young girls. Steve and I both smoked and I felt that I could scarcely forbid Beckie from following our example. I merely asked that she do it at home and not in the street. I also told them both that, if they chose to smoke, they would have to pay for their cigarettes themselves. I imagine that many other households have had such one-way discussions.

Boys came and went in Beckie's life. She was very shy and found it difficult sometimes to converse with them. Quite often, a new friend would be brought home and plonked down in the sitting room with us while Beckie went off to make tea. And eventually I would have to go out to the kitchen and insist that she come back and entertain him. Of course there were exceptions. Dudley and she always seemed to get on very well and I feel that their relationship might have lasted longer had she been more forceful. He was interested in the theatre, they both were. In fact I had known his mother through theatre connections years before.

I found Dudley very easy to get on with. He accepted unquestioningly our insistence that the girls be home at a certain time, a rule that was more a source of amusement than a burden. And when he came round for tea, he cheerfully put the crockery away while the twins did the washing up. There was another boy, Nick, who also fitted easily into our lives. He and yet more friends would often pop round and it was not unknown for me to have ten or more people for tea or Sunday lunch. I used to complain but it was really very nice to have them all there. Both girls had many acquaintances and they kept in touch with school friends when at College. Leanne and Rachael were always close to Beckie. Emma's particular friend was Alison.

After the first experience of losing Richard to her sister, Beckie became very wary of introducing her boy friends to Emma. But it was difficult to avoid the situation. I tried to dissuade them from going out together, which was not always successful, and the stream of visitors coming home made eventual acquaintance with Emma inevitable.

When David Harper left Beckie for Emma she was very upset and I was probably not as understanding as I might have been. I did not like him. But at least it now meant that Beckie spent much more time at home as naturally neither she nor Emma was keen on each other's company. Apart from occasional evenings out with Charlotte and Jo, therefore, who were two more close friends, Beckie would stay in with us. She must have missed the excitement of going to discos but I do think that she drew much comfort from those evenings in. A few nights before she died, there was a programme on the television about a girl who was terminally ill and had only about four months to live. It showed her preparing for death and seeing all her friends. Afterwards, Beckie and I talked about what we would want if we knew that we were going to die and could choose what happened after our deaths. Beckie said that she would like to be buried in a long, white dress in a white coffin to the music of Elton John's 'Candle in the Wind'. She wanted white candles in the Church which would be full of flowers. Her toy panda would be buried with her and an angel would be placed on her grave.

No-one can ever know when death will come but we never imagined for one moment that Beckie's was so close. And we certainly never thought that her simple, innocent wishes would be quite impossible to implement. The strange thing is that Beckie, Steve's sister Julia and I had often discussed life after death. This was mainly because none of us could imagine Elvis Presley, Marilyn Monroe, Henry VIII and Charles Dickens all up in heaven together! We all agreed that whoever should die first would come back, if at all possible, as a spirit. But Beckie has never come back.

I am not sure whether I approve of the idea of coming back. When I die, I want the girls to be waiting for me up there, not down here where I can never see them again, where they will never come back.

On her last night alive, Beckie was not expecting to go out. I do not know why Emma agreed that her sister might accompany her—perhaps it was because a party was planned? Perhaps there was some instinctive need to be together? But we did not prevent her going. "You can't stop me going out, Dad, just because I'm at Tech," said Beckie to Steve. She explained that, after studying hard that day, she wanted some fun and relaxation. And Steve conceded, with more foresight than he knew. "You go against my better judgement."

I find it hard to know what to say about Beckie now. Except that we loved her. Except that she and I argued at times. She was a fine girl with strong beliefs and principles.

At the age of 17 years, both my girls were fit and healthy and had taken part in many sports and activities during their short lives. Water-skiing, absailing, mountaineering, gymnastics, horse-riding, swimming, dancing. They both had trained voices which could be heard distinctly, even in a vast Cathedral like St Paul's. We can never accept that they would not have been able to escape from the danger of a fire. Or that, if trapped, their cries would not have been heard by those nearby.

We do not accept that Emma and Beckie disappeared quietly in a puff of smoke. We will fight to the end to learn what happened and to keep their memories alive in as many ways as possible. Had my girls lived, they would have contributed to the world. They would have found their place in life and would have improved the lot of those around them.

On 23rd January 1991, they were just two ordinary teenagers going out for a good time at a party with their friends. But what happened we may never know. As you read this book then, spare a thought for Emma and Beckie who died as they were born. Together as always.

CHAPTER THREE

January 1991

Vicky:

I don't remember much about the Wednesday which seemed like any other day in the Harper household. Bedlam! I do remember that Beckie and her best friend Rachael came home from the Tech for their lunch as normal, if you can call a plate of hot, chopped tomatoes a normal lunch. And I remember that it was cold and that we had the fire on. Emma sat in front of it, blocking out the warmth for anyone else. She had been given a very long hairpiece for Christmas by her Nan and I worried that it would catch light—"Fussing as usual," Emma told me in no uncertain terms.

I also remember thinking at the time that her omelette looked rather tasty. But I was going to the dentist at 4.30 to have a tooth removed under general anaesthetic and therefore could not eat anything. We were all laughing. They said how funny I was after I had been under an anaesthetic and were generally 'taking the mickey' as Beckie and Rachael went back off to the Tech and Steve came home for his lunch.

Emma had finished her Christmas job and was looking for other work. She was meant to go to the local Job Centre that afternoon but it was so cold outside. Ever the soft touch, I relented and said that she needn't go after all. Setting off later for the dentist, I asked her to be sure to have a cup of tea ready for her Dad when he came home and to lay the table for fish and chips.

And that was the Wednesday.

I vaguely recall two figures later in my bedroom asking yet again to borrow my last pair of tights or use the last of my hairspray. I asked them where they were going, to which they replied that David Harper had invited them to a party. I told them not to be late and that the key would be under the mat. Then they kissed me goodbye and walked out of my life for ever.

Steve:

After work, I had collected Vicky and exchanged the usual jokes with the dentist and anaesthetist about her drowsy state. I was glad to get home and send her to bed to sleep off the after effects.

Emma greeted me with a cup of tea which I drank before collecting fish and chips for our supper. The three of us—Emma, Beckie and I—finished our meal in an hysterical fit of giggles for some reason that I don't remember. And then the girls washed up and disappeared to their bedrooms to watch television while I worked.

At about 8 pm, the 'phone rang and to my dismay it was David Harper asking to speak to Emma. I had been under the impression that their relationship had ended and was rather surprised when Emma declared that she was going out to a party and that Beckie had been invited too. Tonight of all nights, while Vicky was sleeping upstairs, I did not want a row and therefore relented, explaining that I had spent my last cash on fish and chips and would not be able to let them have any money. Emma explained that David was paying for a taxi to pick them up and that, having sold a car, he would be able to repay a loan she had made to him.

The next hour was spent getting ready and eventually a taxi drew up. Both girls shot past me and out through the front door, oblivious to my requests not to stay out too late.

That was the last I saw of them. Two girls looking forward to a night out at a party.

Some party.

Thursday, 24th January 1991

Vicky:

Despite the effects of the anaesthetic, I woke up suddenly at 3 am and got up to check that the girls were safely home. But there were no girls. I was very cross. Beckie had to hand in an exam application at Tech that day and they had both been told not to be late. True, Emma and, on one occasion Beckie, had stayed the night with friends before but I had thought that, just this once, they could have done exactly what they had been asked.

However, I was still not unduly worried—they had planned to go out

40

again on Thursday evening and I was going to punish them by putting a stop to that outing.

Having got up, I couldn't go back to sleep and so I sat and watched early morning TV. By the time I took Steve his cup of tea, I was extremely cross, especially with Beckie who I thought had more interest in her course at the Tech than simply not to turn up at all.

Detective Chief Inspector Gaskins:

It was a cold, frosty morning, one of those lovely winter days when you wish the sunrise would last forever. As I drove into work, I could see a column of thick smoke rising skyward near to the village of Uckington. As I drove through the village, I could see there had been a huge barn fire at Manor Farm. The Fire Service was still there damping down. On arrival at work, I spoke to the Duty Detective Sergeant who was investigating the cause of the fire. At that time it was just a routine investigation.

That afternoon, I was called to the scene of the fire because one of the firemen had exposed some animal or human remains. As I travelled to the barn, I wondered what I would find. Little did I realise that I was about to investigate the unexplained deaths of two lovely girls and the effect this was going to have upon myself and two of my colleagues. Many months of hard work, new ideas, disappointment and emotion were ahead of us.

There was still hay burning in the corner of the barn. I was shown the 'remains'. The police doctor had arrived and together we had a closer look. All I could see was a number of silver coloured bangles. There was no body, nothing recognisable as a human being, but I could just make out part of a hand. I immediately had a strong feeling that there was another body in the barn. Because of this, I decided to have the remaining fire damped down in order to preserve evidence.

Who was it that had died? The doctor thought the 'remains' were those of a young girl, 6 to 10 years. I wasn't convinced.

Who was missing?

Vicky:

During the day, there were several 'phone calls for them including one from the friend who was due to pick them up that evening. I think I told

The burning barn at Uckington, near Cheltenham where Emma and Beckie's 'remains' were found on 24 January 1991.
(*By kind permission of Gloucestershire Police Force*)

him that, as Emma and Beckie had not had the decency to come home the night before, they would certainly not be going out again for a while.

I had already planned to stay at home because I expected to feel a bit dopey after having my tooth out. And I suppose that waiting around made me more annoyed. When Steve came home that evening he was also very cross with them. We decided to do our usual shopping, thinking that the girls would be at home when we returned, ready with some excuse. On the way, we called in at Steve's parents where Eric asked if one of the girls would sit for a picture he was painting at the time. I remember we told him how angry we both were and complained about the youth of today in general.

There was no sign of Emma and Beckie when we got back home. We ate a take-away supper and started to telephone round all their friends.

But none had seen either of them during the day. At about 10.30, we rang a pub the girls had been to before and asked if they were there. They weren't at the pub and had not been seen that evening, we were told. But they had been there the night before.

By now I was beginning to wonder why Beckie at least had not 'phoned us. Emma had no job and therefore might not have been in such a hurry to come back. But Beckie was studying at the Tech and I knew that she had arranged to meet her friend, Rachael. I also knew that the next day, Friday, was the last occasion she could hand in her exam form and felt that she was sensible enough not to jeopardise her career for the sake of a night out.

Steve:

Throughout the waiting, I was quite certain that, if anything had been seriously wrong, one of the girls would have telephoned us. I knew that one of them would make contact if they really needed us. That they would look out for each other.

It never entered my mind that both might be in danger.

Vicky:

Steve and I sat up until the pubs were shut thinking that at any minute the girls would walk in the door. Earlier in the evening, Chris, the brother of David Harper, had come round to ask if either of the twins was at home. I told him that they were not and I gave him a blunt warning to pass on to his brother. Neither Steve nor I liked David Harper's attitude towards our girls: he would not come to the front door to pick Emma up preferring to wait around the back. He had also dumped Beckie for Emma, a recurring problem when you have twin daughters, each of them pretty. It was only in special circumstances, therefore, that we allowed them to go out together with the same boyfriend—and clearly something had gone wrong again on this occasion.

By the time we went to bed, we had decided that things had gone far enough and we intended to telephone the police in the morning—mainly to give Emma and Beckie an unpleasant shock. But I decided to watch Central TV News before turning out the lights and my attention was caught by the first bulletin.

Human remains had been found in a burnt-out barn at Uckington, near Cheltenham.

David Harper lived in Uckington and the thought flashed through my mind that it was Beckie they had found. I called Steve and told him but he did not share my feeling and thought that it was more likely to be a tramp who had fallen asleep with a cigarette.

I admitted to myself that the idea of anything like that happening to us was ridiculous. And we went to bed. Exhausted, worried but still sure that the girls were merely having too good a time to behave responsibly—and that, during the night, they would creep in and all would be well.

Friday, 25th January 1991

Gloucestershire Echo:

"Detectives were today investigating the mystery death of a woman whose charred body was found in a burned out barn near Cheltenham. Firemen called to tackle the blaze made the gruesome discovery as they raked over smouldering hay yesterday afternoon. Two teams of police searchers have been called in to comb through the debris ... but so far the only clues they have discovered are 35 bangles found on and near the body remains. All forces in the country have been alerted and asked to look at their missing persons registers. Officers were making house to house enquiries in Uckington ..."

Vicky:

Woke up this morning determined to call the police if the twins had not come home. Went into their bedrooms. Nothing. Told Steve we ought to inform the police. He agreed.

I don't think either of us really thought that anything bad had happened. Steve went off to the office as normal—he had to go to Cirencester that morning to see a client but would call in at the office first. And when he had gone, I spoke to my Mum on the telephone who had rung to see if the twins were back. When I told her that they weren't, she agreed with me that I should call the police.

I called the main Police Station in Cheltenham and said that I wanted to report my two missing daughters. The officer didn't express much interest when I told him that the girls were nearly eighteen—but when I explained that they had gone out with David Harper of Uckington where there had been a fire, the officer's attitude changed. He asked me for my address and telephone number and advised me to stay where I was. They would send someone round as soon as possible. I 'phoned my Mum who said that she was coming round too.

While I waited for them to arrive, I cleaned the sitting room. And then I cleaned the toilet! I don't know why.

Detective Chief Inspector Gaskins:

Checks for outstanding missing persons revealed that two girls had been reported missing in Cheltenham. Urgent and sensitive enquiries were required and I was beginning to realise that the 'remains' were probably one of the missing girls.

During the early 90's, I had been reading articles about Victim Support for families of murder victims, in particular a report prepared by Liverpool University and Coventry Polytechnic which had identified areas of concern as to how families of murder victims were dealt with by the police. I decided at this early stage that two Detectives should work together with Vicky and Stephen Harper. At the time I was fortunate to have Detective Constables Barbara Harrison and Sarah Morris working on the Department. They were both assigned to the investigation.

That afternoon, I remained at the barn while Barbara and Sarah went to the Harpers' home.

Vicky:

At about 9.50 am, I switched on the television to watch Central News. They reported that the human remains found in the barn at Uckington were those of a female aged between 17 and 20 years. I knew then that it was Beckie.

I telephoned Steve at the client's office and asked if he could call in at home once the meeting was over and he was on his way back to the office. I didn't say anything else because I didn't want him to drive back fast and have an accident. The 'phone call over, I went into the bathroom, crying, asking God not to let it be true.

It seemed ages before the doorbell rang. I must have smoked endless cigarettes and paced the house a hundred times. But the doorbell eventually rang and Women Detective Constables Barbara Harrison and Sarah Morris entered our lives.

WDC Sarah Morris:

I remember that cold winter's day in January 1991, when Barbara and I walked up the steps to the front door of a small but smart terraced home in Tivoli. We were greeted by a woman whom I instinctively took to be Mrs Vicky Harper—perhaps it was her tear-stained face that said it all. This day was to be the first of many visits to a couple who have become very close to my heart.

Barbara and I had been tasked with the unenviable job of obtaining the fullest details of Stephen and Vicky Harper's twin teenage girls, who had been reported to the police as missing—not having returned home from an evening out. The timing of the local barn fire, the findings of human remains and this missing persons report drew suspicions that the Harpers would have to prepare themselves for some horrific news and a life of grieving and pain.

WDC Barbara Harrison:

I had been to the barn at Uckington, a burnt-out smouldering mass, where human remains had been found the previous day.

Today, DCI Gaskins tasked Sarah Morris and myself to go and see Mrs Vicky Harper, who had reported that her twin girls, aged 17, had not returned home last night.

The identity of the 'remains' was not known at this stage, but young female 'remains' were suspected.

It is unusual for two female detectives to attend to take details of missing persons. This task is generally carried out by one uniform officer.

Vicky Harper is an intelligent woman, she noted our dual attendance and it seemed to add weight to her worst fears. She opened the door, her anxious tear-stained face showing disappointment. We had not brought her girls home.

Vicky:

I answered the door as soon as the bell rang and immediately burst into tears telling them that the girl in the barn was Beckie. The two women took over at once. Barbara went to make me a cup of tea while Sarah explained that I would have to fill in a missing person report. Completing the form was very difficult because I had not seen the girls leave the house and did not know what they were wearing. But I was able to tell them that Beckie had two metal braces on her teeth and therefore would be easily identifiable.

The women persisted in asking questions about Beckie's state of mind—which seemed at the time quite irrelevant. But I realise now that they were simply making me concentrate on something other than the thought that Beckie was dead.

My mother arrived and tried to help but, as she had not seen the twins that night either, it all seemed a waste of time. And at that moment I found it difficult dealing with her grief.

After several more cups of tea, Sarah asked if either of the girls had kept a diary. She kept up the pretence that the girls had only run away from home and were actually quite safe. The two Women Constables did not seem interested in Emma and told us that several other reports of missing girls were also being investigated. Eventually Sarah suggested that she look in Beckie's room. I was so ashamed. It was a mess, a typical teenager's room, left in disarray after an unexpected invitation out.

Clothes were discarded on the floor, unsuited to the image she had wished to create. The bed was unmade. Lipstick was on the carpet and endless pieces of cotton wool on the bed. Sarah and I looked to see if Beckie had taken her handbag with her—she kept asking whether Beckie had any distinguishing clothes on or anything like that.

I told her again that Beckie had a brace, the best way of identifying her.

Steve:

I nearly passed out when I received the 'phone message to call in at home on my drive back from Cirencester. Somewhere along the route, a policeman on a motor cycle stopped me. I didn't know what to expect—but it seemed that I had been driving without my seat belt fastened.

When I reached home, Vicky was very calm and made me a cup of tea while the two policewomen read out some sort of statement that she had made. I remember I was unhappy at it. I didn't like the way it had been written. I think I told them to re-write it.

We thought at first that the twins had died in an accident. There was no rage in those early hours. Our attention and our emotions were focused on a situation which was for the time being unclear. It was this concentration that helped us cope with the growing realisation that things appeared rather different than we had first understood.

Vicky:

My memory of the next few hours is very muddled. Steve came home and the women started to question him. At one point while they were asking us whom Beckie had gone out with that night, the telephone rang and it was David Harper's mother. I think she had smelt smoke on David's clothes and had seen the TV news reports. I remember handing over the 'phone to Barbara Harrison who asked her a few questions. And I made sure that Barbara thanked David's mother for telephoning.

Later that Friday morning, two things happened which I believe helped shape my behaviour and self-control from then on.

First, Rachael, who was Beckie's best friend at Tech, came round to see if Beckie was alright. If she had been poorly or unwell, Rachael would hand in her exam form.

I was crying at the time and to be confronted by Rachael was nerve-racking. Whatever I said, Rachael was going to be deeply affected. I made a tremendous effort to stop crying and the practical side of my nature must have asserted itself. I told Rachael that Beckie had not come home and that we were rather worried. It would be best if Rachael returned to her class and asked the tutor to telephone me. I had not been able to find Beckie's exam form and, when she came home, I would make sure she delivered it herself.

And second, another visitor called. Steve answered the doorbell to see Gwynne, one of the physiotherapists I worked for. She had brought me some flowers and a 'get well' card after my tooth extraction. I remember falling into Gwynne's arms when I saw her, sobbing that Beckie might be dead. She was obviously deeply shocked and I think I must have turned away, gone back into the house while Steve stayed talking with her at the door.

Gwynne Tucker Brown:

On my way over to the Forest of Dean, I thought I would pop in to see Vicky who had had a small dental operation for a wisdom tooth. So I went to the house armed with a bunch of flowers and a little card to cheer her up. I parked and went up to the house. I could see people in the front room but didn't think anything of it.

I knocked at the front door which was then answered by Steve who, until that moment, I had not met. I explained why I was there and he said that Vicky wasn't at all well. So I said that sometimes these things take some getting over. He said no, it's nothing to do with the dental operation—and with that Vicky came to the door. She was crying and in a very distressed state. She said that there had been a fire and that the twins were missing. That one of the twins was missing. And that's how it started.

I felt as though I had been hit in the stomach. I couldn't grasp what was being said to me. I went in and two policewomen were there—and Vicky's mother too. The looks on everyone's faces left me in no doubt what it was all going to be about. Even at that stage, there was something very final about the whole thing.

Vicky:

Steve seemed to disappear for a while. It was, is all such a blur. Then he reappeared with a bottle of brandy and the police suggested I drink some. I loathe brandy.

The telephone rang and the call was for the police. Barbara came back from the 'phone and asked if Beckie had worn any unusual jewellery. As Beckie favoured a Madonna style at the time, this was easy to answer. Yes, she had worn about thirty silver coloured bracelets on her arm— which, looking back, I realise was the only clue to the girls' identities.

The Women Constables then left us, saying that they were going to get the bracelets for us to identify. I remember sitting on the sofa and crying out "Oh please not Beckie."

WDC Barbara Harrison:

Sarah and myself took details for a missing persons report and also took a statement from Vicky and Stephen regarding Emma's and Beckie's last known movements and the clothing they were wearing.

The unusual step of taking a statement for missing persons did not go unnoticed by Vicky. Vicky, Stephen and Vicky's mother, Mrs Steele, patiently helped us with the information we required, all the time desperate for news of their girls.

We were all pretending that it was not one of the girls lying dead in the barn but we all suspected the truth.

The telephone rang. I took the call in a separate room. It was DCI Gaskins. He asked me to find out if one of the girls wore bangles on her wrists.

Yes, Beckie did wear bangles.

I told Vicky and Stephen that human 'remains' had been found with bangles. Everything seemed to slow down.

I tried to remain objective. "We can't say for sure yet."

But we all knew.

Vicky:

My mother agreed that I should "have a good cry"—which actually made the tears stop altogether. I got up and made us some soup. It was tomato, I think, and the three of us sat round the kitchen table trying to get some nourishment inside us. It was all quite awful and I don't think I shall ever be able to eat tomato soup again. I was soon feeling sick—a dreadful mixture of too many cigarettes, a glass of brandy and at least twenty cups of coffee.

For several hours, we seemed to talk round the situation, discussing what was happening. My mother was very concerned about Emma's whereabouts although I do not think, at that stage, that I felt Emma might be dead as well. (In truth, it was many months before I really accepted the fact of her death.) I was also trying to come to some understanding with myself about how to react when the police were ready to confirm that the remains in the barn were Beckie's. At some point, the question was raised of calling the doctor to give me a sedative—for Steve and my Mum had already probably deduced that Emma was also dead. But this was a period through which I had to remain alert and in complete control and I would have nothing to do with sedatives or doctors.

When the police returned, they brought with them a plastic bag containing the bracelets from the fire. They did not seem to be very damaged, perhaps because they had been cleaned up first. There was no doubt that they were Beckie's. And I had no doubt then that she was dead—yet still I left the front door key under the mat so that she could let herself in when she came home.

Her tutor from Tech telephoned and I told her that Beckie, it seemed, was dead. But I was still also quite sure that, when Beckie did eventually come home, the college would understand and accept her back. It is difficult to explain these dual, conflicting sensations. Half of me could not possibly accept the fact that Beckie was dead—and yet I had formally identified the bracelets as hers. Perhaps this is the way our brains allow us to continue functioning at moments of unimaginable stress?

Later that afternoon, the police received another 'phone call during which Barbara came back into the room and asked us if the twins were identical. When the 'phone call was over, she joined us once more. "It's both, isn't it?", I asked. And she agreed that it did seem likely.

WDC Barbara Harrison:

DCI Gaskins had telephoned. There may be two sets of 'remains' in the barn. I put the telephone down and stood for about 30 seconds. I did not know how to tell them, I tried to form the right words. It was the hardest thing I had faced in the Police Service. I waited for inspiration, there was nothing.

I went into the front room. Sarah was doing her best to support Vicky and Stephen. I told them the exact details I had been told—not a censored, reduced version. Vicky and Stephen needed to be told things exactly as they were. They had a right to know everything and they were told everything from that moment on.

WDC Sarah Morris:

Barbara, a good friend of mine, was excellent in the way she handled the important issues, the issues Vicky and Stephen needed to hear. I was more of a back-up for Barbara and I tried to provide support and words, perhaps in an attempt to relieve some of the grief. But it was so hard in the first place to actually find words to say.

Detective Chief Inspector Gaskins:

After my second conversation with Barbara, we were satisfied that the 'remains' were probably Beckie, which meant that her twin sister, Emma, was probably dead as well. However, it was always possible that Emma might have escaped the burning barn and could be lying seriously injured somewhere nearby. A thorough search of the area was carried out. Eventually, further remains were discovered and we were satisfied both girls had perished in the fire.

WDC Barbara Harrison:

Sarah and I drank our first of many coffees and tried to answer the first of many questions from Vicky and Stephen.

It was a terrible day. At the end, Sarah took Vicky's Mum home and I delivered her car back to her. Poor Mrs Steele was very upset. Sarah took her inside.

I couldn't get the key out of the ignition. "Help," I said to Sarah. She grinned. Suddenly we both fell about laughing, it was a relief from the day's traumas. Eventually the key came free, there was a button somewhere.

Vicky:

The police faced the grim task of making a fingertip search of the burnt-out barn and its surrounding area. But now they were looking for some part of Emma. We learned later that a JCB digger had been used to disperse the smouldering bales of hay into the adjoining field, necessarily scattering any identifiable remains. The force of the water hoses had further disintegrated whatever pieces were still intact during the fighting of the fire.

Towards evening, WDCs Barbara Harrison and Sarah Morris left us, having taken my mother home earlier, and we were once again alone. The main story had already reached the media and we knew that we had soon to start alerting family and close friends before any more information became public. I decided that we should eat something before we started the dismal telephone calls and prepared some baked beans on toast. But every mouthful was evil-tasting and nearly choked us as we ate.

The doorbell rang unexpectedly and I opened it to see June, another of the physiotherapists for whom I worked. June and her husband had suffered the loss of one of their twin sons years before and this was no doubt why she acted as she did. From that moment, she has been a tower of strength to us both: she came in, cuddled us both and suggested that we stop trying to eat the now congealed baked beans. We all had a brandy and she sat and talked to us. I cannot remember all that she said, only that it made great sense. And later she went, not staying too long knowing how exhausted we both were.

June Kent:

I was going out to dinner that evening when I received a telephone call from Gwynne, another of the physiotherapists at the practice. Gwynne was tearful and distressed. She said that one of Vicky's twins was dead and that they were unsure about the other.

At once, I started writing a letter to Vicky but felt that I ought to call round with it to make sure she was alright. I didn't think Vicky or Steve should be alone and I suspected that they would be. This is because people stay away—they don't know what to say or what to do. Vicky and Steve were alone. Steve answered the door and I went in to see them both trying to feed themselves in the kitchen.

We sat together for about an hour. All we could tell for certain was that Beckie was dead—there was still some hope for Emma but not much as she had still not returned home.

I left later to go to my dinner party. The twins' dentist was also a guest. He had already been given some teeth to examine—which left us all in a state of severe shock.

Vicky:

That evening, Beckie's old school friend, Leanne, telephoned. We had completely forgotten that a school reunion was planned that night and that the girls were all going out together. Leanne asked if Emma and

Beckie had left. All her friends knew that Beckie was always late, yet none seemed to mind waiting about until she caught them up.

Steve did not know what to say and handed the 'phone to me. I told Leanne that the girls had not left but then she asked when they would be ready. I felt that it was far easier to tell her that the twins were missing and therefore would not be coming out that night at all. Leanne was obviously very upset, which decided us that we should ring the parents of the remainder of the twins' friends in order that they might break the news in the gentlest way possible.

We 'phoned round as quickly as we could. It was very difficult for us and some parents rang back in disbelief to make sure that this was not some dreadful practical joke. All Emma and Beckie's friends took it very badly and some were physically ill for some time after.

Next we set about the awful task of telling the rest of our family and close friends. I still do not know how we did it. I rang my father in London who was alone at the time, my step-mother being out at work. I cannot imagine what he felt at the end of the telephone. He was the first to ask the obvious questions how, where, why and when—questions to which we simply did not have the answers: it had been quite enough for us just accepting that the twins were presumed dead without trying to understand what had actually happened. Steve then 'phoned his parents who were so deeply upset that Mary nearly passed out.

There is not much you can say to people at the time and we felt that, however appalling and shocking the news was, it was far better to tell it and then leave them to digest it before contacting them again later.

I rang my Mum to see if she was alright and to explain that we were closing down for the night. She had arranged for a very kind friend to stay with her. And then we were able to sit down ourselves and have a few glasses of wine. I don't think we said much to each other. Except that we simply could not believe what was happening.

Steve:

It seemed that we began to counsel our friends and relatives and not the other way around. To this day, I do not believe I have actually yet been through the grieving process, whatever that may be. Time and time again, I have talked through the facts which next began to emerge. But not the emotions which they raised in me. It was as if we became the people who provided comfort for others as the full horror became known.

Vicky:

It was now some 42 hours after the fire and the police rang to say that three youths were being questioned in connection with it. Their identity was immaterial to us at the time. We understood only that they had been in contact with a solicitor. We had yet to learn that their accounts of what had happened would vary.

Tense and exhausted, we went to bed quite early in the hope of getting some sleep before facing a new and empty dawn. I can only describe that night as horrific. The house next door had been empty for about six months but, during that terrible afternoon, a group of students had moved in. We did not know this at the time and, having left the key under the mat for Emma or Beckie returning, were terrified to hear footsteps mounting stairs. I did so hope that it was the girls coming home but feared some sort of ghost or apparition.

We did not sleep much but lay clinging together like two lost souls on a drifting ship. I must have dozed off later but was awoken by noises on the landing. I had actually forgotten to shut the cats in the kitchen but was unaware of it at the time.

Only half awake, I thought I heard Emma say "Mum, Dad, I'm home."

"Thank God," I called, "come in and see us."

"I can't come in Mum, you can't look at me," came the reply. And so Saturday began.

Saturday, 26th January 1991

Gloucestershire Echo:
"Three youths were being questioned by police last night after the charred remains of a teenage girl were found in a burned-out barn. Police believe the body of a second young woman could still be in the debris after the blaze at a farm near Cheltenham. Police believe they know who the first victim is but they are not naming her until formal identification has taken place. She is thought to be from Gloucestershire and aged between 17 and 20. The second young woman is also believed to be from the county. A police spokeswoman said the blaze was being treated as suspicious..."

Vicky:

As far as I can remember, Saturday was the first time the forensic officers came round. We had been asked not to touch anything in the girls' rooms for a few days but I was beginning to feel uncomfortable: I wanted to tidy up the two rooms so that people could come round and say their goodbyes up there quietly. After all, we had no bodies or anything else to grieve over.

We had still not really thought much about how the girls had died or about the fire. It was bad enough that we would never see them again (yet still the key remained under the mat so that Emma and Beckie could get in).

The forensic men were very kind but I stayed out of the way as much as I could and Steve took them up to show them what they wanted to see. Eventually, they left with a black plastic bag full of stuff to help with their investigation. It was apparently proving very difficult to identify Emma as there was so little left of her. The police had even told us that, during the finger tip search, a tooth had been found. The twins' dentist had actually dropped a note of condolence through the door and Steve went out to speak to him because it was he who was examining the tooth.

But what was a tooth doing lying out in a field? Why wasn't it in Emma's head?

The police came in and out for most of the day. In the afternoon, Steve's parents appeared, obviously very shocked. It was difficult to know what to say to them and in the end we had some inane conversation about the Gulf War which was in progress at the time. Eric remarked how awful it was that Saddam Hussein had set fire to the oil rigs—and as we all found during those months, the word 'fire' crops up repeatedly in conversation. The talk became increasingly silly as we all tried desperately to avoid words linked with burning.

Eric and Mary also had questions for us that we just could not answer. We knew only, from something told us during the day, that the three boys were still being questioned.

Later on, June brought us a meal. I remember it so well—it was a lemon chicken dish from Marks & Spencer, the sort of luxury convenience food that we, with two girls having enormous appetites, had never tried before! It was simple, I just put it into the oven and waited. I think June even brought us a pudding . . .

These gifts of food, which began to arrive regularly from all the physiotherapists, were a very important crutch for us. I was quite incapable of thinking about cooking and, if it had been left to me, I don't think I would have bothered to eat again.

Steve:

The practical support they gave us brought emotional calm. Everyone is capable of offering practical help at times like that—but they tend to think that their emotions are more important and valuable to you and they bring you those instead.

Vicky:

The police rang early in the evening to say that they had two items which they wanted us to identify. They brought them round later. One was a piece of skirt which Beckie had been wearing, charred almost beyond recognition although a tiny scrap of material around the zip had kept its colour. The other item was a belt buckle which Emma had been wearing. There was no material left on it, just the silver buckle.

Looking at these pathetic charred remains, we began to wonder how much the twins must have suffered. Thoughts passed through my mind of a typical, huge Cotswold stone barn with two doors and the twins inside, their hair alight, scrabbling at those doors trying to get out. It did not occur to me wonder how the three boys had survived while the girls had perished. Indeed, the boys' involvement in what had happened seemed almost incidental.

We learned that a piece of paper with David Harper's name on it had been found near the barn. But of the other two boys we knew nothing. The names Daniel Winter and Wisdom Smith were unseen people, just two boys who somehow became involved with the tragic loss of Emma and Beckie.

After our wretched night's sleep, Steve telephoned our doctor to ask if I could take some sleeping tablets that she earlier prescribed for me after a knee operation. When she learned that the bodies burned in the barn were those of the twins, she was very upset. She assured Steve that it would be alright to take two sleeping tablets and she gave him her telephone number in case I needed her during the night.

Until that moment, our world and our tragedy had existed only within us and within the four walls of our home. We now began to realise that the whole of Cheltenham was buzzing with the horror of what had happened. The police warned us that, once the names were formally released after the weekend, the press would become involved and that our lives and our emotions would become public property. They were right. How naive we were not to realise it.

After they had gone, we felt exhausted and quite appalled that the news was spreading before we were ready. Obviously, people were telephoning their friends to tell them what had happened. It made us dread Monday when the names would be released for everyone to see.

And that was Saturday. I could not imagine how I could continue to live beyond it. I didn't want to continue living and hoped for temporary oblivion from a glass of sherry and two sleeping tablets.

Sunday, 27th January 1991

Vicky:

During these first few days, our families rallied round and there were lots of 'phone calls from them. We were invited to Steve's parents for lunch and it was strange to think that we were going outside for the first time in days. We had been assured by the police that the girls' names would not be released until the Monday and, although we went out feeling that everyone knew, we hoped that we would at least be safe from the press for one more day.

I don't remember much about the lunch except that, when conversation flagged, I stood up and went to the fire and said, "There's nothing quite like a roaring fire, is there?" This actually broke the ice and we had to smile at the stupidity of what I'd said. I think it made Steve's parents realise that, although our lives had changed for ever, we were still the people they had always known. Or at least we appeared to be.

We found over the months that followed that sometimes people were frightened of coming to see us as they did not know what they would find. We might be in tears or something. This affected us both to the extent that we always set out to help visitors as much as we could. We would try to get them to talk about their personal memories of Emma and Beckie, some of which we did not know, thereby helping them to remember the twins as pretty, happy young girls and not the terrible remains they had become.

After lunch, we walked back home. As soon as we were inside, we became aware that something was very wrong. Ours was a terraced house and the walls were not very thick. We could hear cries and sobbing from next door and heard the words "Did she say it was both the girls?"

Realising that the news had broken early, we went round next door to see what had happened. Our neighbour, Mrs Spencer, who was a dear lady, and her son, Chris, were visibly distressed. They said that a young woman reporter had been going up and down the street telling people that the twins had burnt to death and trying to find out something about them and us. We were greatly saddened, and still are, that an elderly lady who was very fond of the twins indeed should have been told in such a way. The reporter was not from our local newspaper which has given us wonderful support throughout. And once again we found ourselves offering consolation to other people—but at a cost to ourselves as we were later to discover.

No sooner had we re-entered the house than a girl from our local corner shop came to say that the same reporter was stopping customers as they went into the shop and asking questions about the girls. It transpired that she and other journalists also went to the local pubs and even to the butcher seeking gossip and information.

We had always kept ourselves pretty much to ourselves and there was really not very much that anyone could have told the reporter. But this was a most unpleasant first introduction to the press and, in desperation, we telephoned the police who quickly sent the reporter packing.

It began to dawn on us that, because the news was somehow getting out early, we would very soon have to face a lot of press attention. I felt that, if they were going to say anything about my daughters, I would rather the information came from us. And so, in great haste and with the doorbell ringing, I sat down to write a statement. But it was so hard knowing what to say—what did they want to know?

The police felt that a general background of the girls would be best and perhaps a photograph as well. The photo we chose had been taken at the wedding of Steve's sister, Julia. It is not one of the nicest and it doesn't look particularly attractive reproduced in newsprint. But in our state, it was the best we could come up with. We thought since about changing the photo but decided that, as the public had come to recognise that particular picture of the girls, it was probably better to leave it.

The police sent someone round to pick up the statement and the photo and to assure us that a policeman would be on hand if the press became a nuisance. We gave the statement to Hilary Allison, the Gloucestershire Constabulary Press Officer, who was and still is a great help to us.

The following statement was released by the press office at police HQ on behalf of the parents of Emma and Beckie Harper:

"With regard to the terrible tragedy that has happened, we, Vicky and Stephen Harper, wish to make this statement—
Emma and Beckie were born in Cheltenham. They were educated at Christchurch Primary School and Bournside School and College.
Emma had been studying Child Care on a YTS Scheme and was looking forward to caring for deprived children.
Beckie was studying for a career in nursing, hopefully to work with maladjusted teenagers.
They had both been members of Christ Church Choir for many years and had sung all over the country.
They were both very artistic and caring people, who were looking forward to a full life.
We, as their parents, are naturally devastated and would ask that in these tragic days you respect our privacy and leave us and our families to grieve in private.
We wish to take this opportunity to give our heartfelt thanks to members of the police and fire departments and all those people who worked so hard during the cold weather at the scene of the fire. They have made it more bearable for us. We also thank all our families and friends for their support in these awful times. Once again, we ask for your respect for our privacy and to allow Emma and Beckie to rest in peace."

During the Sunday evening, we had a call from some friends who had moved abroad and with whom we had lost touch. They asked if they could come round immediately. It was getting quite busy as one of

Steve's clients was also going to call. Obviously life was going to be hectic from now on.

The first friend proved almost inconsolable and, although we did our best, we were not able to help. After he had gone, our old friends from Spain turned up. Their names were Mal and Pete. They were both very upset but they talked about the twins a lot and about the fun we had had together. It was so nice to hear their memories of the girls and we were even able to laugh! Mal and Pete offered to do some shopping for us and, before leaving, they even presented us with two tickets to Spain. I don't remember what we said in return. We were so overwhelmed by their kindness that for once we were speechless.

Monday, 28th January 1991

Gloucestershire Echo:

"Two bodies discovered in a horrifying barn blaze near Cheltenham were those of twin teenage girls, it was revealed today . . . their identities were released by police as Emma and Beckie Harper . . . Three men were appearing before Cheltenham magistrates today charged in connection with the deaths. A 19-year old man faces two charges of manslaughter, two of arson with intent to endanger life and one charge of conspiracy to pervert the course of justice. Two 18-year old youths will appear charged with conspiracy to pervert the course of justice . . ."

Vicky:

It was about this time that the guilt started. Why had I gone to the dentist that day? Why hadn't I reported the girls missing earlier? Why, when they kissed me goodnight on that Wednesday, had I not hugged them and told them how much I loved them? Why had I not given Emma the money for a new skirt and why had I refused to lend Beckie a cigarette?

I suppose now that I knew the reason already. I was trying to be a good parent, trying not to spoil them and to teach them that, if they wanted something, they would have to earn it. Easily said. If I were ever granted the opportunity again, I would give my girls the world.

I also knew myself and that I would soon begin to challenge Steve. Why had Emma and Beckie been allowed out that night? Why hadn't he stopped them? Of course Steve had not wanted them to go out but he had not prevented them because they were just two lovely 17-year olds looking forward so much to an evening of enjoyment.

We were well aware that, once the names were released, a number of people would contact us. But I never expected the flood of 'phone calls, full of love and concern, which followed the first radio and television announcements. We saw one of those early TV reports and were stunned to see that the barn had no doors. In fact it was quite open. It was a 'dutch' barn with no sides to it and not a stone Cotswold barn at all.

At least, this new information dispelled the recurring nightmare of the girls, alight, trying to get out—but it also brought fresh horrors to our minds. Why hadn't the girls got out? What were the three boys doing at the time? We did not have the answers to those questions but we did by then know that the boys did not report the fire itself. In fact, it was about 42 hours later that they first contacted the police and then only through their solicitor, Mr Tim Robinson. Why *hadn't* the girls got out? What *were* those three boys doing at the time?

Monday was the day the 'phone calls started. Because of the amount of visitors and calls, Steve and I were taking it in turn to answer the 'phone—and it was Steve who picked it up that first time when nothing happened. No-one said anything. It just went dead. They say that tragedy brings out the best and the worst in humanity and I have found this to be true. Some of the more agreeable calls were from old and forgotten acquaintances, people who for one reason or another no longer featured in our lives. But others were from well-wishers we just did not know. I still do not think we realised at the time how much the public had been affected by the deaths of the girls and the circumstances surrounding their deaths.

I think it was on this day that I telephoned our vicar, Canon John Harwood. He and his family have been friends for many years. I used to work for them and the twins were very much involved with Christ Church, Cheltenham. Canon Harwood agreed to come round . . .

Canon Harwood:

Shall I ever forget those days in January and February 1991? The news of the fire and the terrible death of the twins came as thunderbolt out of the sky.

Emma and Beckie. I had known them as tiny children sometimes coming to the Vicarage with their mother and playing in the garden. Then, to our delight, as members of the Christ Church choir. They were of course inseparable and full of fun. They seemed so much to enjoy church life—on the choir outings and as Explorers and Pathfinders. Emma especially was a keen member of Eureka, the group for older teenagers where, with their peers, they contributed much to church life.

Emma would sometimes speak about faith and they would both read the Good News Bible. Somehow they picked up the essence of faith and enjoyed the Christian life.

They had their own special gifts, in dancing and gymnastics. Emma had done a YTS course in Child Care. She would have been good at that had she lived. Beckie was an artist.

Every vicar has his share of counselling bereaved people. But a child's death is always especially traumatic for the family and friends—and also for the clergy. What does one say to parents who have lost a child? Not much can be said. All one can do is to try to enter their grief and offer love and support in whatever ways are possible.

I shall not forget the pastoral visits to Vicky and Stephen—and the two splendid police officers who were involved in the case. As we sat around drinking mugs of tea, we were reminded of our common humanity in the face of tragedy.

Vicky:

That Monday morning, the two Women Constables, Barbara and Sarah, came round with a bouquet of flowers from the CID. I was so touched by the gesture that I think I burst into tears.

We learned that David Harper had appeared in Court charged with manslaughter and that he was also charged with arson with intent to endanger life. He and the other two youths were also charged with attempting to pervert the course of justice. Words. What do those words mean? I had no idea except that arson meant setting fire to something.

I had thought that manslaughter meant killing someone. But why would anyone want to kill the twins? I was quite puzzled but assumed that the boys would be found guilty that day, sent to prison and that that would be the end of the case.

I could not have been more wrong.

Sometime during the weekend, Barbara and Sarah had asked us if we wished to visit the barn. I was horrified at the thought but was begining to suspect that things were not quite as I had imagined—and the barn, after all, was the place where Emma and Beckie's souls had left their bodies. And so we agreed to go. We would go the next day, on Tuesday.

By now, so many people were calling that I decided to use a visitors' book in order that no-one would be forgotten. Looking at the book now brings strong memories of those early days rushing back and, with them, the enormous surprise Steve and I felt at the love and respect so widely held for the twins. It seems a strange thought but it had never occurred to me what they might be like at school or in college or in their daily work. Understandably, therefore, some of the letters we received still bring great lumps to the throat. It made it even worse to think that two such talented lives had been cut short so tragically.

During the day, the police received a 'phone call at the house explaining that Cheltenham Magistrates had released the boys on bail. I could come to terms with the release of Wisdom Smith and Daniel Winter—but not the release of David Harper. He was accused of the manslaughter of my two girls. I was horrified. The police were horrified. I think the whole of Cheltenham was upset.

The case was adjourned for committal until 22nd April. But why such a long wait? Surely they couldn't allow the boys to walk round the streets during that time? But it seemed that they could.

Detective Chief Inspector Gaskins:

Monday was a long and difficult day. I called in at the barn on my way home to speak to the officers guarding the scene. It was late, about 11 o'clock. The atmosphere was different, it was dark, cold and unfriendly. The search team had finished and I remember thinking to myself how glad I was not to be guarding the scene that night . . .

The burnt out barn at Uckington the day after Emma and Beckie's 'remains' were discovered there.
(By kind permission of the Gloucestershire Police Force)

Western Daily Press:

"Three teenagers appeared in court yesterday following the deaths of identical twins Emma and Rebecca Harper in a barn blaze. David Harper, aged 19 of Uckington near Cheltenham, who is no relation, was charged with their manslaughter ... he was also charged with arson with intent to cause damage and endanger life. He did not speak during the two hour hearing at Cheltenham Magistrates' Court. He was granted bail after after his father agreed to stand surety in the sum of £1,000. He must report weekly to Cheltenham police station."

Steve:

We didn't attend the first court hearing. You accept advice easily at times like these but, looking back, you must never miss that opportunity of watching what happens in court.

What was very useful, however, was meeting the man in charge of the police investigation. We met him on the Tuesday. He wasn't in uniform, he had a frank and direct manner and I felt he was a man I could trust. He invited me to 'phone him at any time I wanted. He would always tell me the truth.

Detective Chief Inspector Gaskins:

Tuesday saw the investigation fully underway. There was no time for emotional thoughts—until the afternoon when Barbara asked me if I could meet Stephen and Vicky at the barn and talk them through what had happened.

I will never forget that visit to the barn. Barbara and Sarah drove into the farmyard and dropped them off. I introduced myself to Stephen and Vicky and walked with them to the burnt-out shell of the barn.

They looked tired and confused. Both were carrying posies of flowers. I talked to them and explained where the first set of 'remains' had been discovered.

It wasn't so easy to describe where the other 'remains' were found, because they had been discovered at a number of locations, both inside the barn and where the residue of hay and straw had been mechanically moved out into the field some 200 yards away.

Vicky:

Today, Barbara and Sarah brought back the things which the police had taken from the girls' rooms for forensic examination. They had managed to identify Emma from a palm print found on a piece of paper in her room. This meant that we were now able to go in there and start tidying up. The flowers that Gwynne had brought on that terrible Friday were on their dressing tables but, apart from that, nothing had been touched.

Today was also the day of the visit to the barn and we had arranged for a local florist, Bloomers, to deliver two baskets of flowers for us to take along. The baskets were beautiful and the people from Bloomers were, and remained, very kind and thoughtful throughout. We had chosen the twins' favourites—pink and white carnations with gypsophila.

Having adjusted to the earlier shock that the Cotswold stone building was in fact an open 'dutch' barn, I was surprised yet again to see how large it was. Its size overwhelmed me. The farmer was too upset by what had happened to meet us but he had given his permission for us to wander round.

It was an incredible experience. I could not believe how close the farmer's house was or how near other houses and telephones were. Why had the boys not gone for help or at least dialled 999? There were cows in another barn quite close by and I was amazed that they had not been burnt.

The police showed us where the first remains had been found, then left us alone for a while. I cannot express my feelings about that place. It did not seem possible that my children could have lost their lives in such a cold place. I remembered that the search for Emma's remains had been called off overnight and had resumed at first light the next day. Had a policeman stayed on guard? Or had my poor little girl lain alone in the field in the cold and the rain?

Detective Chief Inspector Gaskins:

There was a slight breeze blowing and mangled pieces of cladding were swinging to and fro scraping against the steel supports. Vicky and

Stephen looked lost against the huge inhospitable blackened structure that had claimed the lives of their children. I left them alone and they stood in silence for a while before laying the flowers on the ground at the edge of the barn.

That was, without doubt, the most difficult and emotional part of the enquiry and one that I shall never forget.

Vicky:

We did not remain at the barn too long. We just left the flowers and then the police brought us home. This had been our first meeting with the man in charge of the investigation, Detective Chief Inspector Bill Gaskins. He had been waiting at the barn for us. It is odd how he and his team—Barbara Harrison, Sarah Morris, Hilary Allison—and all the other people involved with the case were to become such significant parts of our lives.

Back at home, the police left to allow us time to be alone, to be by ourselves. The postman had called while we had been at the barn and without much interest we began to glance through the mail. The first letter we opened was from the college where Beckie had been a student. I had never imagined that people like that, her teachers, would write to us. In a college that large, I was surprised that they even knew who she was. The letter asked if the course tutor, Gill Benge, and the Head of School, Diane Bennett, could represent the college at the funeral—

—the funeral! My God. It really did seem at that moment that the twins were actually dead. Each day, I kept hoping that it was all some terrible mistake and that, as long as the girls were safe, they would be forgiven for all the trouble they had caused.

There were a few other letters that day, expressions of great kindness that amazed us. Teachers, other bereaved parents and even past employers wrote saying how much Emma and Beckie had been loved and respected. The girls had been a credit us, they said. Oh, how those letters made our day.

The Vicar, Canon John Harwood, was expected soon. He was coming that day to start making the arrangements. But just before he arrived, the doorbell went and we opened it to see June Kent paying one of her fleeting, comforting visits. I think this was also the day we found food left on the doorstep: Nichola Ellis, another physiotherapist, had cooked two meals for us which were so delicious that I am still waiting for the recipes. They were meals that I didn't have to prepare—and they weren't the sort of meals that the twins had particularly asked for. In truth, our eating habits were undergoing a complete change at the time, as everything else was in our lives.

While June was still with us, the doorbell rang a second ime and I opened it to see a young schoolgirl standing there. I have never seen her since but the thought of her brings tears to my eyes even now. She was offering a bunch of dried flowers and a card which she handed to June. And then, saying how sorry she was, she just turned and walked away. Her card was homemade, the sort which Emma or Beckie would have made themselves. It was a happy card with a pretty picture of flowers decorated with glitter. On it were written these words:

Dear Mr and Mrs Harper,

I'm sorry to hear about your recent trauma. I know nothing can stop you grieving but give a little smile for Beckie and Emma's sake.

So sorry,

C–B–

Even now the courage shown by that young girl makes me cry. To come to a house of death and mourning must have taken a lot of willpower and strength. I put her card on the mantelpiece and the dried flowers in a pot on the sideboard where they remain to this day. I wrote her name in the visitors' book so that I could look back in years to come and remember all those who thought of us during those dark, dark days.

Steve and I then sat down to discuss the funeral arrangements. Only a few days beforehand, Beckie and I had watched a programme about a young girl who was dying. It was a beautiful programme. The girl knew she was dying and she had all her friends and family round her right to the end. When the programme was finished, Beckie and I talked about what we hoped would happen to us. Recalling the conversation as Steve and I sat together that Tuesday morning, I told him that Beckie had wanted to wear a long white dress, to have lots of candles and to be buried in a churchyard with a large stone angel on top of her grave. We agreed that Emma would probably have wanted much the same. On visits out to villages and churches in their childhood, they had always admired the angels on the graves—and we decided that this was what Emma and Beckie were going to have too.

Neither Steve nor I had any experience of death at close quarters apart from one cremation we had attended. The thought that we would one day be burying our only children had certainly not occurred to us. It was therefore a very emotional time when John Harwood arrived. He spoke to us about the grief we must be feeling and explained that he shared our pain, as did all the parishioners of Christ Church to whom the twins had given so much pleasure by their participation in church life. We agreed to set a date for the funeral as soon as possible and we began to talk about hymns. He asked us which ones we wanted and whether the twins had favourite prayers or passages from the Bible.

I am afraid to say that, as far as we knew, neither of the twins had particularly favourite passages from the Bible. And although we had been to church several times and heard the twins sing in various cathedrals, we really did not know which hymns they cherished. We told him of our desire for an angel above the twins' grave—and learned that, even in death, the twins wishes could not be fulfilled.

If the twins were to buried, they would have to be buried in Cheltenham Cemetery which did not allow large headstones and definitely not stone angels. Cheltenham Cemetery is also miles away from our home and we wanted the twins to be close at hand where I could visit them frequently.

John then suggested that perhaps permission might be given for the twins to be placed in the Garden of Remembrance at Christ Church itself. But the problem then was that they would have to be cremated— and the thought of cremating their bodies, which had already been subjected to horrors of fire, was unthinkable. He reassured us that he would give us time to digest and reflect upon this new information and to think of hymns for the funeral service. He went on to explain the procedure which would still have to take place at the crematorium.

While this sombre talk was taking place, the police girls arrived with John Coopey, the Coroner's Assistant. It was fortunate that the Vicar was with us because Mr Coopey began to explain that a funeral would simply not be possible for a while as tests were still being conducted on the twins' 'remains'.

This upset me greatly. A week had passed and I wanted the girls home and safe. John Harwood then suggested that a Memorial Service in thanksgiving for their lives would be a genuine step forward in the grieving process. After discussing various dates and times for the service, he then left promising to return later in the week on the Friday.

We then sought Mr Coopey's opinion on cremation and explained what John Harwood had said. Mr Coopey firmly but very kindly agreed, saying that the girls' souls had left their bodies and that only the container was left behind. They would feel no more pain. And so we accepted that cremation was the answer. At least they would be in the Garden of Remembrance near the Church that had featured so strongly in their lives. They would be able to hear the choir singing and their friends could easily visit them whenever they wanted. And of course it was convenient for us. The Church is only around the corner which meant that I could see them and take them flowers.

But there were other practical matters to discuss. We could not bury the twins until Death Certificates had been issued—and this could not be done until the cause of death had been established. As tests were still underway, therefore, establishing the cause of death was impossible.

So began a never-ending circle of red tape which kept us from laying the twins to rest.

The rest of Tuesday is a blur. I believe I rang the *Daily Telegraph* to put an announcement in the Deaths Column. It was hard to know what to say in such a small space and yet I wanted the world to know what a terrible loss we had suffered. In the end we decided on the following:

HARPER—On Jan 24, tragically taken from us, Emma & Beckie, aged 17, of Cheltenham, Glos. Loving and much loved children of Stephen and Vicky. They will be sadly missed by all their family and friends. Born on the same day, died on the same day, together as always. Details of Memorial Service to be announced later.

Next I contacted the local paper to be told that, unfortunately, we were too late for the announcement to go in the next day's edition. I think I was upset over the 'phone but, when I explained who I was, the girl asked if she could ring me back. When she called soon after, she had spoken to the Editor who had agreed to hold the print until our announcement was ready. She also said that there would be no charge for the entry. This was a moving example of the general public wanting to contribute something to the memory of the twins and the gesture touched us greatly. The Editor and staff of the *Gloucestershire Echo* have continued to stand by us throughout and have been a credit to journalism.

During those first few evenings, Steve would settle me on the sofa with a blanket wrapped round me. The physical shaking from the shock had still not stopped and he would take over 'phone duty for the evening. And so it was that the next silent 'phone call again fell to him. This time, there was a slightly longer pause before the receiver was put down.

While this was annoying, we were more concerned that it might actually have been someone trying unsuccessfully to contact us. The 'phone was ringing almost constantly at the time—people calling who had seen something on TV or in the papers, or had heard the radio news and could not believe their ears. They rang us in the hope that it was all a terrible mistake. All of them offered help, love and words of comfort. The offers of practical help we accepted gratefully. Our local deli-catessen, for example, kindly offered to deliver our basic needs such as the milk and so on. I still did not feel equal to facing the outside world and so my employers came and went bringing with them a gift of food, perhaps a homemade cake or some biscuits. I had not been working for them very long and their support and kindness was of the utmost comfort to us both.

Exhausted by the stream of visitors and calls, we went to bed fairly early. The nightmare that night was, I think, the worst one yet. I dreamt that I was in a big empty house and that I had to find the girls before it was too late. The details are vague but I did manage to find Emma. She was trapped inside a black plastic bag and she was on fire. I tried desperately to open the bag but in the end all I could free was one of her feet.

I woke up screaming, my right foot an agony of pain, and did not sleep again for the rest of the night. We had often had family discussions about life after death and about religion, and talked about whether a spirit was able to return to visit its loved ones. Beckie and I and Steve's sister, Julia, had always said that, if it were possible, whichever one of us had died first would visit the others. And now I was terrified that Beckie would visit me. I kept thinking I could see a head peering round the door, some ghastly apparition of flames and smoking hair.

Steve and I decided to get up. We made a cup of tea and waited for the dawn with all its horrors and sadness.

Gloucestershire Echo:

"An inquest has been opened in Cheltenham into the deaths of twin sisters Emma and Beckie Harper, who died in a barn blaze in Uckington ... The Cheltenham & District Coroner was told by Detective Chief Inspector William Gaskins they had been seen in the barn but had not been seen afterwards and a palm print had been matched with documents at the home of the twins."

Vicky:

Today, my father and my step-mother, Pat, were coming down for the day. The date for the Memorial Service needed to be finalised and they had very kindly offered to pay for the flowers, the church and all that went with it. And so we set off to Bloomers again in order that Pat might meet Fay and her staff and discuss what was needed.

We all agreed that the flowers should be as bright and cheerful as possible—after all, the Service was to be a celebration of the twins' brief lives. As we were leaving the florist, a man came running down the road shouting something about another man on a motorbike. We just assumed that he had probably been drinking and we didn't want to get involved. But it turned out that a bank robbery had taken place and two security guards had been shot. What a violent place Cheltenham was becoming.

When we reached home, more letters had been delivered, this time a whole pile held together with a thick rubber band. Steve and I decided to wait until my Dad and Pat had left which would give us something to look forward to later in the day. We all went out for lunch to the George Hotel and ordered a bar snack. Not long after we had sat down with our drinks, a group of men entered the bar and started discussing the terrible tragedy of the twins. Dad and Pat started to cough and make noises in an effort to drown out the men's conversation but we were already shocked that, even in a hotel, the news of the deaths was the topic of conversation.

Nevertheless, lunch was pleasant enough and we returned home talking again about the girls. My Dad still had a lot of questions to which we still did not have the answers. He could not understand how the youths could have been let out on bail and why the case was not going to court again until 22nd April. We couldn't understand it either.

When they had gone, we sat down and opened the cards and letters left earlier in the day. We probably received about 25 cards that day, about 30 phone calls and numerous visitors in between. That was the amount of love and attention we were getting and by about half past eight in the evening we were completely shell-shocked by the volume of it all.

Trying to counsel our callers who were all very upset had the effect of numbing our own pain. And to help ourselves, we made the decision to allow ourselves a certain period of time each day—just for the two of us to express our feelings and to allow the tears which had been held in check to flow.

Thursday, 31st January 1991

Vicky:

I made rather a fool of myself this morning. I had to go to our dentist for a check-up following the tooth extraction and knew that he had been given teeth from the barn fire to identify. I wanted to thank him for coming round that first day with such a lovely note—but on the other hand, I realised that my visit this morning was a professional one and not personal. I decided to write a note of thanks and intended giving it to the receptionist on the way out. The waiting room was empty. I could hear the senior receptionist telling the other one that I had arrived and was very conscious that they were looking at me. They were obviously upset and so I tried not to catch their eye. About two minutes later, however, a mother entered the room with her young son who was not keen to put his coat on. This made the mother very cross—and, for some reason, the child and his mother's attitude upset me and I burst into tears. I wanted to tell her that she should make the most of every minute with her son, that it might be the last. Trying to concentrate on the posters on the wall in a vain attempt to conceal my tears, I stumbled hopelessly around the room. I now realise that tears come at the most unexpected times and that my self-control breaks down over the silliest things.

Steve was due to return to work the following Monday and thought he would have his hair cut. We have a good barber just around the corner but, on his return, Steve was very upset.

Steve:

In an attempt to escape the horrific events and to get away from the continual telephone calls and visits, I decided to go to the barbers. Not only did I need a haircut but it might at least allow me time to myself. While waiting for my turn, the customary chit chat turned to the twins' deaths. In a moment of anguish I told the people that they were my daughters and please not to talk about it. A deathly silence followed. I found myself apologising minutes later. Another example of how the whole town was shocked by their deaths when we imagined that no one else would really care.

Vicky:

Once again, I saved up the bundle of cards and letters that arrived—if there was any high spot in those awful days then it was certainly when the postman called each morning. Sometimes he even had to ring the doorbell if there were too many to fit through the letterbox! As we began to go through them, it started to snow. When the twins were little, we used to tell them that God had dandruff and was washing his hair—another silly memory that made me cry. I could remember their little faces turned up to the heavens as if hoping to see Him actually doing it.

The doorbell rang as I was reading the first card and I opened it to find yet another bouquet of flowers. We were overwhelmed by the amount of people who sent us flowers. We had always loved them and the house was now filled with them. The girls' rooms had several displays and every part of the house contained their scent. All the flowers were cheerful, fresh and young like the girls themselves—freesias, daffodils and many other blooms decorated our home.

Meanwhile, so many other friends were helping and comforting us too. Some were rallying round my Mum, bringing her backwards and forwards to visit us, or staying with her on the nights she could not bear to be alone. Others wrote letters, which affected us deeply—from people I had worked for in the past, from Steve's clients and workmates.

There were some expressing admiration for the twins in their working environment. There was even one from the staff at Coney Hill Hospital where Beckie had completed her work experience:

I knew Beckie for such a short time, during her two work experience placements at the hospital, but found her to be a very caring girl, always keen to work and very warm with the patients. It was a shock to all of us who worked with her at the hospital, but realise that your shock and grief will be with you for ever.

We never saw her at work at Coney Hill, in a hospital where they cared for the mentally ill, but the words of Beckie's superior showed that she would have made an excellent nurse and that the staff and patients loved her.

And there were letters from people who had similarly noticed Emma's love of children. From the headmaster of the twins' senior school. From the staff of the travel firm we always used for holidays. From Benson's Shoe Shop where Emma had worked for a while—

—there were verses in the Shoe Shop card which had obviously been chosen with great care and concern. God forbid that any one else should experience what we were going through but perhaps the sentiment in those verses will help them in the way they helped me at that dreadful time:

When day is done a figure turns and says a last goodbye,
Although we cannot understand where they must go, or why,
But as they leave our sorrow and our sad tears far behind,
They move ahead to seek the peace that every soul must find.
For now they sail a different ship upon a different sea—

A voyage filled with love and hope and new discovery.
And when that journey brings them to that distant lighted shore,
They'll be greeted by the outstretched arms of those who've gone before.
And people they have known and loved and voices from the past
Will be singing out the welcome news that they are home at last.

All these cards and letters were such a source of comfort to us and so, in a way, was the process of replying to them. There was some sadness there, too. Some friends obviously felt that they could not contact us. Some took our statement to the press to mean that we wished to be left alone. Even now some of my dearest friends have not been in touch and some have left it too late to be part of my life again.

Looking back, I suppose that I might not have known how to react had the same thing happened to a friend of mine. The loss of a loved one is something you must experience if you are to have any understanding. And the loss of a child is different again. As one friend said to us: "*When you bury your parents, you bury your past. When you bury your children, you bury your future.*"

CHAPTER FOUR

February 1991

Vicky:

Canon John Harwood came to see us again to discuss plans for the Memorial Service. The family had suggested several hymns and ideas but we were not sure what would be appropriate. There was one thing I was certain about, however—I didn't want 'Rock of ages' or 'Abide with me'. Steve's father, Eric, had suggested 'All things bright and beautiful'. And we agreed. It was a nice happy song that everyone knew and the last thing that I wanted was for people not to be able to sing. My Mum had suggested 'Majesty' from the Mission Praise book and, when John arrived, he told us that this had been one of the girls' favourites.

Christ Church, the choir and the friends of the Church really began to take over plans for the Service. We were so grateful, so much in shock still and unable to think clearly or confidently. And it seemed natural that Emma's and Beckie's friends at the Church would know better than us what the twins would have wanted. John told us that Sarah Haydock, a close friend of theirs from schooldays and also in the choir, had suggested playing one of their favourite pop songs. I thought John would have been horrified but he told us it was an excellent idea. The song which the twins' friend had asked for was called 'With or without you', sung by U2.

Our house had always been full of music. Sometimes it was unbearable because Emma's and Beckie's taste was not always the same—Cliff Richard vying with Iron Maiden doesn't actually sound too good! But 'With or without you' they had both liked and so into the Order of Service it went. Sarah kindly offered to find the tape and set it up. Indeed all the organisation was taken away from us. The Vicar invited the Headmaster from the twins' infants school to read the lesson which was a lovely thought. It had been a Church School and Emma and Beckie had been very happy there. My Dad and Pat were arranging the flowers. And Steve's brother, Chris, and his wife, Rose, offered to print the

Order of Service cards, something which we had just not thought of. All, it seemed, we had to do was to approve the design of the card—and Eric took that away from us, an obvious task for an artist who had exhibited in the Royal Academy!

Things were going along quite smoothly with the preparations for the Memorial Service which had been fixed for 11th February. But if only the same could be said for the rest of our lives. I found the mornings very difficult. When you first wake up, your mind is clear of thoughts—and then it hits you. Back comes that terrible realisation and you're left to face another awful day.

In truth, I had no desire to go on living. I had spent my adult life bringing up the girls and now I was lost, totally lost without them. The only things that kept me alive were Steve and the fact that each day brought with it challenges which had to be solved and more people who had to be consoled.

The silent 'phone calls kept coming too. And it was Steve who each time eased the pain of them. What were these people trying to achieve? Each day it seemed that they'd keep the line open a little longer. What did they expect Steve to say? The only thing that lifted us above that sort of experience was the love shown by complete strangers as well as by our friends. And, goodness knows, we were to need this love in the future.

Saturday, 2nd February 1991

Vicky:

Another of the 'phone calls. It woke us at half past six in the morning and Steve went to answer it to hear just heavy breathing. How sick these people must be.

Once we had been disturbed, it was impossible to get back to sleep again. And so we got up and tried to make a start on tidying the girls' rooms. We had talked for several days about what to do with the rooms—we didn't want to turn them into shrines but we did want to keep the house filled with Emma's and Beckie's belongings. Beckie's room, we decided, would become a study as it was the smaller of the two. For the time being, we would keep their things in Emma's room.

With the exception of the forensic examination, neither of the rooms had been touched since the girls went out that Wednesday night.

Beckie's was very cluttered, full of Marilyn Monroe and the usual teenage mess, and it was hard to know where to start.

I picked up her nightie from the bed. Holding it up to my face, I could smell a faint hint of deodorant and rather a lot of hairspray! It was terrible to think that Beckie would never wear that nightie again, never listen to her tapes, never do anything again. As I stripped her bed, I noticed that during her last period she had leaked a bit ... cleaning the mattress, I felt as though I was somehow washing away the last vestige of her life.

I started on her bookcase and came across what appeared to be a Will. It said that, on her death, she wanted all her clothes and make-up to go to Emma and me—and that, if there was anything worth selling, the proceeds should go to her Dad as she had nothing else to leave a man. Any money she had saved was to be given to Cancer Research and the Aids Foundation—and also to Cystic Fibrosis sufferers, the same shadow which had darkened both their early years. Her wishes in respect of those charities have been carried out. Beckie also asked that we should not grieve for her because she believed in reincarnation and that she would die peacefully and not in a violent way. How wrong she was.

It was only later that I found that this 'Will' had been part of some school exercise—but perhaps she also had at the time some premonition of an early death?

I cried all the time while I sorted through their things. In Beckie's private box, I found photos I had never seen before, photos of Steve and me. And of her best boyfriend, Pat, in America. Letters from Pat. Her identification wristband from the time she'd had two teeth taken out in hospital. All sorts of things that had meant something to her. I wanted to keep everything but in the end felt that all schoolwork had to go except for certificates and reports. Even if Beckie came home now, I knew that her teachers would understand and allow her to copy up the missing subjects ...

This continuing belief that Emma and Beckie were not dead saved me, I think, in those first few weeks.

We had already agreed to give their clothes to the local homeless project. The girls had donated clothes before and it seemed better that some needy teenager should wear them rather than us throw them away. But I have lived in dread ever since of seeing someone walk down the road dressed in their clothes. I washed everything, even the clean

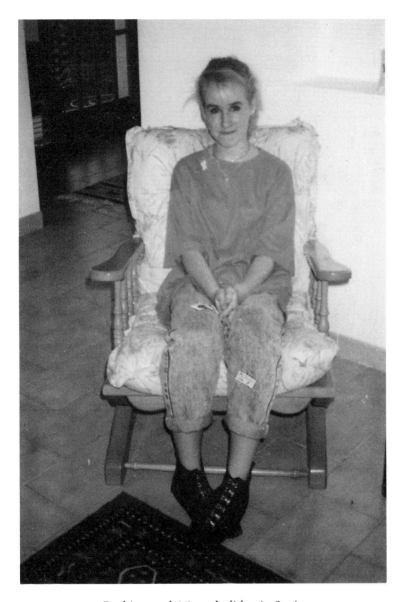

Beckie, aged 16, on holiday in Spain.

clothes, and began packing them in plastic bags. I was working faster. It seemed urgent to get things straight. People said I was wrong. That I shouldn't clear things out so soon—

—but I still feel it was right for me at the time. I separated out all Beckie's photographs and put them in boxes so that I could make scrapbooks of their short lives. I discovered awards that I had forgotten about. And I realised how talented they had been from the dozens of their drawings stuffed away in boxes everywhere. I did so long to tell them how much I loved them both.

Steve's brother and his wife planned to take us out to lunch that day so that, with Steve's parents there too, we could all discuss the Memorial Service. Pulling into the car park of the pub near Cheltenham where we'd agreed to meet, we saw Chris and Rose getting out of their car. We saw also that their two children were with them. This made me burst into tears. I don't know why: I am not exactly the 'earth mother' type and other people's children have never really interested me. But seeing these two young ones was suddenly a real kick in the teeth.

During the meal, it seemed as if the two children never stopped saying "Mummy!" and "Daddy!" Nevertheless, we spent a comforting lunch-time with their parents and with Eric and Mary. Without their combined help and expertise, the Memorial Service would not have been the memorable event it was.

After lunch, we all returned home to Cheltenham where the younger boy, Simon, passed the time with his finger in the cat's mouth while his brother, James, became quickly bored with grown-up talk. In desperation, I went into Emma's room remembering that she kept a drawer full of plans and distractions for the time she would have her own nursery school. Among the handwritten worksheets and homemade reading cards, I found a set of snap cards in a plastic case. Each card had been lovingly designed and made by Emma and they so fascinated the two boys that, when James asked if he might take them home, I agreed. Emma would have been happy to think that her children's work was being used.

When the family had gone, Steve told me that Chris had brought some photos of the twins and a video taken at James's second birthday party. Each year on his birthday, the whole family got together and the twins were always keen to look after the assembled children. But I wasn't sure whether I was ready to see my dead girls alive on film. Steve poured two glasses of wine and, with cigarettes to hand, we set the tape going.

What joy and, oh, what pain I felt as I watched them care for those toddlers. Emma forever fiddling with her hair, Beckie pulling her skirt down all the time. I noticed their feet—how big they were! There were moments, too, when they came across to talk to us or to other members of the party ... how beautiful they seemed.

That video is a source of great comfort to us both and we often watch it, to see them running and laughing in the sunshine of that day.

Sunday, 3rd February 1991

Vicky:

In the morning we went to Church. I knew it was going to be hard but John Harwood, our Vicar, felt that it would be wise for us to go and face the people before the Memorial Service on the 11th. He told us that several of the very young members of the choir had asked to sing at the Service which worried Steve and me. Some of them were very young indeed. How would they react? But the older girls in the choir had offered to stand by them and would be ready to take them out if they got too upset. I was touched that so many people wanted to be there.

As this morning's service was a Communion Service and neither of us is confirmed, I suggested to Steve that we should sit quietly at the back of the church and perhaps even leave when everyone else went up. As we entered, I felt very nervous—but everyone was so kind. We sat in the corner at the back and settled down for the Service to begin. By coincidence, one of the hymns that day had been a favourite of the twins and I found it hard not to cry. It was then that I noticed that in the row in front of us a young girl was quietly sobbing, too. I wondered what terrible thing had happened to her to make her so unhappy and she continued to cry as the Service progressed.

During the sermon and prayers, John announced the time of the Memorial Service and asked the congregation to pray for us. And then, at the point when you wish peace upon those around you, the young girl in front turned to us—and I knew her. She was Lizzie, a great friend of the twins. It had never occurred to me that she had been crying for them. Turning, I saw Sarah, another good friend of the girls and she too gave me a cuddle, the tears running down her face.

Many of the congregation were weeping and, as the others left to go to the altar, I finally broke down. I could not hide my grief any longer and felt it better to leave them. I shall never forget the feeling of love present in that church that day.

83

Trish Helps:

My husband, Ken, and I were in the congregation when John Harwood spoke of the terrible deaths of Emma and Beckie. We didn't know the twins but have since recognised them from the portraits and photographs in their home. We were appalled, like everyone else, and perhaps more so—because news of the death of any young person would trigger emotions associated with the death three and a half years earlier of our own seventeen year old son, Roland.

After the Service, we asked Canon Harwood if there was anything we could do. He agreed to let us know if Stephen and Vicky would like us to visit them.

Vicky:

At lunchtime, close friends from Wales came to see us. It was an emotional reunion during which we went out to lunch at the nearby Lansdown Hotel. Beckie had worked at the Lansdown for some months and it seemed strange that she was no longer there. The Lansdown was also where we had held our last Christmas lunch together, a celebration at which I had wanted to be waited upon for a change. Today's was a quiet lunch in contrast. Afterwards, Steve took George to visit the barn in order that he could lay some flowers there. I believe that other baskets of flowers had been left and I am grateful to the farmer for allowing people to visit. On their return, George and Lynn went up to the girls' rooms which I had tidied in readiness.

And then they left after a cup of tea. Alone again, Steve and I were mentally exhausted and I remember nothing else.

Monday, 4th February 1991

Vicky:

First day on my own. Very scared. I tried not to let Steve know—and, as soon as he was out of the door, I collapsed in tears.

I am not sure why I was so scared but suddenly the house seemed very quiet.

I decided to tackle some more of Beckie's room and started going through the dozens of tapes scattered around. There were several without any names on and so I took pot luck and put one into the cassette player.

Immediately, the room was filled with the sound of Beckie's voice. She must have been taping a record and thought that she could do much better. How eerie it was hearing her singing. Suddenly in the background, I could hear a commotion: obviously fed up with Beckie's warbling, Emma had decided to play Queen at full volume. Quite an argument ensued as Beckie set about telling off Emma in no uncertain way, but without switching off the recording. Eventually, I heard myself intervene and the argument stopped, only to be replaced with more uproar as they then ganged up on me! At this point, Beckie must have remembered that the tape was still running and turned it off.

I have to admit that hearing them again, so unexpectedly, was making me laugh and cry at the same time. It was typical of them—sometimes they couldn't stand the sight of each other but any threat or telling off and they would form a united front.

As I continued with my work that morning, I found many taped conversations between them. I also began to notice a peculiar smell in the room—it was a mouldy smell that was not unfamiliar. Every day, I used to ask Beckie what she wanted for her packed lunch. I would then leave something made up on a tray in case she and Rachael came home and I happened to be out working. On the days when I was at home, the sandwiches and yoghurt (or whatever it was she had asked for) would be eaten up. But on other occasions, when the lure of her favourite tinned tomatoes proved too much, I would sometimes find more normal lunches discarded in her room. I was more or less certain that the smell that morning was yet another unwanted meal—and there it was, hazel-nut yoghurt and a doubtful looking sandwich left down at the side of her wardrobe.

The significance of finding a mouldy sandwich is probably quite meaningless to outsiders but, to me, it was very hard to cope with. Each thing that I came across and threw out seemed to be erasing from the world a little bit more of the very little that remained of Emma and Beckie.

There were several visitors that day and each offered to help with the sorting out. My Mother particularly wanted to be included but I felt that this was something for me. Something that I had to do. Steve did not help much because he was shattered when he came home from work and I wanted him to relax during the evening. If he didn't, I could even see him cracking up. With hindsight, however, I think we both regret that he was not more involved.

While looking through Beckie's things, I found a favourite piece of clothing, an old black top which I had had to forcibly separate her from whenever it needed washing: the day it finally went missing, Beckie had accused me bitterly of throwing it away. And then I found hers and Emma's cameras, each of them with a film in. I was suddenly very anxious to see what pictures had been taken and was most grateful to Gail and Brian, parents of a close friend of the twins, who sensibly arranged for a number of films to be discreetly developed outside the Cheltenham area.

I realised that it would be some time before I could face sorting out all the girls' personal things and so I gathered them into storage baskets to be dealt with later. In fact, those baskets are still there now. Next, I set about taking down the posters that covered the walls. I think that Rachael visited me that day and I gave her the first choice of the posters. The rest I folded away neatly. The wallpaper suffered badly because Emma and Beckie had used sellotape to stick things up. Redecoration— and therefore more removal of something linked to the girls—was necessary.

I found a diary that Beckie had briefly kept after watching Anne Frank on the television. One entry showed that she had been thinking about her friend, Pat, in America who had not written for some time. I remember that she had come to me in tears and that I think I said that romance from such a distance was hard to sustain. Pat was also older than Beckie and perhaps best remembered as her first love—she would meet plenty of other boys. She must have been very upset with me and wrote in her diary that I didn't understand at all. And then I found an entry where I had been very cross with her for something which had hurt me greatly. I felt I should look no further for, elsewhere in the diary, the love we shared as a family shone through clearly enough.

As I worked, I began to understand what a strong faith in God they each had. There were lots of books on faith and growing up with God. It pleased me that that they had found comfort and reward in their dealings with the Church although my own feelings were far less certain.

Lots of letters were delivered that day, some from people we did not know and one from a family whose daughter had died very young. We

Emma, aged 17, just before she died.

felt an affinity with these people because no-one can imagine what grief the loss of a child brings unless they too have experienced it. Once you are involved with the death of a child, you notice how many more murders or tragic deaths of youngsters there seem to be every day. I often write now to the parents of children who have died violently offering advice and help. Some reply, some don't—but I hope that my letters bring some comfort to them.

That afternoon, the police came. They brought with them Beckie's leather jacket.

Apparently one of the boys, Wisdom Smith, had actually been wearing the jacket when they all went to the police with their solicitor. It had been examined for signs of scorching but there was very little to see. However, this didn't seem to fit the idea of being close to 30 feet sheets of flame which he said he had been trying to put out. Inconsistencies and the different accounts which were to emerge made us more and more doubtful. We came to the early conclusion that none of them was true.

In Beckie's pocket was the exam report ready to hand in at College the next day. She would have no need of it now—

—why did the boy have her jacket on? Didn't Beckie need it? After all, it was January and very cold.

Apart from the exam form, there was just a piece of tissue in the pockets, with some lipstick on it. It was of no use to anyone but the fact that Beckie had used it made it very hard for me to discard.

Another of those stupid 'phone calls tonight. They are very upsetting. In one, a woman even played funeral music and whispered "It's Beckie." The people who do these things must be very sick. I'm sick, too. Sick of living in this horrid world. I just want to die and be with Emma and Beckie...

Monday, 11th February 1991

Canon John Harwood:

The Memorial Service was painful yet strangely triumphant. A packed Church, complete of course with the choir. We tried to make it special with hymns and songs by request. 'All things bright and beautiful' somehow summed up the twins themselves. 'Praise my soul, the King of Heaven' spoke of our thanksgiving for what they had meant to us all. 'Majesty' was one of their favourite choir pieces.

I did not find it easy to give the Address—save to remind us all of the love of Jesus for children. To remind us of His own premature death upon the Cross and our hope for Emma and Beckie caught up in Christ's resurrection.

Vicky:

Woke up this morning, after an appalling week, to appalling weather. Rang my Dad who said they would not be able to come because the snow was 12 inches deep—they couldn't even get to the end of the road on foot. This was a great disappointment to me as I had very much wanted him and Pat to be there. We promised instead to ring that evening and would try to take some photos of the flowers.

I was getting very worried about other people not being able to get through. And my fears were confirmed later when my Auntie Joan called to say that she and her son, David, could not get down from Manchester. Chris and Rose, bringing the Order of Service cards from Maidenhead, reported that the weather was bad there, too, but that they would struggle through.

On opening the front door first thing that morning, however, there was a lovely sight outside. On the doorstep was a beautiful arrangement from the physiotherapists I worked with: miniature daffodils, irises, a tiny spruce tree and ivy, all in a basket. So fresh and pretty. Flowers and cards arrived all through the morning. A basket of flowers from Beckie's College. Flowers from family friends. Flowers left by neighbours—and even a 'phone call to say that flowers would be delivered later, sent from those we knew in Spain. To know that, even that far away, friends were thinking of us meant a great deal.

But I still continued to panic that people themselves would not come and that the church would be empty. Our acquaintances from Wales did arrive quite early and, after a cup of tea with them, Steve and I set off. Everyone else we were meeting at the church, a deliberately late Service so that any of the twins' friends still at school could attend if they wanted to without having to miss any lessons. The Vicar had offered to man the doors of the church so that we would have a list of everyone who had been at the Service—a wonderful idea that I would never have thought of.

As I got out of the car, the snow was crisp under my feet and the sun had not yet broken through. I didn't know what to expect, I still didn't know if anyone would be there. We went inside. There were some people already there but I didn't look at them. The front two rows had been reserved for the family but the bad weather meant that they stayed fairly empty.

I did not want to turn round and I did not know how many were

ORDER OF SERVICE

'With or without you', a song much loved by the twins—sung by *U2*

Introduction

Hymn 116 *'All things bright and beautiful'*

Vicar We meet today to give thanks to God for Emma and Beckie. We want to praise God for their lives and all that they gave to their family, to this Church through their membership of our Choir, to their schools and to their friends. We also want to pray for their parents and to all who mourn their loss. But above all, we want to affirm our faith in the Lord of life and death—Jesus Christ, their Saviour and ours, who lived and died and rose again—and to pray that we might live in the light of His resurrection with hope in our hearts and His strength in our lives.

So hear the word of God in these promises of Scripture:

Jesus said: I am the resurrection and the life. He who believes in me though he die, yet shall he live, and whoever lives and believes in me shall never die.

He also promised: Blessed are those who mourn for they shall be comforted.

St Paul wrote: I am sure that neither death nor life, nor angels, nor principalities nor powers, nor things to come, nor height nor depth nor anything else in all creation, will be able to separate us from the love of God in Christ Jesus our Lord.

A verse found among Beckie's and Emma's papers—from the Revelation of St John: I am the alpha and the omega, the beginning and the ending, saith the Lord, which is and which was and which is to come, the Almighty.

ORDER OF SERVICE

As our Saviour taught us let us pray . . .
Our Father in heaven,
Hallowed be Your name,
Your kingdom come
Your will be done,
on earth as it is in Heaven.
Give us today our daily bread.
Forgive us our sins as we forgive those who sin against us.
Lead us not into temptation
but deliver us from evil.
For the Kingdom, the power
and the glory are yours
now and forever.

Amen.

The Lesson   Part of 1 Corinthians 15 (from ASB page 312) Mr Colin Harding, Headmaster of Christ Church School

Hymn   *'Majesty'* Mission Praise 151

The Anthem   *'Make me a channel of your peace'* Mission Praise 153

The Address   Canon John Harwood

The Prayers   The Revd. Richard Inglesby

Hymn 192   *'Praise my soul, the King of Heaven'*

The Blessing

Choir   *'Gaelic Blessing'*

eventually to join us. But gradually the church filled up. The music changed and the choir entered from the back of the church: there were forty two of them who had made time to sing at the Service, some of the men must have taken time off work and even the little ones had managed to turn up. Tears filled my eyes but I tried to be brave for everyone else who was there.

We all sat down and the Vicar welcomed us. He asked that, for a few minutes, we sit and listen to the twins favourite pop song—and, strangely, as the first strains flooded through the church, two shafts of light shone through the church windows bathing the Cross in sunlight and creating a kind of mist over the flowers and the altar...

Canon John Harwood:

We meet today to give thanks for Emma and Beckie. But there's no denying also the shock and the grief we all feel about their loss and the manner of their deaths. Especially we feel for their parents, Vicky and Stephen, who have been through so much these last weeks.

It seems such a short time ago that their cheerful selves were with us, coming to church and making music with the choir. Ever since they were tiny things of about seven, and for the last ten years of their lives, they were with us. And when some of their friends laughed at them for going to church, they had their answer in a growing faith which clearly meant so much to them. Not only were they confirmed two years ago at Christ Church but they were genuinely interested in and committed to Christ. Indeed, on a 'thank you' note sent to a friend were verses of Scripture—we had one at the beginning of this Service. And another was a quotation from the Second Epistle of John: "*Grace be with you, mercy and peace from God, the Father, and from the Lord Jesus Christ, the Son of the Father, in truth and love.*" And in their bedrooms at home were many, many Christian books they had read.

But not only the choir. Like many others, they were helped by our Explorer and Pathfinder groups—and then by Eureka, which meant so much to them for its Sunday evening fellowship. What a challenge to us all. Many young people are totally dismissive of Christian faith. But here were two enthusiastic young things who went through the usual ups and downs of childhood and teenage years—for whom Christ was real and important. And they found Christ through this Church which nurtured their faith.

They looked forward to the years ahead, too. Emma had done a YTS course in child care. Beckie hoped to do nursing. The question we all face at times like these is—why did it happen? Why does God allow tragedies of this kind? There is no simple answer to that—at any rate not in a short sermon. But two things need to be said.

The first is that Jesus himself had His life cut short—just in His prime. To be crucified on a cross because of the wickedness of other men meant a terrible death. Nobody came to His rescue in that burning sun on Calvary's hill.

So the God we worship is not an unfeeling, celestial tyrant who knows nothing of human pain and death: He went through it all and He knows how we suffer because of human sin. And because He has gone through it in His own experience, He understands ours also.

The second thing is that, for Jesus, death led on to resurrection and life beyond the grave. "*I go to prepare a place for you,*" said Jesus to His disciples not long before He died. A life which will not be lived out in this same flesh and blood for all of us, has to perish. But a new, spiritual body is given to us on the other side. As St Paul put it in that lesson: "*This perishable nature must put on the imperishable, and this mortal nature must put on immortality ... death is swallowed up in victory.*"

Perhaps then, that must be our final thought. Our Christian faith looks beyond death. For Emma and Beckie, who were born together and died together, there is a further togetherness not only between themselves but with Jesus, our risen Lord and theirs. It is that togetherness with them and with the Lord, that we are called to believe in and to share. And when dark moments of grief attack us, as they undoubtedly will, to remember them both with thanksgiving. For at the end of the day, it is not the length of life but the quality of a life that counts.

"*I go to prepare a place for you,*" said Jesus—and Emma and Beckie will forever have a place in the memory of this Church and in the hearts of all of us. Even better, they forever have a place in the heart of God.

Vicky:

When the Vicar's voice became choked, we all understood. And when, during prayers, the Curate stumbled over his words, it was all accepted as a display of love. There was expression and meaning in the Lesson. Joy and pride when they sang 'Majesty'. And gentle tears during the Anthem as the teenage girls began to weep steadily—and the little ones

Emma (*2nd row, fourth form left*) and Beckie (*2nd row, fifth from right*), aged 13, with the Christ Church Choir, at Saint Paul's Cathedral, London.

touched their sleeves and comforted them. So much emotion, the church was charged with it.

After the choir had sung the 'Gaelic Blessing' and started to lead us out, the Vicar passed us and asked us to join him. We were not to be afraid to look up as we turned into the aisle.

So many people . . . so many dear faces . . . so many unknown faces . . . I could not believe my eyes. Steve was obviously taken aback and, for a second, we both just stood facing the congregation. And then John led us out.

I had thought it would be a nice idea to to thank everyone who had come although I realised now that it was going to be a difficult and upsetting experience. But, with tears falling, we took up our places in the foyer of the church.

Eric (from a letter written by Steve's Dad to a family friend, Mary Nash):

Hello.

In our youth, you and I have listened to hundreds of tedious and lengthy Services in Church—but we also became connoisseurs!

Monday's Service at Christ Church was one of the finest I have ever been to—it was remarkable and very moving.

Canon Harwood was inspired! Beckie and Emma have gone on their journey with all our blessings—Vicky and Stephen have now come to Hill Difficulty.

Thank you for helping them.

Vicky:

We calculate that there must have been about 350 people at the church that day. The whole Service was a wonderful, uplifting experience and it all came from the congregation and the choir.

We returned home in control of ourselves. In fact, we felt elated. Some people came back to the house while others went to visit Steve's parents. My Mum returned to her home with some of our relatives, too. Steve and I were having a large glass of sherry each when the doorbell rang and there on the doorstep was the most enormous wreath of pink and white orchids and dozens of pink and red roses. It was from our dear friends in Spain and was absolutely gorgeous.

But a problem lay in knowing what to do with it. There were no graves to put it on and all I could do was to display it on the dining room table. At night I kept it in the bath!

After we had made a last tour of the family that day, to say our thank you's, we were on such a high that we stayed up late talking over the events of a truly extraordinary day. My last thoughts were once again that it could all be a great mistake—that people would forgive the girls if they would only just come back home safely to us.

How I wish they had done.

Tuesday, 12th February 1991

Vicky:

Came down to earth with a bump this morning. After feeling so good yesterday, I just wanted to die today. The police came round before I was even dressed—and there doesn't seem much point now in hurrying to face the day.

The police told us that Daniel Winters and Wisdom Smith had also been charged with Manslaughter and Arson. I just don't understand what is going on. How can three individuals all decide to go off leaving two young girls behind to burn to death? Surely one of them must have been concerned at Emma and Beckie's plight? Apparently, the accounts varied and I have to know what happened. We understand that they are saying now that there was a huge sheet of flame and that the last they saw of the twins was the two of them, standing together and backing away from the flames. Well, why didn't they go round behind the barn then to see if they could get them out? They also said that they heard no screams or any noise at all from the girls. I can't believe that. If you were trapped in a fire and burning, I am certain you would scream.

The boys appear in Court tomorrow. I still cannot understand how any magistrate can grant bail to anyone who is charged with killing two people. I am supposed to be going in to work today but I really do not think I can face it. God, I hate this town. I just want to sell this house and move away.

Tried to sort out some more of the girls' belongings, underwear, bikinis and so on. How awful I feel, throwing away their things. I still cannot believe they are not coming back. How will I cope with life without them? The answer is simple: I don't want to cope with life without them—if I could be sure that Steve would get the insurance money and meet some nice girl, I'd kill myself now. I've got the means, I've looked up a medical book and I know that thirty sleeping tablets plus some alcohol should do it. I just want to be with Emma and Beckie in heaven.

Perhaps I should go and see a spiritualist and see if we can contact them? I feel as if I want to be wrapped in cotton wool and protected from all that is going on.

Listening to their tapes upstairs, as I carried on with clearing out their rooms, I found more conversations between them and several bits of singing. It's very odd to have the house filled with their voices—I would give the world to see them again. June arrived while I was crying upstairs, she is so understanding and kind. They have all been kind at work, bringing me food and gifts and generally making sure that we are alright.

June Kent:

Remembering is so important. We still talk about Jonathan, the twin son we lost twenty four years ago from meningitis. I started to keep a diary when he died because I thought I might forget some of the things he said and did—but you don't forget.

People stay away from you, too. They don't know what to say or do. And initially, you just want to talk about the child you have lost. That's what other people find so difficult. The mornings are the worst. Every time you wake up, you have to make yourself believe what has happened all over again.

And when you are in shock, your body shuts down, too. Physical things, like eating, become unimportant. But you need your extra strength to be able to carry on.

WDC Barbara Harrison:

I didn't know Emma and Beckie during their lives but, during the course of the investigations felt that I got to know them well. I found that when speaking to Vicky and Stephen, we all forgot that Sarah and I had not met the twins.

Vicky and Stephen always tried to make our job as easy possible. I admire their strength. They have welcomed Sarah and me into their home, patiently compiled statements, made us coffee, and fought through terrible grief and its resultant illnesses.

Vicky:

By second post, we received a lovely letter from one of the students on Beckie's course at Tech. It must have taken a lot of courage both to attend the Service and to write to someone he had never met and we were both very touched by his feelings. I hope he will not mind but I have shared his letter with you below. I wrote back, as I did to most of the letters we received—I still find it helpful to reply to people who took the time and trouble to write.

> *Dear Mr and Mrs Harper,*
>
> *I really hope you don't mind me writing to you, but I felt I wanted to.*
>
> *I was in the one half of the Preparation for Nursing Course with Beckie. Although I didn't know her for very long, it was obvious she was a very happy and caring person. Everybody really liked her, she was ever so popular as she was always so happy and caring. I'm just so sorry I knew her for such a short time. I never had the pleasure of meeting Emma but I am sure she was as nice as Beckie.*
>
> *I attended the Thanksgiving Service at Christ Church this afternoon. I thought it was a lovely Service but I couldn't help shedding a few tears. I really felt so much for you, to lose both of your caring daughters. My mother and I are so very sad for you.*
>
> *I know we on the Preparation for Nursing Course are going to really miss Beckie, especially Rachael. It won't be the same without her and I know Emma will be greatly missed too.*
>
> *I am just so pleased that I met Beckie.*
>
> *Best wishes*
>
> *Gary*

Sarah telephoned—Sarah who had been so upset at that first Church Service—to say that she had collected together some things that the twins had left at her house. She had also got some photographs of them in the choir and had some tape recordings of hymns and anthems they had sung. Sarah promised to come round when she was at home from college and bring the bits and pieces with her. In the meantime she was sending me a copy of something that Emma had written to Sarah when Sarah had been fed up with the Tech. Emma's words still hang on the noticeboard in the kitchen and have been a great comfort to us, too. We have shown them to many other people who have been ill or who have lost loved ones. I don't know where Emma got it from but the message is very true as I was beginning to find out.

One Day at a Time

There are two days in every week about which we should not worry—two days which should be kept free from fear and apprehension.

One of these days is Yesterday with all its mistakes and cares, faults and blunders. Yesterday has passed forever beyond our control, all the money in the world cannot bring back Yesterday. We cannot erase a single word we said, for Yesterday is gone.

The other day that we should not worry about is Tomorrow with all its possible adversities, its burdens, its large promises and poor performances. Tomorrow's sun will rise either in splendour or behind a mask of cloud—but it will rise. Until it does we have no stake in Tomorrow, for it is yet unborn.

That leaves us only one day—Today. Anyone can fight the battles of one day. It is only when you add the burdens of these two eternities, Yesterday and Tomorrow, that we break down. It is not the experience of Today that drives one mad—it is the remorse and bitterness for something that happened Yesterday, or the dread of what may happen Tomorrow.

Wednesday, 13th February 1991

Vicky:

The boys are in Court today. The police have told us that all three are now to be charged with Manslaughter plus Arson and Perverting the Course of Justice. I don't really understand what these words mean. My daughters are dead, that is all I understand. The boys' accounts continue to vary but none of this will bring Emma and Beckie back to us—and I still cannot understand why the boys didn't call the Fire Station or make any attempt to get help for the girls.

Once again, they have been granted bail. It is all so confusing.

I am pretty sure that this was the first day that Norma, an old friend of mine, came round for lunch. She was shaking and obviously very frightened. I tried to show her that I was still the same Vicky Harper although of course I had changed in some ways. And I tried to put her at her ease, joking and being as familiar as we'd always been. As soon as I mentioned Emma and Beckie by name, however, she seemed visibly relieved that I could talk about them. I said that it was much easier for me to talk about them than for other people to brush them under the carpet as if they had never existed.

And then Norma started to tell the memories she had of the twins. There were some I had never heard before, from times when Norma would look after them while I was off somewhere modelling. Norma was very down to earth and, once we'd started to talk, did me a lot of good. I had not realised my own influence over the way she had brought her own daughter and later her own (unidentical) twins.

Steve and I were beginning to feel that it was now time that we started doing things for ourselves. Everyone had been so supportive—from the local delicatessen who had kept on delivering things, to the police, family and friends who fetched and carried whatever was needed. But we could not face going to the local Sainsbury's where all the family had regularly shopped and where we were known to the staff. And so we went to another supermarket where no-one would recognise us.

Cooking for two proved a bit of a nightmare because I had spent all my adult life feeding four enormous appetites. Furthermore, neither Steve nor I could face any of the dishes that the twins had liked and we had never tried things from any of the other shops. And so we wandered among the unfamiliar shelves not knowing where we were going or what to look for.

I kept imagining that everyone knew who we were and, when some-one bumped into me with their trolley, I was very upset. I know now that it was an accident but, at that time, I was feeling very ashamed at being seen and identified. I felt as if I were the one in the wrong and not the youths charged at the time with causing their deaths. I even felt that people might want to hurt me.

In the end, I think we bought some toilet rolls and cat food. We simply couldn't find anything else to spend our money on. We didn't even need washing powder or things like that because we had been to Sainsbury's the night the twins died. I was actually finding it hard to get a full washing machine load together. Only three weeks earlier, I was doing at least two loads a day and, rest assured, that final piece of clothing which the girls urgently needed but which I had overlooked. What I wouldn't give for an argument about a lost sock now. No, not an argument. The girls always used to say we were having a fundamental discussion about life!

And then we came home, with cat food and toilet rolls, to another meal which had been lovingly prepared by some friend. To a quiet house and nothing to do or to look forward to—except another sad and lonely day tomorrow.

Thursday, 14th February 1991

Vicky:

Woke up this morning, hoping that no Valentine cards would arrive for the twins. That would have been too cruel. I needn't have worried. There were just some other cards—and some bills, too. Life had to go on it seemed.

After the boys' Court appearance yesterday, today seemed something of an anti-climax. Steve was at work and I returned to the sad task of clearing out Emma's and Beckie's bedrooms. We were increasingly concerned that the press would try to sift through rubbish bags outside the gate and we became just as devious in return. Unable to go the council tip ourselves, we began smuggling bags out of the back gate where Steve's father, Eric, would use his old commando skills to sneak them away unseen—except for the day that we locked the back door and he had to climb over the fence, attracting the attention of the entire neighbourhood!

It was while I was sorting through the girls' rooms and what remained of their lives that, for a split second, the mist that had surrounded me for the last two weeks or so lifted. I saw with frightening clarity that the twins were really dead. This sensation lasted only very briefly but it was a most terrifying moment for me. I collapsed as all the shock and the physical shaking returned. I think that, had I known exactly what the coming weeks and months were to bring, I would have ended my life there and then.

101

This shattering experience must have been the brain's way of coping with the terrible shock and the cloudiness, the mists as I called them, was a protective device. But unfortunately, the mists don't last very long.

I don't think I went to work that afternoon. I think that I rang Steve and that he came home from work to be with me. He had not yet experienced the feeling that the girls were really gone and so he was able to support me. It seemed that we never had bad moments at the same time, which was just as well. God knows, we needed each other...

Steve:

I was not to need Vicky in quite that same way until November 1992 when far more than just the deaths of twins was to hit me. That later experience was a violent explosion of emotion after nearly two years of supporting her in her grief. Mine must have been as terrible a reaction as hers was now.

Vicky:

As the days passed, I think that Steve was extremely worried about my being on my own and very grateful to our friends for keeping an eye on me. In fact, I felt very safe and secure alone in my little house. I could talk to the girls and do my grieving quietly and alone.

I relived all the memories of Emma and Beckie. Their different characteristics. Their relationships with each other and with Steve and me.

Beckie had very firm ideas about her appearance and great determination to live her life her way. She had enormous strength of character but could be a pain in the neck as well! Her best friend, Rachael, spent hours waiting for her in the mornings while I tried to chivvy Beckie along and remind her that everyone was waiting. But it was never any good. Only when Beckie was ready would she come sailing down the stairs quite unconcerned and, pausing only to give me a dirty look, exit the house with Rachael in tow.

Emma, in contrast, was always punctual. If anything, she would be ahead of time. On many a Saturday night, she would be waiting, neat and pretty, at the bottom of the stairs and pleading urgently with her sister to hurry up—only to lose her temper and threaten to storm off if Beckie wasn't ready in two minutes.

How I longed for the house, which seemed so very quiet and still, to ring with their noise again.

Before long, Gail and Brian brought back the developed films which I had found in the twins' old cameras. We were delighted by them. Some showed Beckie in her Police Cadet uniform or with friends at school or as a care assistant in the old people's home. And there were pictures of Emma with her group of children at the nursery school where she trained. Perhaps some of those friends or children will turn up some day? Each photograph means so much and I am glad that we were the sort of family who liked to record everything on film. It helps to look back on the happy times we had together. Times which, of course, are gone forever.

In the days that followed, I continued to agonise over why the girls had died and why Steve had allowed them out that terrible night. He suffered the worst of my depressions. I treated him as if it was his fault and, as I sank deeper and deeper into self pity, I blamed him for Emma and Beckie's deaths. I would become angry—why couldn't I get hold of the boys and find out what happened in the barn that night? And the next moment some other thought or connection would drive me under dreadfully.

I saw a television programme with a wedding scene in it. The enormity of our loss had not hit me until that moment. We would never see either of the girls as brides, radiant and beautiful on the best day of their lives. We would never see either of them with their chosen love. How often we had joked about their having a double wedding to save money! Now there would be no weddings at all. It also occurred to me that we would never be grandparents either. It was the end of the line for us. Nothing to save for, no-one to work for and nothing to look forward to.

I wished I had never watched that television programme. When Steve came into the lounge, he found me sobbing bitterly. We talked about our bleak future. We switched off the lights and went to bed with heavy hearts.

CHAPTER FIVE

Profit & Loss

Vicky:

I have felt so numb and yet still so awful that I haven't been able to write or even think. Everything is confusing. I don't know whether I am coming or going.

Last Wednesday, John Harwood arranged for a couple we had not met to come and see us—Ken and Trish Helps. It seems that they lost their son, Roland, in a climbing accident three years ago and John thought that that they might be able to give us some help and advice. We were rather nervous about the meeting but felt so miserable that speaking to someone who knew what we were going through would be a release. They came round in the evening.

Trish Helps:

We sat in the car outside their house plucking up the courage to knock on the door. Knowing, and still feeling, the terrible grief caused by the loss of our youngest of three children, we didn't know what we would say to two people who had lost all their family at once.

Ken Helps:

I didn't know what to expect or how we could help, but we felt drawn to meeting them. We paused in the car thinking of the horror that had happened to them. Inside the door they made us welcome. Vicky hugged us and Steve shook hands.

"I'm not the hugging type," he said. We had not been hugging types either until our son died. They took us into a front room.

Before we even sat down, Vicky asked Trish, "When does the pain stop?"

Trish Helps:

I think that one of the things that I had resented most when Roland died was being told by misguided people that I was not to mind, that I would get over it, that time would heal. My reply to Vicky was therefore rather bald.

"It doesn't. The pain never goes away but it does get easier."

Vicky:

After finding the meeting difficult at first and not knowing where to start, Trish and Ken turned out to be very easy to talk to. They told us about the death of their son and described how it had affected them. Some of things we spoke about would only seem relevant to people with similar experiences. Whether or not I should have kept the girls' rooms as shrines. Whether I should have given their clothes away to homeless teenagers. Trish and Ken shared their feelings with us. They also had some interesting thoughts about the press. Apparently the media had not been kind to them. And at the inquest into Roland's death, they had felt sufficiently inhibited at being under the spotlight that they had not asked all the questions they might have wanted to. Steve and I had not paid too much attention to the media. We had certainly put out a press release but, by doing it through the police, we seemed to have been saved a lot of bother—apart from that one woman journalist, of course. She had gone up and down the streets and into the local pubs and shops trying to dig up any sort of dirt until the police moved her on.

Now it seemed that we ought to think about what lay ahead for us—especially when it came to going to Court. But we still didn't want to because it seemed too much of an admission that the twins were dead. I suppose, too, that I was also hanging on to the idea that it was all a ghastly mistake and that Emma and Beckie would eventually come home to us.

Trish Helps:

It takes a very long time to accept that your child has died, to really believe it. You may know it intellectually but your whole being tells you that it can't be true.

Sometimes, I would hear Roland's voice calling "Mum!" so plainly. Other times, I saw him out of the corner of my eye, running past the window. One day, I saw a young man in town who bore a striking resemblance to Roland and I followed him, telling myself that perhaps it was Roland and that he had simply lost his memory.

Vicky:

When Trish and Ken left, we felt exhausted. I am sure they did, too. Trish had very kindly asked us round to their house for a meal the following week—she fully understood my complete aversion to cooking and my inability to do anything but cry. We were very grateful for their kindness and compassion.

Such heartwarming gestures and offers of support continued to come to us from many other quarters. We were trying at the time to get away, to organise our trip to Spain. Some old friends, Marilyn and Peter Quigley, came to see us as soon as they heard the news. Marilyn and Peter lived in Spain but were back in England visiting their son. They came round immediately, their arms full of things they thought we might need. They even brought us two tickets to Spain and they invited us to stay with them at their home after we had visited our normal holiday haunts!

It was a question really of reorganising ourselves. We had already booked a family holiday for May but this had had to be cancelled—we didn't know when we would be allowed to have the twins' bodies for burial or when the next Court appearance would take place. Eventually, we decided to go towards the end of March and spend the girls' eighteenth birthday in Spain. I simply did not feel that I could bear to be in Cheltenham on such a day. We had planned to give them both driving lessons for their birthday and that there would be a celebration. But now there would be nothing. I felt cheated.

If we were going to go away, there was much to be done. Having my legs waxed for one thing. This was actually quite important to me. It was part of going out into the world again.

I found a new person in the telephone book because I couldn't face going back to the people I had known before. I was nervous but Linda was very pleasant and we chatted easily. We were taking a holiday, I told her, and she said how nice it must be to be able to go for three weeks so early in the year. And then, of course, I told her. She was deeply

Drawings by Beckie which have been reproduced as Christmas cards by Vicky and Stephen Harper.

shocked but once we had got over that particular hurdle it helped me a lot to be able to talk freely to her. It turned out that Linda's cleaning lady's grand-daughter had been at Broadlands where Emma had completed her Child Care Training. The cleaning lady's grand-daughter, whose name was Laura, had actually seen Emma's picture in the newspaper and asked why Miss Harper, her favourite teacher, was in the news? Even stranger still, Emma had spoken to us about a little girl at school called Laura who had been one of her favourites!

What a small world it is. How comforting it was to learn that other people were still talking about the girls—and remembering.

The experience of talking to Ken and Trish, and then to Linda, had increased my determination to speak about the twins to people I met. I realised that some would be worried and fearful that I would start crying. But I found that, once initial awkwardness had passed, they too wanted to talk about Emma and Beckie and to share their special memories.

The twins' friend, Sarah Haydock, came to see me again. She had rung to say that she had some more of their belongings and that she had gathered together some photographs of them taken at choir rehearsals and other events. As Sarah had been so very upset at the Church Service, I was a little worried about her visit but everything was fine. She had obviously spent a lot of time rounding up the photographs—and a lot of money having copies made. Some of the photos I had not seen before: the girls rehearsing at St Paul's Cathedral, the girls at St David's in Wales. Sarah also brought all manner of bits and pieces that the twins had given her or left at her house over the years! There were a bracelet, a Spanish phrase book and many other items. Sarah had even thought to collect Emma's chorister's badge, her Dean's Badge, which is awarded when a certain level is reached and appropriate tests passed.

Christ Church choir is a member of the Royal School of Church Music and the choir had to take exams regularly. Membership of the School even meant they could be invited to sing at Royal occasions. Although we knew of Emma's achievement, however, I don't suppose that in the circumstances at the time we would have remembered to ask for the badge itself.

Sarah also brought me a copy of a tape the twins had made with the choir. It was called 'Parish Praise' and we had been unable to find it in the local shops. Sarah explained that, because the twins had been standing in front of the microphone, you could actually hear them singing! I thought it unlikely but agreed to listen to it later with Steve. And as if this wasn't enough, Sarah had also been trying to obtain a video of the choir performing in BBC's Palm Sunday Service but had so far been unlucky. I was so pleased with the things she had brought and very touched by her love and devotion to the girls.

After she had gone, I had a sneak preview of the 'Parish Praise' tape and was amazed. Sarah was quite right. The room was filled with the sound of the choir and its music but, sure enough, two voices sang out clearly above the rest. These were lovely songs they were singing and to hear the girls' voices was wonderful if a little eerie! You could even hear Emma about to have a fit of the giggles and both of them competing to see who could outsing the other.

How very fortunate we are to have a small part of their lives preserved in this way.

Gwynne Tucker Brown:

I remember when Vicky had to sort out all their toys and clothes. Things like bras and knickers, little things that make up part of a young wardrobe, the child's self, their jewellery, their bracelets. Those all made it more poignant and somehow so real, it was all that was left of them. It just seems as though they were—and then they never were.

Vicky:

So many people were ringing us at this time offering help or suggestions for tributes to the girls. We went for advice to Colin Harding, the Head of the Christ Church Primary School, who had read the the lesson at the Memorial Service. We really had no idea and needed guidance.

Evidently Mr Harding had discussed the question at length with his staff. When the previous Head had died, they had placed a plaque and a seat in her memory in a small garden at the back of the school. They had wanted it to be in a place where the little ones could have stories read to them in the summer. His suggestion to us was that we should plant a flowering cherry tree so that the children could sit under it. We thought this was a lovely idea, one that would have immediately appealed to Emma and Beckie. We agreed, too, that a plaque should go at the foot of the tree.

Colin Harding was very helpful to us. We had found some old school photographs of the twins but could not date them—and so he suggested that, when we were ready, we take away the school albums in order to try and find the dates at our leisure.

From Christ Church Primary, it was then on to Bourneside School and Sixth Form Centre to see Mr Watts, the Headmaster. The Parents Teachers Association had sent us a lovely letter in February explaining that funds had been set aside to plant bulbs in the school grounds in memory of the twins. However, we wished to put something ourselves into the school. Mr Watts had previous experience of setting up Trust Funds in memory of deceased pupils and felt that a Fund was not the answer for Emma and Beckie. We agreed that we didn't want to ask people for money either. We were prepared to consider something like shields and trophies until it became apparent that Mr Watts and his staff, some of whom had taught the twins, had a very different and original idea.

It seemed that the school possessed a picture of Sir Winston Churchill and that they wanted to create a Hall of Fame in which similar people, who had contributed a great deal to the world, could also be remembered. The twins' caring qualities recalled Mother Teresa, he told us and wondered if we would care to donate the nun's picture which could then be placed in the Hall with a brass plaque in memory of Emma and Beckie. But we had an even better idea. Steve's father, Eric, was an accomplished painter—perhaps he would consider doing an oil painting of Mother Teresa and we could contribute that. It would be a valuable asset to the school and an everlasting tribute to the twins.

Much heartened by the visit and determined to ask Eric, we returned home—and I went off shopping at Sainsbury's, determined to learn for myself once more how to do tasks which had always involved the twins.

I went with Steve's sister Julia, and her son Alex, but still felt as if everyone was staring at me. In fact, concentrating on new foods took my mind off things although I would walk away if anyone came up to speak to Julia—I couldn't have faced a conversation which led to baby talk and what would I have said if someone were to ask if I had children too?

Denying the twins' existence was unthinkable to me but so is telling someone in the middle of Sainsbury's that your daughters have died in circumstances which no-one will explain. So I would avoid that sort of situation. It was another example of the way in which my life had been abruptly changed while the lives of those involved seemed largely unaffected. It's six weeks now and there is still no news about when we can have the bodies. No girls to touch or grieve over. No final cuddle or goodbye.

June Kent:

It is sometimes very hard to cope with other people around you, even those close to you. People say emotionally difficult things—a girl wondered how they died. You can't lash out at these people, they are trying to help you but it's very hard. At times like these you have to be strong and controlled. It's an unbearable strain. But I think it actually gives you inner strength.

Vicky:

The undertaker came to see us, Ken Stephens from Selim Smith. Never in our worst nightmares had we ever imagined needing the services of an undertaker and certainly not for the funerals of our girls. Once again, I felt that things were moving too quickly—what if the girls were still alive? What if they came back when we had arranged their funerals. Oh God, it is all too awful to bear.

When Ken arrived, we tried to put on a brave face and to make him feel as comfortable as possible. He actually told us, once we had got to know him, that for the first time in 42 years in that line of work he had been nervous: it was such a rare and awful tragedy. That first visit, however, we didn't know what to ask him or what to expect. We explained the problems of getting the twins' bodies and how we were thinking of having them cremated so that their ashes could be interred at Christ Church where so much of their lives had been spent. He seemed very relieved when we asked him for his advice.

Apparently, he had managed two other funerals where the deceased people had been well-known for one reason or another. He had even buried a particularly famous pop singer, a household name, and told us how the media had been very much in evidence during the ceremony. He felt they had intruded on the grief of the relatives and he advised us to keep Emma's and Beckie's funeral as quiet as possible. It was Ken who suggested too that, because there was so little left of the twins, he should arrange to have the cremation conducted privately and for us to attend a simple interment at Christ Church.

We still had doubts and uncertainties about the thought of cremation and were greatly upset to learn that so little of the twins remained. What exactly did this mean? Contemplating what had happened to Emma and Beckie was horrible, we had no experience of death or fires and we could only imagine what might happen to a human being under such circumstances.

We were grateful for Ken Stephen's suggestion and for his advice about the press and the need to keep things quiet. We also agreed to speak to Canon John Harwood once more and would contact Ken again as soon as we knew when the bodies would be released to us. The following day at work I broke down for the first time but could not explain the reason why to my workmates. I did not want to upset them by telling them there was not much to bury.

They were as kind to me as ever. As were the countless people who called or visited us in those dark days. And as were Ken and Trish Helps to whom we turned for food and understanding.

Ken Helps:

We began to have meals together every couple of months—either at their place, usually with Steve doing the cooking, or at ours. I think they meant to ask us more often but it was easier for us to invite them. They would always come by taxi so that we could drink two or three bottles of wine over a slow meal. We would talk about what happened and about our children. Sometimes, in spite of everything, we would laugh about the crass things people said.

Vicky:

On 9th March, we had arranged to go to Willets, the stonemasons, to arrange for a stone to be made in preparation for the interment. It was a very sad morning. We had driven by their yard so many times before, never dreaming that one day we would stop there to order a stone for our own children.

The staff were very helpful and took from us the drawing that Eric had prepared, showing what we wanted on the stone. We knew there were rules and regulations about the size and colour of the stone and

John Harwood had recommended that we used Willets as they had done similar work for Christ Church before. We decided on the following:

EMMA and BECKIE HARPER

3.4.73—24.1.91

CHORISTERS

TOGETHER AS ALWAYS

And so, one more part of the whole terrible process was completed.

We knew that the arrangements were going to cost a fair amount of money and so we turned to our mortgage to raise it. Both Steve and I were surprised to learn that there was not even a Death Grant and that, despite the twins' deaths being suspicious, no help would be forthcoming. We didn't begrudge the money but it did seem a bit ironic that that we should have to take out an extra mortgage to pay for the privilege of burying our children.

We were very depressed by the time we reached home but more upset was to come. I had planned to go into town that afternoon to buy some photo albums so that I could start putting together the pictures of Emma and Beckie. When we got out of the car, it suddenly struck me that everyone in Cheltenham was preparing for Mothering Sunday the following day. There seemed to be little children everywhere, and some not so small, clutching posies of flowers or counting their pennies to see if they could afford a card as well as a hamburger in MacDonald's!

In fact it was dreadful—I just wanted to get out. As soon as I had bought a card for my own mother, we returned to the sanctuary of our home.

In previous years, my Mum and I would have gone to the Mothering Day Service at the Church where the twins and all the other young children would be given a tiny bunch of flowers to take back to their mothers. How proud I had been when the girls came down from the choir and presented me with their two bunches. I would also always give one to my own Mum—but tomorrow I would have nothing.

Mum came down briefly in the morning with some flowers for me. She didn't stay long, she could see that I was too upset to do anything but cry. Steve was very good, however, and did his best. But I just felt too tired and depressed to care about anything.

In the afternoon, I just lay on the bed upstairs and thought about the bleak future ahead. About the mothers of the three youths and wondering what they were thinking that day, whether they spared a thought for me. Their lives hadn't really been changed in any way by the twins' deaths. They still had their sons and their children while I had nothing.

I felt very bitter and tried to pull myself out of it. I don't want to become a nasty person, wallowing in self-pity and hating the world.

I just want to see the girls and find out what happened to them. I wish I could go to sleep and never wake up again in this world. But I know that I have to stay alive to fight for Emma and Beckie and to feel that justice has been done. And yet sometimes it is so hard.

I long to give them a cuddle and tell them how much I love them. Sorry, loved them. Sometimes I still talk about them in the present tense and then I feel I have to correct myself. Speaking on the 'phone the other day, I said I was the twins' mother. Then I corrected it. I said I had been the twins' mother.

The person I was talking to said that I had always been the twins' mother and always would be. He said I should be proud of the fact. I am, but it doesn't help overcome the loss.

Barbara Steele—Vicky's Mother:

Mothering Sunday

Never forget you are their Mother still,
however bereaved, however bereft;
forget misunderstandings of the past
for they occur in everybody's life.
Their love is still with you
their love surrounds you;
they watch with pride
your fight for their good names.

Never forget you are their Mother still
with a Mother's pride and
a Mother's anguish at their fate.
They are with God
and he is with you.
Carry your sorrow with pride
for their love surrounds you.

Ken Helps:

What parents of children who have died away from them want desperately to know is the truth. What exactly happened? No matter how awful the death or deaths must have been, a parent will want to know how it was. Nothing brings the dead back, but at least Steve and Vicky should know what really happened to Emma and Beckie on that terrible night.

Vicky:

On the Monday, Wendy was coming to cut my hair. She was a friend and had agreed to come to me because I couldn't face going to the salon. Her fiancé, Dave, came too. They had both known the twins well and Dave had helped us with work on the house. Steve and I were willing to talk about what had happened and relieved that Wendy and Dave felt able to share their feelings too.

We told them about a visit earlier in the day from John Harwood who had called to discuss funeral arrangements and dates and so on. We had explained that we still had no idea of when the twins' bodies would be released. We wondered whether to ask the Coroner's Assistant, Mr Coopey, if he had any more idea than we had—but were reluctant to trouble him.

And so we chatted on, talking over our reactions to events, as Wendy cut my hair ready for Spain. It was a pleasant evening. It played a part in enabling me to keep going although, at work, I seemed to be functioning on autopilot only—able to do my job but quite numb all the same. The majority of patients had no idea who I was and therefore talked quite normally, which was a help too although by the end of each afternoon I would be exhausted by the strain of holding normal conversation. I was always glad to have a day to myself—or at least time to think about the girls and to have a good cry. Steve kept his emotions under control very well—he had to, being at work every day. But there were times when it just got too much, even for him. One thing did seem clear, however. We were both strong enough to help the other when things were bad.

Some days are a great strain.

Steve:

From time to time, Vicky 'books an appointment' with herself, as she calls it. She still does it. It helps her. But I continue to this day to fear for her ability to keep going.

Vicky:

Having decided to use Beckie's room as a study, we had bought a new carpet for it. The fitter was due to call during the week but I was once again nervous of talking to strangers and was not looking forward to it. The house was still filled with flowers from well-wishers and I had not yet taken down the sympathy cards—would the carpet fitter know that this was the twins' home before he came or would it come out? He didn't know and it did come out.

Having started to lay the carpet, he commented on different wall-papers in the airing cupboard and I explained in turn that we had felt it was time to change the teenage décor. Then he asked if our daughter had left home yet and so I had to tell him. He was appalled and seemed quite angry.

While he was there, Barbara Harrison, one of the women constables, telephoned. Apparently, they had found a small piece of material in Beckie's hand and they wanted to try and identify where it had come from. My heart froze. Immediately, I pictured Beckie tied up, unable to help herself and unable to escape from the fumes—I couldn't think of any other explanation.

Not knowing what had happened was very hard to bear. Your imagination runs riot and fills your mind with unspeakable images.

Trish Helps:

As we grew to know Stephen and Vicky, they revealed more of their doubts about the deaths of Emma and Beckie. They desperately needed to know what had happened to them. From our own experience, we understood that it is indeed a desperate need.

Drawings by Emma made into Christmas cards.

You can begin to deal with what you know—even if it is very terrible. But if you don't know, you can't make the picture in your mind. It slides away and you cannot grasp it and you cannot begin to cope with it.

Vicky:

Barbara called to talk to me about the piece of material which the forensic people wanted to know about. Originally, they had thought that it might have been part of a scarf that one of the boys had been wearing. But all three had denied it.

Steve had found it difficult to describe what the girls had worn when they went out that evening and, as I had been semi-conscious, I couldn't help either. The police believed the scrap to be from a wool-based garment, possibly black but they couldn't be sure. As nearly everything that Beckie wore was black, this was not much help. I thought that they would both have had tights on and suggested that perhaps it could be part of those. But Barbara thought it was more likely to be from a woolly jumper.

Neither of the girls was into woolly jumpers and so I ran upstairs to check that my own big, black jumper was still in the drawer. It was. And while I was looking more carefully through the other drawers, I found the tights that Steve thought they might have been wearing. I racked my brains trying to think of something black and woollen that Beckie might have worn. Of course, the garment could have been something that the boys had had with them.

After much searching and thinking, I rang Steve and he remembered that Beckie had been wearing a cardigan that my Mum had bought her at Christmas. It had a net effect, almost like crochet. I imagine that if it had been pulled or put under strain it would have made a strong material that might just have survived the fire.

I was very anxious to know whether the police thought this was a significant find but they were not willing to speculate. It seemed so sad that Beckie had held this in her hand as she died, a dreadfully upsetting thought which it took all my strength to rise above in the face of a daily stream of visitors and their frequent invitations. Going out was just too difficult to cope with.

And so we carried on somehow, continuing with our false lives and longing for the time when we could get away to Spain.

Vicky:

At last we were going.

Flights had been difficult to book and the route we chose to follow involved a long, unknown drive. But we didn't care. The flight itself proved traumatic. We were both suddenly scared of dying before we got to our journey's end, which I didn't mind provided I could see our friends in Spain first. On the runway as the plane was taking off, Steve and I held each other's hands. We said we loved each other and the twins—and we made it to Spain.

I sat next to a very nice lady who lived not far from where we would spend our holiday. She chatted away and asked all sorts of question and, in the end, I pretended to fall asleep so that I wouldn't have to answer them. But she did also give us some advice about the best route to follow as a particular fiesta was likely to disrupt our progress.

On arrival, just as the sun was setting, we were given different advice by the car-hire man and followed his suggestions instead. Not a good move. It was a hair-raising journey in and out of floats and processions in Cartagena and round and round the town, avoiding celebrating Spaniards. I never want to see that place again and do so wish we had followed the advice of the lady on the plane!

It seemed hours later, after a fast and hazardous drive, that we eventually reached our destination. But our friends had all given up and gone to bed except for the barman, Antonio, who welcomed us with a glass of wine. In our room, they had placed flowers in all the vases to make our arrival a real home-coming. And then they began to call, one by one, reminding us of the love that I always knew was there. We have known these people for years but only see them for a few weeks at a time. Not long really but they have all become such very good friends.

Peter called. He is an Englishman but has been resident in Spain for many years. We sat up with him until 3 o'clock in the morning. He is one of the kindest, most sincere men I have met and his friendship and support for us is a great blessing. We talked about Emma and Beckie and sat for hours looking at their photographs, some of which Peter asked if he could have for his own collection.

He was also the first man to talk to Steve about the anger that was felt among our male friends. One expects women to show grief at the loss of two such lives but, for men, it's anger. Desire for revenge. Loathing of cowardice.

Those few weeks brought back many happy memories for us. We were surrounded by love and by people who cared for us and for the twins greatly. There was shock and sadness too, especially among the young people who had known Emma and Beckie. But there was also unforgettable generosity. Chris, Carlos, Sally, Andy, Fiona, Peter, Mal, Pete—they were all so kind that we wondered how on earth we should ever repay them. They allowed us to recharge our batteries and to face once more the looming Court dates, the prying eyes, the telephone calls and everything else.

There was a taste of what was to come when a French couple took a great fancy to Steve and me and would not leave us alone. They meant well, I know, but asked so many questions that, when they were told what had happened, the knowledge of our experience proved more shattering for them than us. It taught us how much conversation with strangers revolves around describing your family.

April 1991

Vicky:

I did not want to leave our other 'family' in Spain. One of our last visits was to a church in Santa Faz where a piece of cloth with the face of Christ is kept. We lit some candles for the twins and said a prayer for them.

It seemed so odd when their birthday arrived on 3rd April. We should have been preparing a great celebration for them but instead we were playing Trivial Pursuits and drinking wine on Mal and Pete's boat. I still felt it was all a terrible nightmare and, as the day passed, I felt worse. I spent the night crying, coughing and generally feeling lousy. In the end they took me to a local doctor who diagnosed bronchitis and doled out the antibiotics. Things did not improve and I think that our hosts must have been relieved when it was time for us to go.

Back at home again, I was meant to return to work the following day but felt so awful that I doubted I would be able to get there. And so I went to the doctor once more. She told me that I had a virus which did not respond to antibiotics.

Great. As if I didn't have enough to cope with. The next day, I had pains in my side and suspecting pleurisy, made yet another trip to the surgery. This time the verdict was a cracked rib! Just what I needed.

We were beginning to attract a lot of interest from the press. They wanted to write our story and to know more about the girls. At first we turned them away. We were just not interested. But as time went by, we realised that it would be far better if the papers printed the truth and not some story that they had made up.

I had a friend who was a journalist and telephoned him to ask which newspaper he thought we should deal with at the time of the trial. After some 'phoning around and much discussion, he recommended the Mail on Sunday. He had already called a journalist he knew there who had experience in preparing this sort of article—and so it was that Fiona Barton came into our lives.

It is very difficult sharing private and personal things with a stranger when you know that, at the end of the day, that person has a column to write and a newspaper to sell. However, Fiona was very pleasant and talking to her became easier than we had expected although the whole process was exhausting. We could not discuss much about the Court case because it was *sub judice*. But Fiona told us that she would be attending the Court hearing and the trial and that she would update her notes at the time.

It was a relief for us to be able to tell other newspapers that we had committed ourselves to just one. They left us alone after that. The question of payment had not been mentioned and at first we had not wanted any money. But we hadn't realised then how expensive the business of death can be—and so we accepted the £5,000 offered to us. It helped pay for the extra mortgage to cover all the costs.

We also hoped that, by telling the twins's story, we would help ensure that their memories lived on for a little longer in the minds of the public. It was only after I had lost the twins that I began to take more notice of other violent deaths reported in the papers. Two particularly affected me.

The first was the death of Raymond Kelly, a twin who was shot in the back by armed raiders at a garage. Perhaps it was because he was a twin, or because his life had been taken needlessly by cowards, that I felt I wanted to write to his parents. I wanted to tell his family of my sorrow at their loss. Although I had not expected a reply, I did eventually receive a lovely letter from Raymond's mother, Annette, with whom I still correspond to this day.

The second death shook me even more as it happened in Cheltenham and was therefore more alarming for being physically nearby. On his way home from a disco, a young man called David Nock had been stabbed and had later died in hospital. It was terrible to think of another young life wasted. Once again, I wrote to the parents expressing my sorrow—which was even greater when I realised that David, too, had been a twin. Gloucestershire police provided a team to help the family in the same way that Barbara Harrison and Sarah Morris had supported us. I find comfort in recognising that the policewomen's experience with us would have been immediately valuable to Kath and Peter Nock.

Someone was arrested for David Nock's murder and placed in custody awaiting trial. Meanwhile, our case was progressing very slowly and with a good deal of uncertainty about the charges which would eventually be laid before the Court. The three boys continued to lead their lives unrestrained—while we suffered in dreadful torment.

Life goes on however and it means that we became 'walking wounded'. Only Steve knows what I go through and he, too, is suffering so much. Will we ever be normal again?

early May 1991

Vicky:

Every Wednesday, except in the school holidays, my dear friend Norma has come faithfully round to see me, to eat my ham rolls and to suffer two hours of ear-ache while I pour out my moans and groans. And never an outward sign of strain on her part.

I am very grateful to her and to those other friends who came and went, some unable to cope with their own emotions, others strong enough to help us with ours. There were so many invitations, too, that Steve and I scarcely seemed to have time for ourselves. The most difficult occasions were when people avoided mentioning the twins. They did it with the best of intentions, I am sure, but it was so hurtful. By the end of such evenings out, I was screaming inside that Emma and Beckie were dead and all that I wanted was for people to acknowledge it.

However, some of our acquaintances found it natural to mention Emma and Beckie by name in the conversation. With two good old friends, Carrie and Simon, we were even able to laugh for example about Beckie's crush on Simon and about how the twins would always give Carrie a goodnight kiss while being marshalled upstairs to bed. Eventually Beckie plucked up the courage to give Simon a kiss too!

But others who had been similarly close and involved with our family could not, or did not want to, face us. The person I regarded as being closest to me has never made contact. I accept that she no longer feels a part of my life and that hers away from Cheltenham with children of her own is now quite separate. I wish her well. But I have to say how thankful I am, too, that there were some friends, from whom we had parted over some silly disagreement, who chose to return to us bringing back their memories of the twins' early days. How we laughed and gained pleasure from sharing such recollection and reunion.

Thursday, 9th May 1991

Vicky:

Emma and Beckie are coming home from Cardiff today, from the forensic laboratories where the police sent them. Steve and I wanted to go and get them but the experience might well have been too much for us.

Ken Stephens 'phoned from the undertakers to say that there were more 'remains' than he had expected. This meant that we could have coffins for the girls and a funeral service. Steve and I talked it over late into the night. The Memorial Service had been so special, so filled with love, that we each felt it would be better not to try and recreate the occasion. And so we decided not to invite anyone else at all. We would say our farewells alone to Emma and Beckie and have a small interment attended by the family on the following day.

We both continued to work and to function but both of us, Steve and I together, were totally preoccupied with thoughts of the funeral. I supposed that seeing the coffins would bring it home to us that the twins were really dead—no more doubt, just the awful certainty that we would never see them again.

Vicky:

Well, after all the fuss and bother over the funeral arrangements, today is the day and we are still not going to tell anyone else. We both feel that this must be our private farewell to the girls. We also feel that we could not cope with anyone else's grief at the service.

The cremation service was to due to start at 11 o'clock and we arrived at about quarter to. We left Roland Helps's flowers in the car intending to find his grave and have a walk round after the funeral.

We had never been to the crematorium before and did not really know what to expect. But as we drove up the driveway, we were impressed by how pretty it was and how nicely kept. We went into the main building to wait for John Harwood and were reassured by a very serene feeling to the place. There was music playing in the background—I think it was from the Hovis advertisement. On the notice board were the names of those being cremated that day but, at the request of the police and with our agreement, the twins' names did not appear. This would keep the press away.

Flowers surrounding Emma's and Beckie's grave.

Ken Stephens from Selim Smith arrived with Rev. John Harwood. We told them that we were ready and Ken asked us whether we wanted to walk into the chapel with the coffins or whether we would like them to be already in position when we went in. I felt that it would be more bearable for me if the coffins were placed on the platform beforehand.

We had been told that the coffins would not go into the cremation room until we had left. I did not want to think of the girls going into the flames again even though I knew they had to. After a few moments, we were taken out of the waiting room and towards the Chapel. A man was standing outside the door, to stop anyone else going inside. The door was open. And there they were—

—two beautiful coffins side by side on the platform, flowers laid neatly on the top. We had asked Bloomers, the florists, for a basket of pretty flowers and they had provided pink roses, carnations and gypsophila, the twins' favourites.

We were shown to a seat and Ken Stephens remained with us, a gesture which we appreciated. I don't remember what was said or whether we sang or whether we prayed. It was all over very quickly and then Ken and John left us alone for a few moments.

I approached the coffins wanting to see which was Emma and which was Beckie. Their names were on the top and I went to touch them trying to imagine how they had been before the fire had reduced them to charred pieces. When I had my hands on both the coffins, such a wave of pain hit my heart that I had never experienced anything like it before. The grief welled up inside me and came rushing out uncontrollably.

On hearing my anguish, the Vicar returned, took me in his arms and comforted me. I think that Steve said his goodbyes to Emma and Beckie and, with one last glance over our shoulders, we were led away.

And that was how my girls were given back to me the second time.

My pounding heart began to steady, I brought my sobbing under control and we managed to compose ourselves. Thanking Ken, John and the coffin bearers, Steve took my arm and we went out into the cemetery collecting the flowers for Roland's grave on the way. It did us both good to have a breath of fresh air and to be distracted while we looked for him. We poured water into the vase and arranged the flowers. And then we paused for a moment thinking of this young man we had never known but whose parents had been such a help and comfort to us in recent weeks. And then we started back towards the car—and we looked up, inevitably, to see smoke rising from the crematorium chimney.

Whatever remained of the girls had now been reduced even further to dust. The smoke spoke for us and told the heartache and sorrow that we felt. With the news later in the day, that the cause of the twins' death could not be 'ascertained', and that the inquest had been adjourned, I went, once again, to the bottle of sleeping tablets and found a few hours peace.

Gloucestershire Echo, Thursday 16th May:

"The inquest into the deaths of two teenage girls whose bodies were found in a burnt out Gloucestershire barn after a blaze has been adjourned indefinitely. And it will not be reopened unless an order is made by a judge instructing further investigation into the deaths of 17-year-olds Emma and Rebecca Harper. The inquest has been adjourned because of criminal proceedings and also because forensic tests failed to establish the cause of the twins' deaths."

Thursday, 16th May 1991

Vicky:

We started the day at Christ Church School at half past 9 where we presented a commemorative plaque to Colin Harding, the Headmaster. It was to go under the cherry tree in the children's garden and the inscription was simple:

In memory of

EMMA and **BECKIE HARPER**

3.4.73—24.1.91

Pupils at this School

1977–1984

We put the plaque under the tree which I hope will flourish and give shade and comfort to the young children whom Emma and Beckie loved so much. Then it was back home for a quick cup of coffee and some cigarettes. Our consumption of the dreadful things had increased as you might imagine.

And then we set off for the Church. Only a few people were coming to the interment which would be a very short service—my Mum and cousin Chris, Ken and Trish Helps, Marilyn ('Mal') and Peter from Spain, Steve's sister Julia, and ourselves. Because of the short notice, my Father and Pat were not able to get away and Steve's parents were in France.

Ken Helps:

I remember the small service of interring the twins' remains at Christ Church. The burial place was almost under the eaves of the church. It was a small gathering of just family and close friends.

Vicky:

We were very worried about the caskets which someone had told us would probably be made of plastic. We weren't sure either whether flowers would be in order and we had asked that people didn't bring them—but no-one took any notice!

Ken Stephens arrived as did John Harwood. John had actually moved away from Christ Church since the Memorial Service and we were greatly touched and honoured by his agreement to return to Cheltenham and stay overnight to help us through these last two rites.

And then Ken brought out the caskets from the car. They were beautiful caskets—tiny wooden things with lovely brass handles and the twins' names on plaques on the top. We had not thought about what should be put on the plaques but Ken had inscribed their names and that they were 17 years old. That seemed to us to say it all.

The caskets were lowered side by side into the ground as John read a psalm. Then we said a few prayers—and it was over. Once again, Selim Smith and John Harwood had brought dignity and warmth to a sad occasion and touched the hearts of all there. People went to their cars to fetch their flowers and many more tributes were laid in the course of the day. Ours were brought from the cremation service yesterday and the stone was laid once we had all gone.

The local press had been warned about the cremation and interment but we had asked that no information be released until it was over. They were very considerate and took the problem of what to announce, and when, away from us. We knew that at 11 o'clock that Thursday morning, the radio stations would play 'With or Without You' by U2 but we had not expected such gentle, sensitive treatment as the announcement which accompanied it. We had all gone back for coffee and sandwiches when the telephone started ringing—people calling to say that a report had been on the radio and how beautifully it had been done.

BBC Radio Gloucestershire, 11 o'clock news, Mark Tulip reporting:

The remains of teenage twins, Beckie and Emma Harper, who died in a barn fire on the outskirts of Cheltenham, have been interred in a service in the town within the last few minutes. The girls who were both 17 years were trapped in the barn on Manor Farm in Uckington when it caught alight on January 24th. They would have celebrated their 18th birthdays last month.

This morning's service for close family was conducted by Canon John Harwood who returned to Christ Church in Cheltenham especially for it. The girls' mother, Vicky Harper, said she hoped the Memorial Gardens at Christ Church will now be a place where their friends can come to terms with their grief after several traumatic months and can pay their respects. She asked BBC Radio Gloucestershire to dedicate Emma and Beckie's favourite record to them . . .

Gloucestershire Echo, Friday 17th May:

"The parents of tragic identical twins, Rebecca and Emma Harper, paid a final farewell to them at a private burial service at Christ Church in Cheltenham. The 17-year-old twins who sang with Christ Church choir died in a barn fire at Uckington in January. Only parents Vicky and Stephen Harper of Cheltenham attended the service yesterday. Burial was at the Church Memorial Garden. Mrs Harper said: 'We want people to know that the girls have been laid to rest and to let their friends know where they are if they would like to say a final goodbye or take flowers.'

Three teenagers are due to appear before Cheltenham magistrates on May 20 charged with the unlawful killing of Emma and Rebecca Harper."

Vicky:

We wrote to thank the BBC as we did to everyone involved in this chapter of our lives. We felt particularly that the Fire Service should be thanked. Theirs had been such terrible job, a nightmare as the TV pictures of the fingertip search at the scene made shockingly clear.

And later, in the evening, we went back to the church alone. Someone was inside playing the organ and the late evening sunlight shone on the newly laid stone. The words looked perfect, saying everything that we had wanted. Flowers lay around the stone—and so it was that Emma and Beckie were laid to rest.

There was no doubt now that they were gone. Never again would we see their faces, nor hear their laughter, nor touch them, nor feel their love in return.

How, in God's name, would we cope?

CHAPTER SIX

Kind Hearts and Coronets

late May 1991

Vicky:

We learned that, while we had been at the funeral, the inquest on the twins' death had been adjourned until after the trial. If only we had known, we'd have gone. We would have wanted to go.

It's the coroner's job to decide the cause of death but it cannot be easy when the boys' accounts continue to vary. We were told, too, that there was a lot of talk around the town about how the girls had died—and tales were even being spread about the College. I wanted to tell those concerned to make proper statements to the police or to shut up. It was horrifying to learn the detail of some of the rumours in the local pubs. Some of the stories were very cruel.

It was very, very hard to keep calm and to wait for the police to investigate. There must have been people out there who knew much more than was admitted. Why won't they come forward? What is so wrong with us in this country that we won't get involved?

I was amazed that more could not be done to find out the truth and yet I knew that Inspector Gaskins was working hard to cover every angle that he could. He had arranged for a scale model of the barn to be made so that the jury in the court trial would be able to see the seat of the fire and where the girls had last been seen. He had also arranged for test fires to be recreated at the Fire Brigade Training School at Moreton-in-Marsh so that more might be understood about why two girls had died and why three young men got out.

Bill Gaskins tried to explain these things to us. And, in turn, we struggled to understand why a fireman's fire-proof gloves should be

The reconstruction of the barn at Uckington. *(By kind permission of Gloucestershire Police Force)*

burned when David Harper's hands escaped blistering when fighting the fire unprotected. But how could anyone stay in the barn, we wondered, when the test in the mock-up barn showed that the smoke became so thick that it was impossible to remain inside.

We could only hope that these things would become clearer.

Detective Chief Inspector Gaskins:

During the investigation, I visited the Harpers' home on many occasions—sometimes on my own and sometimes accompanied by Barbara. Vicky and Stephen were given updates on a regular basis. Some of the visits were lengthy, especially when it was necessary to explain police proceedings and the law.

Vicky was very inquisitive and usually had a long list of questions meticulously prepared prior to my visit. Some of the questions concerned Emma's and Beckie's 'remains'—and I had to decide at an early stage how I was going to explain that we did not find complete bodies, only badly burnt 'remains'. I realised that Vicky was not aware of this when she asked me certain questions about body positions and teeth. It was then that I had to gently explain that nothing found was recognisable as a human being, apart from Beckie's hand.

Police officers are not trained to deal with situations like this but I tried to imagine how I would feel if a police officer declined to tell me the truth about my dead children. I felt they had a right to know how it really was.

mid-June 1991

Vicky:

Went to have my legs waxed this morning. Very exciting.

Actually Linda who does my legs is easy to talk to and it's a pleasure going to see her. Came back and had just got in the door when the Police rang. Could they come round in the afternoon?

Steve came home at lunchtime and we both waited nervously for the arrival of Detective Chief Inspector Gaskins. When he arrived with Barbara Harrison, he said that on advice from the QC dealing with our case they had decided to go for a murder charge! We were thrilled—although 'thrilled' is scarcely the right word. We were told that the boys would be arrested that evening and would appear before a special Magistrates sitting in the morning. We said that we wanted to go. We knew that the boys' solicitor would apply for bail and, in view of the new charge of murder, were wondering what decision the Magistrates would make this time.

Mr Gaskins then explained that Beckie had no soot in her windpipe. This was important. Had Beckie been alive at the time of the fire, she would have inhaled smoke and soot would have been found. Had she been dead at the time of the fire, she could not have inhaled smoke and no soot would have been found.

It had also been puzzling me why, if Beckie's windpipe was sufficiently intact to be tested forensically for traces of soot, could they not identify her from the brace on her teeth? A sudden thought occurred to me while Mr Gaskins was talking. Taking a deep breath I asked him if Beckie's head had been attached to her body. No, he said. Beckie's head had not been attached to her body.

The shock of hearing this was enormous. It was to have a profound effect upon me for some time. He explained that parts of Beckie's body had been found in a scattered area about the size of our front room—I suppose about 12 feet square.

I do not remember much else of the conversation that afternoon because I was once again in complete shock. It was arranged that the police would pick us up the next morning and take us to Court, for which we were very grateful—it is frightening to sit in full view of the accused and their families, some of whom seemed to hate us for some reason. The police said that they would keep us informed of the re-arrest of the boys during the evening. Wisdom Smith was arrested when signing in at the Police Station, David Harper some time later. Only Daniel Winters proved elusive and I think it was the following morning before he was detained.

So with great dread in our hearts about the following day we went off to bed.

Gloucestershire Echo:

"Three teenagers were today charged with the murder of 17-year-old Cheltenham twins Emma and Rebecca Harper.

David Harper (no relation), 19, a carpenter ... Wisdom Smith, 18, unemployed ... and part-time student Daniel Winter, 18, ... appeared during a special sitting of Cheltenham Magistrates' Court. The three sat handcuffed together in the dock during the hour long hearing. They were already charged with manslaughter, arson with intent and conspiring to pervert the course of justice in connection with the deaths of the twins...

Mrs Rita Crane, prosecuting, outlined the new charge during a 25-minute address to Magistrates.

An application for bail for the three youths by Mr Tim Robinson, defending, was turned down by the bench.

The three remained impassive as they were remanded in custody until June 20. The hearing was attended by more than 30 of their relatives and friends and the family of the dead girls..."

Vicky:

The police picked us up at about 9.45 ready to be in Court for 10 o'clock. We went in through the back entrance of the building and, thankfully, arrived early enough to avoid having to walk through the families in the waiting area. They were still arriving but the boys, of course, were already in custody. On entering No. 1 Court, we were stopped by an usher who asked where we thought we were going. Barbara explained who we were and he showed us in to our seats.

The Court began to fill up. I recognised David Harper's parents. Daniel Winter's family I did not know. The rest were the family of Wisdom Smith. The people there looked very intimidating and seemed to be making as much noise as possible—some of them not very polite noises.

Then the Magistrates came in and the Clerk ordered the boys up from the cells below. How different they looked. Untidy, unprepared and for once looking slightly nervous. I cannot truly describe the feelings I had, sitting there seeing three young men charged with the murder of my girls. They were handcuffed together and accompanied by two uniformed policemen. I began to hope that perhaps they might realise the seriousness of the situation and explain in simple terms what actually happened. But the prosecution spoke first which gave the defence solicitor the last word—and what a lot of words he used!

Rita Crane, our Crown Prosecution Service lady, gave a clear and concise resumé of what had happened so far and explained that, although there was no new evidence, clarification of certain points had led to the decision to go for a charge of murder. She reminded the Magistrates that the boys had been drinking heavily in the course of 23rd January and that, during the evening while the twins were still in the bar, had assaulted another youth outside. This, she said, showed violent tendencies. As Rita Crane sat down we thought that she had put the case very well.

Mr Robinson got up and spoke for quite some time. I found his way of talking confusing. He reminded the Magistrates that the boys had previously been given bail of £1,000 each by a wise and sensible bench and that really nothing had changed. He seemed to be suggesting that, without any new evidence, the Crown Prosecution Service was clutching at straws.

Next the boys were taken back down to the cells and the Magistrates retired to consider their arguments. But it did not seem too long before the boys were brought back up again and stood ready to hear the decision. The Magistrates said that in view of the seriousness of the charges they were going to remand them in custody!

Oh, what relief! To know at long last that someone would be held responsible for the deaths of two young girls. The Magistrate actually said "Take them down!" The boys would be taken to Bristol jail until another Court appearance on Thursday of the following week. I was in tears trying to thank everyone concerned but the boys' friends and families were not so pleased and said so in blunt language.

We were allowed to go out of the side door so that we did not have to pass by the others. And we came home again with the police feeling so reassured that, after a cup of tea, we set about ringing around with the good news. The law was not an ass after all. The boys were locked away. Justice would be done. We went to bed feeling that now we really had something to fight for and that the Magistrates had helped us very much.

The reconstruction of the barn at Uckington with the roof removed.   (*By kind permission of Gloucestershire Police Force*)

<u>*Sunday, 16th June 1991*</u>

Vicky:

What a terrible night. It was filled with visions of Beckie's head dancing around, followed by other dismembered parts of her body.

How they must have suffered. What terrible things must have been done to my girls before they were released from pain into death. Even looking at a photograph of Beckie on the dressing table, her head seemed to fall off.

I cried most of that Sunday, the euphoria of the day before gone. It was the realisation that people now thought that the girls had been harmed before they died that set my imagination running riot. Had they been cut up and set fire to? How much pain had they felt? Oh, how they must have cried for me and I wasn't there. I hadn't been able to help them. It was all my fault.

Steve too was very depressed. We went and bought a few papers and there it was in all of them. Murder! Murder!

I thought about the boys spending their first full day in prison. What had gone on in their minds that night and why would anyone want to kill the girls? Steve suggested that I should get on with the decorating and this was how I spent the rest of that long, hard day.

<u>*Thursday, 20th June 1991*</u>

Vicky:

Woke up this morning with a feeling of impending doom. We now know that the boys' solicitor has one more chance to obtain their release on bail. And we have been warned that he intends to do just that.

The police picked us up as usual and we were in Court ready at 10 o'clock. By half past, it transpired that the boys had not left Bristol jail yet and would therefore be late in arriving. Rather than leave us sitting in the Court or the waiting area, the police very kindly took us to an empty cell which they sometimes used as an office. While Barbara went to get us a coffee and Detective Sergeant Gibb was checking on progress, we were joined by a uniformed constable who asked us what we were waiting for. When we told him we were there for the barn fire hearing and that we were the twins' parents, he said how sorry he was and what an effect the deaths had had on everyone at the Police Station. Detective Sergeant Gibb returned and the young PC left.

We asked the Detective Sergeant if the constable had been involved in the inquiry and it was explained that he had been one of the team involved in the fingertip search of the burnt ashes. No wonder he had seemed affected by the tragedy. How awful for someone so young to have to search for the remains of human bodies.

Barbara came back with the coffee and said that the boys had left Bristol jail and were expected in about an hour. It seemed such a long wait. Having tensed ourselves for the Court appearance it was dreadful sitting there, just hanging about. We drank endless coffees and smoked far too many cigarettes. Eventually we heard the prison van arriving and then the banging of cell doors. The boys had arrived.

We had assumed that they would have been taken to Gloucester Prison but apparently it was felt that the nature and seriousness of the charges required the boys to be treated as Category A prisoners. This means that they are held in solitary confinement and are under surveillance at all times. They are escorted by two guards wherever they go. It felt good to know that the charges were being taken seriously.

Eventually it was time to go in. This was a different courtroom and we were not segregated from the other families at all. They were behind us and to both sides. The room seemed hostile—some of it directed, I think, at the police but most at us. I couldn't understand why. We hadn't wanted our daughters to die. And we certainly were not to blame for their deaths.

As we were being seated my Aunt came in. She is about 80 and had asked if she could come. I hadn't thought it a good idea at all but she had turned up anyway and Barbara suggested she came to sit in the front row with us. There were people from the press there, too, and another case was being heard first. It concerned a break in a community service order and I did wonder whether it was right that Magistrates should be hearing such a trivial offence and then a double murder. Still, that was the law. At last it was our turn.

You are shocked and never forget that, after the initial reading of the charges by the Clerk to the Court, the names of those who have died are never mentioned again. Emma and Beckie became known as 'the remains'. I found this very hard and thought it equally wrong that two human beings who had been physically destroyed should also be legally reduced to a few bones and a bit of skin.

Rita Crane got up first and gave her usual concise summary of what had taken place on the night of the 23rd January. Next it was Mr Robinson's turn to speak. On rising he announced that it was lunchtime and that, as he was calling character witnesses for his clients and had a lot to say, it would be better if the Court adjourned till after lunch. After all that waiting, to be dismissed in such a fashion by a mere solicitor was most hurtful. It also meant that by the time we returned to Court the Magistrates might have forgotten the things that Rita Crane had said. Barbara drove us home for a sandwich, more coffee and cigarettes and to try to relax us for half an hour. As we left the Court the Chief Magistrate was setting off into town—I sent a little prayer with her asking her to remember the twins and all that they must have suffered. Steve said good afternoon to her as she passed and briefly she replied.

On our return I suddenly realised that I had left my Aunt sitting in the middle of the other families in Court. But when we got there she was not in the least perturbed and had gone over the road to a local hotel for a sandwich! What a marvellous lady. We sat down and prepared ourselves for the worst.

The defence solicitor, Mr Robinson, started by saying how impeccable the boys were, how they had co-operated with the Police in every way. I could hardly believe my ears. Was I perhaps in the wrong court? Surely he could not be talking about the same three boys who, only a short time earlier, had been shown to have been drinking and violent on the night of the girls' deaths? Next he said that he was going to call David Harper's father to the stand to give a character reference. I found the picture painted that afternoon very difficult to stomach—it did not tally with my experience of him. As his father was leaving the stand, he turned to the Magistrates and said that the twins were David's friends and that he would never have done anything to hurt them—

—rubbish! Rubbish! I was so incensed that I stood up and said that that was not fair. That it was not right for him to be able to say things like that. I was furious and, knowing it, Barbara asked me if I wished to go outside. The responsibility for supervising me was all hers as Bill Gaskins was away on a course and Sergeant Gibb was unwell.

I sat down again feeling very angry and hurt. What kind of legal system allows these things to happen in Court under oath? Next came Daniel Winter's mother. Such stupid questions were asked that she even

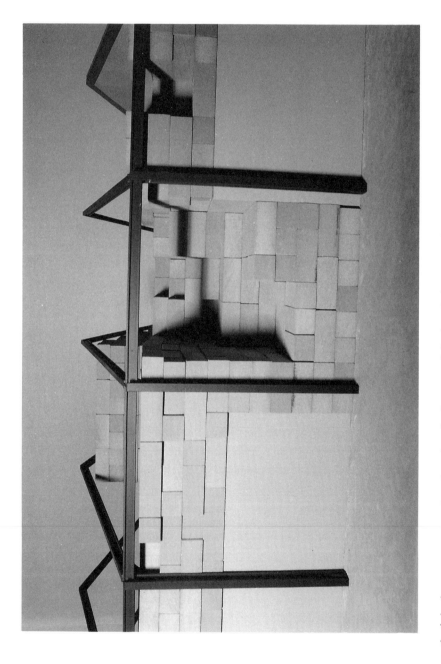

Detail of the barn reconstruction showing the lay out of the hay bales.   (*By kind permission of Gloucestershire Police Force*)

appeared not to know how to reply—except to say that, like David Harper's father, she would be very willing to sell her house and pay £50,000 if Daniel ran off. When asked how it would be for Daniel at home, she told the Court that a 10.30 pm curfew had been imposed upon him. But if that was the case, I wondered, why did the police have difficulty arresting him?

Mr Robinson then asked her how her daughter would feel if her mother sold the house to pay for Daniel's bail. I interrupted saying she was very lucky to have a daughter. And so it continued—worse and, I thought, a farce. By the end, I was fuming and finding it very difficult not to shout at them all. The three boys were the most wonderful things since sliced bread and my girls were forgotten. The whole horror was forgotten.

As the Magistrates retired to consider their decision I pointed out to Rita Crane a discrepancy I had noticed in the remarks of the defence solicitor. She said that, as I had noticed it, hopefully the Court would have done so as well. With the Magistrates gone, the boys were taken back down to the cells and the waiting began. Eventually, the Clerk to the Court was called in. She is legally qualified and advises the unqualified bench on points of law. After a few more minutes the Magistrates sent out to get the boys brought up. When they came up they looked at us and, I felt, were laughing. However the smile was soon wiped off their faces when the Magistrates once again refused them bail.

One of the people behind us called out "Don't worry, Danny, they won't win!" Steve turned round and asked who they were but there was no reply. We were so relieved and grateful, however, that I could have kissed everyone. The boys were taken down again and, this time, it was ourselves who were ushered out through the front entrance.

I am sure to this day that our presence in Court reminded the Magistrates that the 'remains' had once been two kind and loving girls called Emma and Beckie Harper. I would urge anyone in the same position to attend court if they can. If we had attended the first hearing, who knows perhaps bail would not have been granted and the whole affair might have taken a different course: if the boys had gone to prison at an early stage maybe the experience would have encouraged them to explain what happened. Anyway they were now on their way to Gloucester Prison having been reclassified as Category A prisoners. God, how relieved I am.

Once again we rang round friends and received many calls of congratulations. We went to bed that night well pleased with the way things had gone. What silly, naive fools we were...

Saturday, 22nd June 1991

Gloucestershire Echo:

"Three teenagers charged with murdering twins Beckie and Emma Harper have been beaten up while on remand in Gloucester prison.

Solicitor for the three teenagers Mr Tim Robinson said they had been assaulted by other inmates at the prison...

Mr Robinson said he found out about the attack after speaking to the father of one of the men. 'I sent one of my assistants to the prison to see them but he was denied access. We now have an appointment to see them on Monday.'

Principal officer at the prison Mr Mike Pratt said: 'The men were assaulted by unknown people. One received minor cuts and the other two received bruising. I carried out an investigation immediately but was unable to to discover the assailants and my report was given to the duty governor. They asked to be put in solitary cells, which is normal in this situation, for their own protection.'"

Vicky:

Up early this morning. Lots to do in town, buying frames for some of the girls' drawings and so on.

After breakfast we went out to the car but as soon as I sat inside I realised that the glove compartment was hanging open. Steve noticed that it had been forced and as we looked around it became clear that someone had broken in. At first, we could not think how they had done it until we noticed that the window had been slashed. It was a soft top sports car and the window at the back was only plastic.

Fortunately Steve has a security key which makes the car unusable and so the thieves had not been able to drive it away. Nevertheless it was very upsetting on top of everything else—the car had stood outside our front for 6 years without any problems at all. We reported it to the police at once which proved a bit disconcerting. The policeman I spoke to on the telephone thought I was Mrs Harper, the mother of David . . . Eventually the confusion was cleared and we set off for town.

Having bought all that we needed, we could not wait to return home. Being in town was always an horrendous experience—I constantly felt that everyone was looking at me and wondered what on earth I would do if I came face to face with one of the boys who were seen in town from time to time. On that day, of course, they were in prison but it was still a relief to reach home.

As soon as we got in the door, the telephone rang. It was Steve's mother, Mary. Obviously she was upset and it was difficult at first to understand what she was trying to say. From what I could gather, she had been told that the three boys had been beaten up in prison, one of them so seriously that he needed emergency hospital treatment. It appeared that the attack had taken place yesterday within hours of their being put in their cells. We thought we ought to ring the police straight away to see if this was true. We were beginning to learn that rumours spread very quickly and are not always based on fact.

I cannot describe my feelings when the police confirmed that there had been an attack on the boys. In some way I wasn't surprised—we had been told that they would be classed as child molesters and would certainly not be very popular with the other inmates. But it was still quite a shock. At first, reports were mixed about how seriously they had been hurt. The police rang up the prison but the Governor would only say that an attack had taken place. It was a prison matter, would be dealt with internally and, therefore, they did not have to give a report to the police.

Mr Robinson had apparently heard from one of the parents and on applying for a visit himself was refused entry. He next appeared on television saying how awful it was and that he would be demanding a full inquiry. But in the newspaper that evening, it seemed that the boys had in fact only received cuts and bruising. And that they had asked to be put in solitary confinement for their own protection.

I think deep down inside I was glad that they had suffered—an awful thing to say, I know, but nothing compared to what the twins must have endured. At least the boys would now know that even prisoners in jail despised the crimes they were accused of. I continued to hope that this might make them realise the seriousness of their position.

Throughout this period, we had been advised to focus on one explanation of what happened to the girls, one that we could live with. But this was very difficult when each time that police interviews took place, the accounts that emerged were different. There were just too many inconsistencies and anomalies for the boys' statements to be truthful. For example, all three said that they had heard no noise from the girls while they were supposedly burning to death. But as soon as the implication of this became clear to one of them, he would change his version of events: yes, he had heard the girls call out while they were burning to death. Unaware of this new information, the two others continued to insist that, no, the girls had not called out . . .

I wondered if we would ever really know the truth about what happened that night. Forensic tests had shown that Beckie had no soot in her windpipe and yet at one point David Harper had said that he was standing with her at the time of the fire. He later complained of a sore throat from inhaling smoke—so why hadn't Beckie been inhaling anything at that point in time?

It also appeared from the statements of Wisdom Smith and Daniel Winter that, on leaving the barn, they would have had to have passed by one of the girls. But they made no attempt to get her out. Later on, in fact, they said they had not seen either of the girls for some time. Yet in another statement, Wisdom Smith said he had sex with Emma in the barn. It was all very hard to understand. Clearly not all the different accounts of what had happened could be true. But, nevertheless, I clung to the simple idea that somehow it would all be sorted out.

Tuesday, 25th June 1991

Vicky:

Working all day again. It keeps my mind busy I suppose and everyone here is so very kind and thoughtful. They have obviously talked about the best way to behave when I am around and have decided to be themselves and talk as normal. That is by far the best way.

I am waiting to hear from the police. It seems that a last attempt is to be made to get the boys bail, mainly on the grounds that it is not fair that they were beaten up in prison. I begin to wonder now about the origin of the stories that were circulating. One headline even said 'Youths battered in cells, three teenagers savagely beaten up'—when it transpired that there was hardly a scratch on them.

Mr Robinson is going to the High Court in Bristol where his plea will be heard in Judge's Chambers. We think it will happen tomorrow and the judge's decision will be final. I cannot really believe that any Judge will overturn the Magistrates' decision now. Surely the boys could be kept in solitary confinement if they are that worried? Nevertheless, I am very despondent that Judge Scheiman is to hear the appeal. The Judge dismissed a case at Bristol Crown Court recently where one man even admitted shooting another. Will there be any justice for Emma and Beckie?

Tuesday, 25th June 1991

Vicky:

Working this morning. Norma came round at lunchtime. She has been such a help over the last few weeks and, to thank her, Steve and I are going to ask if she would like to have the twins' bikes. They are just going to rot in the cellar and I would rather think of Norma's husband, Paul, who is very good with his hands, making a decent bike from the two for their daughter, Sandy. When we asked Norma, she seemed very pleased by the thought and I am going to get the bikes cleaned up ready for the next time she calls.

Went shopping with Julia as usual. Then we came back for a cup of tea and to see if there was any news on the radio about the bail hearing. This afternoon, I'm due to visit Mrs Nock whose son, David, one of twins, had been stabbed to death in Cheltenham in April. But I would like to know the result of the hearing first. Eventually on the four o'clock news it was reported that Judge Scheiman had granted the boys bail of £50,000 each on condition that they live at home and report once weekly to the police station.

So that's it. They are out now until the trial. And God only knows when that will be.

Went to see Kath Nock. She cannot believe they have been let out. David's killer has been in custody since his arrest and did not even ask for bail. How can defence solicitors sleep at night knowing that people charged with such serious offences are out on the street?

Had a good talk to Kath. It is such a help to talk to someone else who knows what I feel. She is very upset of course but I believe we help each other. It is not all doom and gloom when we meet—we do laugh about our children's ways and in so remembering them keep their spirits alive.

Steve is very upset by the news and very, very angry. I would like to get at the boys myself sometimes but I can guarantee that, if I did, I would not get bail. Probably life instead. Bad evening all together. People constantly ringing up to ask why and how it could be allowed to happen? I wish I knew the answer. When this is over I intend to do all I can to get the Bail Act changed. In the meantime I have to go to sleep with my friends, the sleeping pills, and face another night.

Barbara came to tell me at work the news we had heard on the radio. I still do not understand how people accused of murder can be granted bail. It is bad enough that Emma and Beckie are dead, but for us to know that the men accused of their killings are walking free on the streets is almost too much to bear. The burden it puts on us and our families is enormous. What if I met them in the street, how would I react? The whole justice system is a farce. What about the danger to other people, or what if the boys decide to leave the country?

Late this evening, we received a phone call to say that one of the boys had been out bragging about getting out of jail. I can't write any more. I'm too tired and too depressed.

July 1991

Vicky:

Eight hours at work today, a full working day instead of my usual part-time. I know that is what everyone works but it tires me greatly. I think it is probably the strain of trying to be cheerful and normal in front of the patients. I would not like them to know who I am which is why I don't wear a name badge or tell anyone my surname.

I don't remember much else during the day except that when I got home and talked to Steve we were both very upset and fed-up. Just one of those days, I guess, when the world is too much to cope with and we want to hide away. We were sitting moping when the telephone rang. Steve answered it. It was Dr Giraldi, the twins' doctor. He asked Steve if I could listen on the phone as well.

We knew from the police that Dr Giraldi was going to be asked to make a statement concerning the girls' health—and I must confess I was a bit worried about what he was going to say. Perhaps he was going to tell us that the girls had been on the pill or something like that. But he began to talk about the twins' work in the caring profession. And then he went on to say that he and some colleagues had come up with the idea of a one-stop clinic for the elderly to be held at Charlton Kings in Cheltenham.

It all sounded a very good idea but neither Steve or I could see where this was leading. Then I thought that possibly he wanted me to do some reception work or maybe Steve to drive the elderly to and from the clinic. I was about to tell him that, unless the people were very agile and liked being squashed into a sports car, helping out would not be possible when Dr Giraldi took a deep breath and asked if he could name the clinic The Harper Clinic in memory of the girls!

It took us a few seconds to take in what he was saying and then with tears in our eyes we understood. We were so overcome by this tribute that I cannot remember what we said except yes, we would be delighted. Dr Giraldi asked us if we wanted time to think about it but we both knew instantly that it was a lovely idea. He said he would be in touch when everything had been sorted out and that mention of the opening would be made in the *Echo*.

Gloucestershire Echo, December 1991:

"Elderly people in Charlton Kings can get free advice and tips from British Gas officials on keeping safe and warm this winter. Avoiding the cold is the theme of the monthly Harper Clinic to be held on Monday at St Mary's Church Hall. As in the first clinic a month ago, there will be a doctor, dentist and social workers on hand to provide all the information the elderly might need.

'The first clinic attracted 60 people and we are hoping to keep the momentum going by having a different theme each month,' said social worker Chris Moxham...

Each of the clinics—from 2 pm to 4 pm on the fourth Monday of each month—is free to attend. The clinic gives information on a variety of topics to the over-60s and was named after Emma and Beckie Harper who died in a barn blaze in January. It was set up by staff at the Sixways Health Centre, where the twins were patients, and by the County Council social services with help from St Mary's Church, police and voluntary groups."

After such a dark and dismal day, Dr Giraldi's phone call revived our spirits. Once again our hearts were gladdened by people's kindness to us. And so, on this occasion, off to bed with joy in our hearts knowing that the twins were being remembered with love by the most unexpected people.

We had found other ways of recording Emma's and Beckie's existence. Our friends in Spain, Mal and Pete, had suggested finding photos which would make good portrait paintings. This we had done and were looking forward to seeing the results. But we were learning too that other friends had still not discovered what had happened in the first place. I saw an old acquaintance, Mrs Ellis, quite by chance at the Clinic—it was good to talk to her again but, not knowing, she asked after the twins. It was very difficult telling her. Thankfully, that doesn't happen too often.

I also learn that one of the three boys has been granted leave to go on holiday. But I still cannot understand how people charged with a serious offence can be allowed to walk the streets and have fun. To me the Bail Act is a farce and sooner or later someone is going to die as a result of it. Meanwhile the killer of David Nock has been charged and not given bail. This comforts me and, I hope, the Nock family too. On their twins' birthday, David and Sally, I sent two bunches of flowers—one for Sally because she is a living, vibrant pretty girl and one for David who never lived to celebrate that day.

Monday, 15th July 1991

Vicky:

Back to my normal hours this week, thank goodness! I had promised to go up to my Mother to help her start sorting out the spare room in case she took in a student later on in the year. It was a job I did not relish but felt that it was the least I could do. Unfortunately I was not in a very nice frame of mind and started off by upsetting her as soon as I walked in the door.

We started to sort through her chest of drawers, a task that I had always enjoyed as a young girl, as had the twins. The bottom drawer was full of things put by for Christmas and birthdays. All sorts of pretty bits of pieces and as a child I remember that there was always the chance of a small gift if I was good.

But today the job was a chore. There were things that she had put by for the twins' Christmas stockings. It made me very cross and upset and, in my grief, I could not see beyond my own sorrow and realise that Mum must be feeling the same. It was then on to the top drawer where under lock and key were the family pieces of jewellery and such like. Some of the things Mum had promised to me on her death. The remainder, with the exception of a few bequests, was to have gone to Emma and Beckie. Mum was at a loss to know what to do about these things now and I could be of no help. There was little point in her leaving them to me. I had no children to pass them on to and anyway had more than enough rings and pieces of my own.

It was very sad sitting there with the accumulations of generations, all destined now to finish with us. This brought us round to the subject of wills and what would now happen to my Mother's possessions. I was getting crosser by the minute and after some rather selfish words I left as soon as I could. It was only when I got home and sat down and talked to Steve about it that I realised just what a heartless bitch I had been. He rightly pointed out that, after her divorce from my Father, my Mum had worked very hard to make something of her life and gather together enough money and assets to ensure my future. Once I was settled with Stephen, she had made arrangements for the twins to be given the best start in adult life and now all this had been taken away from her.

I have tried not to be selfish in my grief but must admit that, once Steve had talked to me, I felt awful. Instead of giving help and advice to her I had shouted and been cruel. I rang her at once to say how sorry I was and for once she forgave me and the matter was dropped. It was a lesson to me that I must realise that others were suffering too—although not as greatly perhaps or in the same way that we were.

My Mother has also been trying to decide what to do with some money she had put aside for the twins. She asked us which charities we thought the girls would have liked. What a dreadful thing to have to think about. But I suppose, if it helps their memories to live on, a donation like that is a good idea.

In the end we decided on three for Beckie—the Cystic Fibrosis Society, a charity for Aids sufferers called Aidsline because Beckie had done a project on it at College, and the Cobalt Unit because she had often expressed an interest in their work. My Mum received very nice letters of thanks from them all. In memory of Emma, we chose her favourite charity, the National Children's Home to which she had so often written and contributed. We had a lovely letter from them expressing their sadness at her death. Mum also gave to the NSPCC, the Cancer Unit at Cheltenham General and the Young Homeless Project here in Cheltenham. It was a nice thought by my Mum and her way of keeping their memories alive.

People continued to be very kind to us all. Friends rallied round Mum and all came to our help—although some of our friends found it difficult to contact us. But once the initial ice was broken all was well and we would chat freely. A friend from Solihull, Amanda, whose birthday is the same as mine, rang up to say that she was having a party and would we like to go. She was hesitant in asking us but thought that it might do us good to get away from Cheltenham and see different people. We gladly agreed. It would be something to look forward to after the next Court appearance of the boys.

After the girls' deaths I wrote many letters including one to Margaret Thatcher. During a speech on leaving her position as Prime Minister she had made some reference to the legal system in Britain. It was a favourable comment and in my distress and pain I felt bound to write informing her that my impression of the system was not quite the same. I never expected her to reply, in fact I doubted whether the letter would even be read by her. But on 16th July I did receive a reply. She had answered not as a former Prime Minister but, as one Mother to another and her words brought great comfort. She also opened the door for further correspondence from me, a brave and compassionate thing to do bearing in mind we had never met.

It had not been a good morning and when the postman came I was not eager to look. I can only say that Mrs Thatcher's words to me renewed my faith in the human race.

Dear Mrs Harper,

Having read your letter, and having children of my own, I feel for you, greatly, and can fully understand your every comment.

Please let me know when the trial comes up. I should like to follow what happens. Words are so inadequate—comfort will elude you. Every mother who knows will share your sorrow.

With kind regards.

Yours sincerely,

Margaret Thatcher

CHAPTER SEVEN
Daylight Robbery

early August 1991

Vicky:

August has arrived and I feel awful. When we got back home from shopping at Sainsbury's today, there was a beautiful girl standing opposite our house looking at it. She had long blonde hair and was wearing sunglasses. When she saw us arrive, she walked up to the top of the road and continued watching from there.

I had a strange feeling that it was Emma—I don't know why but I have often felt that Emma was not dead. I knew that Beckie was dead as soon as I heard about the fire on TV. But, somehow, Emma was different. I know that Inspector Gaskins has assured us that two sets of remains were found but, on occasions still, I feel her presence.

We are going to the christening of Steve's nephew this weekend. He's going to be Godfather. I am dreading it but I have found some comfort and reassurance in talking to my Victim Support volunteer. I just wish that Steve would talk to someone, too. He can talk to me but the pressure on him is intense, I know. He is unhappy at work and I wish I could do something to help him.

Little Alex's christening turned out to be a lovely service on a lovely, warm day. There were several people we knew there including one lady who had twins just before me. I watched them, pretty girls sitting with their mother—she caught my eye and looked as if she understood. It was difficult but I made a point of chatting to her for a moment, wondering inside what it might have been like to have my own grandchildren christened. Lunch afterwards was very pleasant of course but we soon slipped away, quietly, to the silence at home.

A week later, while out for a meal at a friend's house, I became ill. Panic set in and I was powerless to fight it. Emma and Beckie are dead: I cannot go on: I want the girls to come home. Two days of misery followed as I wandered round the house crying and shouting: I am going to see the doctor: something must be done—

—I went to see the grave at the church instead and, as I approached, a boy was standing there, his head bowed over the stone, his hands clasped. We drove round the block and when we returned he was gone. I have no idea who he was but in some way that boy brought me to my senses. I have to be strong because to give in now would be to fail Emma and Beckie. At least until the court case I will survive.

Shocks and jolts keep coming though. In the hospital, I mistook Gwynne's white-coated daughter, Verity, for Beckie—and they saw my distress and were disturbed by it. Out in the street or in some shop, there also continued to be times when, suddenly, I would notice one of my girls. But when I looked closely, it was never them at all.

late August 1991

Vicky:

On one day, I worked in the main hospital, which I quite enjoyed although I did get very tired. Everyone is nice and makes me feel most welcome.

When I got home, I remember, Steve was standing just inside waiting for me. I knew instantly that something was wrong but I couldn't imagine what. He said that I wasn't to be upset but someone had been in the house. When he returned from work a few minutes earlier, a neighbour had come to tell him that she had just seen someone in our garden, a youth whom she had shouted at but who had run off with something in his hand.

Gloucestershire Source (now the Independent), 29th August 1991:

"An impassioned plea has been made by the parents of the Cheltenham twins who died in a barn fire six months ago, after heartless thieves burgled their home.

Heartbroken Stephen and Vicky Harper made their appeal after discovering that some of the items taken included jewellery that had belonged to their 17-year old daughters, Emma and Rebecca. '...they belonged to the girls and to me they are irreplaceable,' said Mrs Harper."

Vicky:

Steve had a quick look round before we called the police and set about trying to discover what might have been taken. The sitting room was fine, the bits of silver and the video still there. The camera was on the hall table and the dining room looked untouched. I was beginning to think we had got off lightly.

In the kitchen, the contents of my wallet had been strewn across the table but luckily I had had my credit cards with me. A plaque, to be presented to Broadlands Nursery School, was on the work top where I had left it—but it had only been unwrapped. A packet of twenty

Emma (*left*) and Beckie, aged 16, at Julia's, Stephen's sister, wedding, February 1990.

Marlboro cigarettes had been taken but some Gauloise left. Evidently our thief didn't like French cigarettes.

Our petty cash had not been taken either although it was in an obvious money box. And my collection of antique coins was undisturbed. The thief wasn't an expert then. However, he had forced open the downstairs bathroom window and known enough to unlock the backdoor as his escape route.

By this stage, so little seemed to have been taken that I began to fear that damage might have been done to the freshly decorated girls' rooms. But no—all Steve's computer equipment and the girls' TVs were in place. It was only when I went into our bedroom that I realised it was my jewellery they'd been after. The bedroom was littered with empty jewellery cases and a pillowcase had been taken from the bed to carry our possessions away. Because I had been working that morning, I had merely pulled back the bedding before leaving—and it felt awful now to think that someone had been sitting on my bed and going through my things. The drawers were open and they had even looked through my underclothes.

When the police arrived, we didn't recognise either the young woman constable or the 'scene of crimes' officer, and they didn't know us. We told them who we were and they were visibly shocked that this could have happened on top of everything else. In truth, I wasn't quite sure how I felt. After the girls' deaths, the theft seemed unimportant. It was only on examining my main jewellery case that I realised they had removed nearly everything. Lots of worthless paste jewellery from my modelling days had been taken but, thank God, they'd missed a gold sovereign of my grandmother's. My father's second wife's jewellery had gone too—he'd given most of it to me when she died and there had been much of sentimental and real value. Things I had collected over the years had also gone—rings, presents, an antique wedding ring, a cameo, a hand-carved ivory necklace. None of it could be replaced.

But it was only as the police were dusting for finger prints that I realised that a tiny mother of pearl box had been taken, too. The box had been on another dressing table and its theft was the most terrible shock imaginable. The box had contained two crosses that had belonged to the twins and a silver locket which Steve had bought for my birthday containing photographs of the girls wearing their choir cassocks.

I was very angry. First my daughters. Then the car. And now nearly every piece of jewellery including my most precious possessions. What more could people want from me?

That evening, we both felt very much aware that our home had been violated. We kept finding things in the wrong place or that another piece of jewellery was missing. I had to strip the bed and hoover it, too, to get rid of any traces of the disgusting parasite who had been in my home. Now I know what people mean when they say they feel dirty after a burglary.

Gloucestershire Echo:

A businessman has offered a reward for the return of treasured jewellery stolen from the home of barn death twins, Emma and Beckie Harper.

The man from Cheltenham—who did not want to be named—has put up the undisclosed amount of cash to prompt the return of two silver coloured crosses and a silver locket. He said the twins' parents, Steve and Vicky Harper, had suffered greatly and the belongings had been part of their precious memories…

Vicky:

We were taken aback by everyone's generosity and kindness—the newspapers, the television, tradesmen, neighbours. And, of course, by a family friend who offered a reward for information. But what price can you put on a locket containing a picture of Emma and Beckie and on their two small, silver-cloured crosses?

During the month, someone wrote to the Echo asking why people did not do more to keep crime off the streets. He complained that he was afraid to walk out in the town late at night. I thought his criticism of the police unfair and I wrote a reply condemning among other things the failure of the Bail Act to keep the community safe from people charged with violent crimes. Tragically, on 28th August, my worst fears were confirmed when a young Gloucester woman, Anna McGurk, was murdered on her way to her car by a man who had been granted bail by Cheltenham Magistrates.

The judicial system must carry responsibility for Anna's shocking death. The man who did it had been allowed to live in a Bail Hostel in Gloucester where he could watch workers leaving their offices and walking the short distance to their cars. That day, he'd already aroused suspicion watching people—but poor Anna's fate was already sealed. I hope that those who enable these things to happen gain some understanding from this book of the terrible blow they deal the bereaved families. And I hope that others will join me in demanding that the Bail Act be reformed.

We fled from Gloucestershire for the Bank Holiday at the end of the month, misguidedly seeking some calm in Cornwall, a place that Steve had always loved. But even that had changed and we were glad to leave. August was finally over when we returned but it still had a kick in its tail. While playing his first game of cricket for some years, Steve was bowled out for a duck and fell down a rabbit hole, dislocating his shoulder. Goodbye and good riddance August!

September 1991

Vicky:

We had intended to go to Spain in mid-September but Steve's father, Eric, is very poorly. I don't know whether we ought to go. He and Steve are going to see the specialist on 6th September so we will just have to wait until then.

The twins' bikes, which we had promised to Norma, were duly collected—but both Steve and I were horribly upset when she'd taken them away. In fact I cried. Pathetic, isn't it, to cry over two bikes? But they were part of Emma's and Beckie's lives, a part that would never be needed again.

I must confess that we each drank a lot that night. I have also started to sleep walk again. It is a frightening experience waking up and discovering from odd signs around the house that I have been wandering about at night. I wonder, and worry, what would happen if I went outside or hurt someone. If there is anything to smile at in my sleep walking, it's the recollection of once babysitting a hamster and two lovebirds belonging to Mal and Pete. Because we had cats, the 'visitors' had to be segregated in the dining room—but on one morning, we found everything undone and the hamster gone leaving just a few scraps of fur and some tiny piles of food around the floor. Emma even suggested that I must have eaten it in my sleep but, with one hour left before their owners arrived to collect their menagerie, she found the poor little thing sheltering in a corner of the room under the dresser!

The 6th arrived and Steve went to the specialist with Eric. Mum came down and other people popped in—but I felt that Steve and I ought to be by ourselves when he returned. The news was bad. Eric had cancer and would have to undergo a colostomy. I cannot imagine anything worse for such a proud and dignified man. We went to see him that night—but he did look ill and was so obviously in distress. He tried, gamely, to be his normal self and insisted that we took our holiday. He was quite right—without a break to recharge our batteries Steve and I would be no use to either of them. The holiday helped but it was more difficult than ever coming home again.

October 1991

Vicky:

During October, the boys made a couple of Court appearances. Each time they appear, they are very well turned out and noticeably contrite—unlike our experience of them. David Harper applied for a change to his bail restrictions to enable him to see a psychiatrist in Nottingham, which was agreed. Why he should need psychiatric help I cannot imagine. I should have thought the best treatment would be to explain what happened, something so elusive but which we all desperately needed to be told.

I found it very hard to see the boys in Court and, as I found the atmosphere hostile, I was reluctant to go again. And so the police called frequently and kept us up to date. But Steve and I just want it to be over: once the Court case is finished, we shall be able to put the boys out of our minds and concentrate on thinking of Emma and Beckie as themselves and not as 'the remains'.

I had my own appointment with a psychiatrist at this time. I felt very nervous but his reputation was good and off I went to the Doctor's Surgery where we had agreed to meet. The psychiatrist looked very pleasant, shook my hand and invited me to sit down. I had thought carefully about what I wanted to say but he started asking for background information and this annoyed me. I could not see the relevance of what had happened to me in my past life to what had happened to me since January 1991. After about 30 minutes of questions about my parents and boyfriends, he sat back and asked how I thought he could help. This was the last straw. I tried to explain my feelings of suicide but he just told me they were unacceptable—at which point I knew that there was little point in continuing.

Of far greater comfort was discovering that the girls' headstone had been covered with flowers and posies on the occasion of their eighteenth birthday. Being invited by Dr Giraldi to the formal opening of the Harper Clinic in Charlton Kings. Being invited to Broadlands Nursery School to the opening of the 'Baggy Pants' activity centre with its plaque and photograph of Emma. And being present when the Beckie Harper Memorial Plaque was first presented to a student at the College.

How sad it is to think that Emma's and Beckie's many gifts were not observed and understood by us until it was too late to tell them how proud we were of their achievements. I hope that, one day in the future, we shall be reunited with them and can explain how much we did indeed love and admire them both.

Throughout the police continued to call, keeping us up to date with events. What strength they have brought us—Barbara and Sarah have become old friends and we welcome their visits. It helps particularly to be able to talk freely about the case which we are not allowed to discuss with anyone else. Nevertheless, people do ask and people do put forward their own opinions. But there was so much gossip, often overheard in shops or pubs or commented upon to my Mum, that it was hard to focus on facts.

Some rumours were particularly distressing. That Beckie had been tied up. That Beckie's arm had been broken. That the boys had always been fascinated by fire. That drugs had been given. That the boys had been sniffing glue. That the girls had been beaten. That Beckie had died during forced sex. These are terrible, terrible things to hear and we had to make deliberate efforts to distinguish Emma and Beckie as we knew them to be, from the dreadful tales of horror and distortion that came our way.

The police tried to shield us but soon realised that we had too many questions that needed to be answered.

Vicky's Victim Support volunteer:

I have been involved with Vicky Harper in a rather strange way—intimately privy at times to Vicky's feelings about the deaths, the criminal proceedings and the final outcome of the court case, and yet not directly or personally affected since I did not know either of the twins. I only learned of them through the eyes of their parents, relations and friends.

Victim Support volunteers have two main roles. The first and perhaps the more important, although its value is more difficult to assess, is as an emotional support—a befriender rather than a counsellor, someone who listens in an objective, non-judgmental way to the thoughts and feelings of the 'client' we are to support. Frequently, those who have been bereaved, especially in violent circumstances, do not feel able to unburden themselves to people close to them for fear of adding to their stress. And also because they see their own reactions as being strange, different from those of the other person and therefore perhaps difficult for them to understand. Having an outsider, to whom they can confess their feelings, is an essential help.

The second role is to provide practical help to the client, including obtaining information. This can cover a number of matters but mostly concerns the progress of the criminal case. We use our contacts with the police, the Crown Prosecution Service, the Coroner's Office, the Magistrates' Court and the Crown Court to find out what is going on.

One of the great difficulties for the family involved with a serious criminal Court case is that it takes a long time for the case to come to trial. In Vicky's case it took 21 months to come before the Crown Court. Throughout this time, the family of the victim is in a sort of limbo, wanting to know what is happening, grasping at every new piece of information, needing to know what the eventual charge will be.

By the time I became involved, Vicky had already built up her own links with the police and the Coroner's Office and did not need to go through me to obtain information. On the contrary, it was often Vicky who told me about the charges and evidence being built up.

I was able to provide her with a copy of the 'Victim's Charter' which is a Home office publication setting out the rights and expectations of victims of crime. Occasionally, I was able to find out about Court dates and once went along myself so that Vicky would not need to go. I was also able to obtain information about the Compassionate Friends organisation, with its offshoot 'Parents of Murdered Children'.

Vicky:

Woke up this morning with a hangover. And stomach ache. One of those days when I just want to be wrapped in cotton wool and not have to think. Due to see Kathleen Nock this afternoon and then out again tonight in a foursome. But I don't think I can do either. Spent the morning lying on the bed feeling really sorry for myself and prayed that, when Steve came home at lunchtime, he would say that I didn't need to go out at all. In the end I settled for Kath's.

I always enjoyed talking to Kath. It was interesting. We had things to share. We each believed, for example, that a local woman whose son had recently been stabbed in the stomach had emerged from the experience quite lightly. The man responsible had already been tried and sentenced to two years imprisonment—and the mother still had her son and seen justice done. But she was dissatisfied and was demanding publicly that more police patrol the streets.

It worried me that, if her son's attacker had been imprisoned for two years and the three boys charged with Emma's and Beckie's murder did not get sent to prison, we should feel even more bitter than she did. Some robbers were given up to 10 years and yet we gathered from the police that they'd be satisfied if our three youths get five years. To my disbelief, it seems that anti-establishment crimes get far higher sentences than those relating to human life.

Eventually persuaded to go out for a drink that evening, I realised yet again how upset our acquaintances are by all that has happened. Everyone knows about the 'barn blaze twins' but not all had associated them with us. They don't know what to say about it either.

Vicky:

In the films when someone is arrested, you hear them being cautioned. They are told they have the right to remain silent but that anything they do say will be taken down and may be used in evidence against them—

—personally, if I was accused of doing something I had not done, I would not be interested in the right to remain silent. I would be shouting my innocence from the roof tops. What I had simply not grasped until now is the real meaning of the caution given to people who are arrested. It means that they needn't say anything and, more importantly, they don't have to explain what has happened. How naive I have been! I had always assumed that the purpose of Court hearings and the subsequent trial was to get at the truth. I am wrong.

Over the months since the twins' deaths, the boys have altered their accounts but now settled on one. They have had plenty of time to get it right. On the other hand, we have just learned of something called the Disclosure Act which seems to me a very biassed thing indeed. Apparently, the police and prosecution have to reveal every shred of evidence to the defence before the trial. All notes and pieces of paper relevant to the case have to be sent to the accused's lawyer. In return, the defence is not obliged to reveal anything to us. Not until we go to trial will we have any notion of what their plea or evidence will be. This means that they have the element of surprise as well as the last word in Court.

We have heard a lot of words in Court so far—rambling waffle which, by the time it's over, has probably made everyone forget the facts raised by our own solicitor. On talking to the police, I learn that one of their main complaints is that they have to give the defence a list of witnesses to be called. Apparently, this results in witnesses including police officers sitting around the Court building for hours, even days, only for some to be told that they are not required after all. What a waste of police time and the country's money! Even material which is not to be used in the prosecution case must be made available to the defence, resulting in the squandering of even more police time and resources. Think of the thousands of pounds that could be saved if the defence's intentions had to be made clear at the outset. Think of the costs of a solicitor, barrister and his assistant—all provided by Legal Aid to the accused. I know there have to be safeguards in case an innocent person is sent to prison—but think of it.

After all the waiting around, I couldn't bear it if the judge threw out the case at the beginning of the trial for lack of evidence or something like that. But I have every faith in Inspector Gaskins and his team and I am certain they will do their best. We have also been impressed with the work of Rita Crane. Apparently, our barrister will be a man called Pat Curran—he will take over from Rita when the case reaches the Crown Court. The Queen's Counsel is called Chadd who they tell us is a bit of a Rumpole of the Bailey.

As long as he is good, I don't care. We have to rely upon these people whom we have never met and who are fighting for our two girls who never met them either.

God help us.

Vicky:

On 6th December, I received a second, lovely, handwritten letter from Mrs Thatcher expressing her concern that things were taking so long. Her letter brought tears to my eyes. She felt that by writing this book I would be helping others—she even offered to put us up if ever we needed to go to London! That such a busy and important person should make such an offer was quite overwhelming and Steve and I are deeply grateful to her.

I had been writing many letters of my own expressing my fears and my disgust at the way the legal system and the Bail Act are misused. I wrote to everyone—from the Queen to my (then) local MP, Sir Charles Irving. Many kind replies have been sent to me, including letters from John Major, Neil Kinnock and Paddy Ashdown. My concerns were forwarded to the Attorney General and to the legal spokespersons of the various political parties. But the (late) Sir Charles Irving was so upset at my last letter that he passed it on to the Home Office and sent me a copy of the Home Secretary's reply. The Rt Hon John Patten MP left me nonplussed:

"...the decision as to whether an accused person should be released on bail is a matter entirely for the courts in the exercise of their judicial discretion, subject to the provisions of the Bail Act 1976. You will appreciate that it would not be right for me or any other Minister to seek to comment on, or intervene in, decisions taken in individual cases.

"In general terms, I would explain that although the Bail Act establishes a presumption in favour of the grant of bail, it also provides that a court need not grant bail in certain specified circumstances. In particular, a court may withhold bail in the case of a person accused of an offence punishable with imprisonment if it is satisfied that there are substantial grounds for believing that if the defendant were released on bail he would abscond, commit an

offence, interfere with witnesses or otherwise obstruct the course of justice.

"Having to decide whether to remand a defendant in custody or on bail can be one of the most difficult decisions facing the courts. Nevertheless I accept that there is a legitimate public concern over cases where people accused of serious crimes are granted bail. For that reason, section 153 of the Criminal Justice Act 1988 provides that a court must now give reasons when it grants bail to a defendant accused of murder, attempted murder, rape, attempted rape or manslaughter, when the prosecution has objected to bail being granted."

I don't remember the reasons given for granting the boys bail. In fact I don't remember any reasons being given at all. It just began to dawn on me what difficulties lay ahead and how much attitudes to those involved in violent death varied. For example, I noticed in an article in *The Mail on Sunday* that the mother of the murdered Oxford student, Rachel MacLean, expressed her forgiveness for John Taylor, the killer, and her sorrow that two lives had been ruined by his actions. I understand that John Taylor had become ill, that something had changed the person known and trusted by the MacLean family. But I cannot ever imagine feeling like Mrs MacLean.

We had some very bad nights at the beginning of the month, beset by terrible nightmares and the constant question, what had happened in the barn? Terrible scenes passed through our minds. Nothing could be discounted and yet nothing could be proved. We were waiting too for the photographs of the remains of Emma and Beckie. We felt we needed to see them to understand why more tests could not be done—to understand just what we had buried at Christ Church.

The Minister's letter continued:

"I have taken careful note of what Mrs Harper says about the right of silence and juvenile witnesses. On the first issue, the Royal Commission on Criminal Justice has been specifically asked to look at the potential of this rule for miscarriages of justice and Mrs Harper may be assured that the Government will look very carefully at the case for change in the light of whatever the Royal Commission may recommend. On the second point, I think that there may be a misunderstanding here about the legal position of

young persons who are wanted as witnesses. In general, if a witness is competent to give evidence, he can also be compelled to do so. This, in general, holds true of juveniles as much as any other category of witness. You will understand that I cannot comment on this particular case however."

'Competence' was not something I had thought about. But 'compelling' the boys, all adults, to explain how the three of them could escape from an open burning barn while two girls did not was certainly at the forefront of my mind.

"Mrs Harper also makes a more general point about offences committed by people on bail. I share her concern and accept that it is disturbing when an accused person who has been released on bail is later arrested for allegedly comitting further offences. It is obviously important to get an accurate picture of the pattern of offending and whether there have been any changes, particularly in view of recent reports from some police areas. Home Office researchers have conducted a review of work in this area, including analysis of recent research studies undertaken by police forces, to establish whether patterns of offending have changed. We are looking carefully at the results of this review and considering what further steps may be needed."

Steve and I began to have rows. The added strain of Eric's illness told on Steve and his mother's reliance was also wearing him down. And yet I found myself still being very unsympathetic and saying some dreadful things to him. On many a night, racked by guilt, I would come downstairs and pound away on the typewriter to relieve my feelings. And on reading it the next day, would feel even more ashamed.

To me, the loss of a child has to be the most awful experience in the world. And, therefore, the loss of a parent is insignificant in comparison. Having lost neither of my parents, I have no right to pass judgements but I do feel that it is natural to lose older relatives—that while grieving for them, we can draw comfort from their long and hopefully fulfilling lives. But children? And in such circumstances?

I was very jealous of Steve's Dad—I desperately wanted to die and felt it was just not fair that he should be going to join Emma and Beckie first.

Ken Helps:

Steve and Vicky were torn apart at this time with distress at the whole legal process which was not geared up to finding out the truth about what happened. I admired Vicky for her campaign to get politicians to do something about the inadequacy of our legal system, in which the closest relations of the dead in a murder or manslaughter case have no status in the trial or any right to know what is happening.

They knew we attended services at Christ Church and were just about clinging on to the Christian faith. They said they might come to a service—we hoped it would be Communion. One morning, we saw them in Church and sat near them. However, we cringed at the grievous words of the Psalms and Canticles. There is so much in them about God protecting people and so much about death. But they all seem empty promises. We wondered what on earth Vicky and Steve were thinking. I don't think they've been to a service since.

Vicky:

During this time, letters went backwards and forwards to various publishers. Some dismissed the idea of a book out of hand. Others expressed an interest but felt that publication would depend upon the outcome of the court case. It seemed impossible to take things further for the time being although I perservered in the hope that someone somewhere would recognise what I was trying to do.

One publisher suggested that I read the book by John Ward about the search for those who killed his daughter, Julie, in Kenya. Some publishers felt that the story of Emma and Beckie was just too sensitive an issue altogether. Yet looking back on this dreadful year, I still felt that the ordinary person in the street should know what to expect when their child dies violently—especially as I had read with astonishment the Victim's Charter which Pat, my Victim Support volunteer, brought me. It bore little resemblance to our own experience.

Christmas is drawing closer and I dread it. I quite understand that Steve wants to be near his father, Eric, but I want so desperately to be far away. I feel as if I am in perpetual shock, shaky and unable to do much more than weep, be cross and be bitter. And I am so very bitter. About everything. When people moan about trivial and unimportant things I could scream at them. Why don't they shut up and be grateful for what

Vicky and Stephen Harper by the birch tree as seen in the cover and
the frontispiece photograph of the twins.
(*By kind permission of the* Mail on Sunday)

they have got? And then, when I have stopped being bitter about them,
the guilt comes back: so many of our friends have had upsets since the
twins died that I must have the kiss of death.

Went to the park where they have been cutting down the branches of
the willows to enable the twins' trees to be planted.

While I was there, a squirrel dashed out in front of me, stopped and
scampered back again towards the biggest tree. There it sat looking
cheekily at me and so I moved towards it. Up and around the trunk it
went, always staying out of sight except for the tip of its tail. I began
chasing it around the tree until I realised that a lady and her dog were

watching me with a rather curious expression on their faces! At least with a squirrel playing round the twins' trees, there will continue to be some life about.

Went to the grave where the flowers looked so beautiful. The girls have had so many visitors that the grass seems almost worn away. But I am not complaining. I want to go to Church again before Christmas and to meet the new vicar—but I couldn't face a Communion or a Family Service.

I don't want it to be Christmas at all unless the girls are here.

I have so much love and no-one to give it to. No presents to buy and no stockings to fill. I miss them so very much.

Tuesday, 10th December 1991

Vicky's Victim Support volunteer:

The committal proceedings, to be held at Tewkesbury Magistrates' Court, were originally expected to last up to a week. It would be an old-style committal in which witnesses were called and questioned and the evidence tested for the case to be committed for trial by a higher Court. More normally, the Court considers written statements only.

Such a hearing can be, and often is, a traumatic experience and we were concerned about a whole week in which Vicky and Steve would find themselves in close contact with the families of the defendants—if not the defendants themselves. We were anxious to minimise this possibility and to make the experience as bearable as possible. And so we visited the Tewkesbury Court to see what arrangements could be made.

Vicky:

Pat and Felicity, Mum's comforter, had been over previously to Tewkesbury to make themselves known and to arrange for us to visit. They had obviously taken a great deal of time and trouble to find out everything they could, right down to the car park and what restaurants would be open at what times. They had met the Usher and several of the legal people, and they had introduced themselves to the Clerk of the Court and her staff.

When we arrived, Pat showed us the various waiting rooms and introduced us to the same Usher who had attended us in Cheltenham at that terrible first hearing. He greeted us warmly and took us to meet his two assistants, Ruth and Margaret, who overwhelmed us with their kindness. Their office-cum-kitchen was evidently the heart of the Court, warm and inviting with a kettle permanently on the boil I should imagine. Ruth's two dogs snuggled by the radiator and I found it very hard to believe I was actually in a court-house. We were offered the use of various offices if we needed to be alone during the proceedings—a great source of comfort knowing that there was a refuge there if we wanted it.

People who don't know may think it all very trivial to be given such domestic details, to be shown where the back stairs are and to have permission to use them. But knowing what to expect and being confident that there would be a friendly face waiting to guide us, gave us the strength to face what lay ahead. Our gratitude goes to those people at the Tewkesbury Court.

On the way back, we passed the barn now refilled with hay and straw. And once again we were struck by the closeness of houses, 'phone boxes and the busy main road. This was no barn stuck out in the middle of nowhere, miles from civilisation.

I went on to work that afternoon but the strain of the visit to Tewkesbury had taken its toll. When I left the clinic, it was dark and foggy—and I cried all the way home. It is strange how one lives through nightmares like ours without any outward display of grief. And then the terrible situation hits you. Hard.

Tuesday, 17th December 1991

Vicky:

Spent most of the morning getting ready for the Hospital Christmas lunch. I don't really feel like going and I am frightened of spoiling it for everyone. But they've all made me feel so welcome that I'll try. I tried with my contact lenses too—and for the first time after having them, they went in successfully!

On arrival at the lunch, we were given a glass of sherry and shown into the dining room which was very nicely laid out. There were crackers, fruit, sweets and other goodies on the tables—and games, wine and a marvellous lunch which was a credit to the staff. It occurred to me that, if Beckie had still been alive, she would have been at the lunch too, but probably not sitting with her old Mum. It felt odd, too, not taking home the spare crackers and novelties—those pleasures belonged to people who still had children to enjoy.

When I finally left work that evening, the wind had picked up quite a lot and I was worried that the flowers on the twins' grave would blow away. So I rang Steve at his Mum's and asked if he could pop round to make sure they were alright. Something was wrong however and, when Steve came home, he was obviously very upset. Eric's condition had deteriorated and the doctor had been called. He had confirmed what we had feared all along.

There was nothing now to be done for Eric except to make his last few days as comfortable as possible. Eric himself was shocked and desperately upset—we all were. Even though we knew he was poorly, there had always seemed to be a chance that he might have pulled through.

I feel very strange about the whole thing. I shall be upset when Eric dies. I wish he did not have to suffer—but I am jealous. He will soon be in Heaven and can talk to the girls. Can find out what happened. I want to send a message with him but I can hardly say: *"Oh, Eric, when you get up there, tell the twins I love them, will you?"*

This is going to be a shit of a Christmas.

Friday, 20th December 1991

Vicky:

The police were due round again tonight to go through the box of evidence including the photographs of the remains of the twins. I am dreading it but we need to know exactly what had been recovered. Having read the list, I still find it hard to believe that more tests could not have been done or some reason for death established.

Barbara called in the morning to say that Mr Gaskins had been taken ill and would not be able to join us in the evening. She brought us a Christmas Card and a framed goodwill message from Pam Ayres. I gave her lockets for Sarah and herself and a bottle of whisky for Bill Gaskins. We also sent a box of biscuits for the CID to eat on Christmas Day.

Barbara and I sat in the sitting room drinking coffee when she explained that the final forensic report had come through from Dr Hill and that it contained some very bad news. The murder charges were based on there being no sign of soot in Beckie's windpipe—but now it seemed that Dr Hill had found something consistent with soot.

This was entirely the opposite of what we had hoped for and expected. I continued to believe that the girls were dead or unconscious at the time of the fire—because if they had been alive they would have escaped, or if they were burning to death they would have screamed the place down. No-one can tell me anything different.

I was very upset by Barbara's news. It means we have to start all over again trying to understand what terror the girls actually suffered and what agony they must have endured. But the news still did not explain why the boys left two girls behind without raising the alarm and apparently ignoring the 'phone box, house and main road just ten yards away.

I rang Steve when Barbara had gone. He came home straight away thankfully, but with more bad news. Eric had been very ill in the night and the doctor had been called yet again. I suggested that we go round to stay with Mary, to cook her a meal and for Steve to be available through the coming night. Pat from Victim Support called in—I could not discuss Dr Hill's report, which was still not official, but talking about Steve and his father made me feel stronger and determined to help support the family that remained.

Saturday, 21st December 1991

Vicky:

It was about 4 am that Mary woke me asking if Steve and I would like a cup of tea. She said that Eric was having a very bad night and I think she was frightened. She had had very little sleep for some time and had coped marvellously but I felt she was getting to the end of her tether.

I offered to make the tea so that she could stay with Eric. And, assuming that Steve was getting up, I went downstairs. When I had made the tea I took Mary and Eric a cup each and was about to go down to have mine in the kitchen when Mary said that she wanted to fetch Eric a hot water bottle. He was shivering with the cold and making sounds over and over again.

When Mary had gone I did not know what to do. Eric said he was very cold and so I told him that Mary was getting him a bottle. I just kept talking to him. He was shaking under the blankets and I started to rub his hand to comfort him and reassure him—and in that moment all my fear left me. I knew I could and would cope.

The noises he was making continued for some time, along with the occasional humorous remark. His sense of humour was with him right to the end. At one point he said: "I've got a frog in my throat" and I replied: "I know, I can hear it. It sounds like a bloody great toad." He smiled and the noises in his throat changed to sad, distorted laughter.

At one point he said something about someone standing there and I wondered, if I had looked around, whether I would have seen the twins standing waiting for him to join them in Heaven. I think the thought that he was going to be with them was a great consolation for us all.

Eric complained only once, saying how ridiculous it was not being able to get warm in one's own house. Mary and I talked to him and to each other. Occasionally he would reply or make some comment. We had left Steve to sleep realising that he must be very tired. After about two hours the noise changed again and Eric began to call for Steve. I went in and gently woke him saying I thought it was time for him to come. And then I went back to tell Eric that his son was on his way.

Mary and I even giggled at one point because after the first half hour I realised that I had not been stroking Eric's hand at all but merely a lump in the special mattress the nurse had brought him! I soon found his hand however and Eric responded several times to my touch.

It was the eeriest feeling in the world. The dawn coming up through the open shutters. The occasional whirr of the machine at Eric's bedside as it dispensed its soothing drug. And the slow intaking of breath and noise. Watching Mary tending him, I realised that she was watching over 43 years of married life slip away before her eyes. The pain in them was hard to bear.

As soon as Steve came in and took my chair, holding his father's hand and stroking his forehead, Eric seemed to relax and be at peace. Eventually the noise stopped and there was just the rattle of fluid in his throat as his body expelled its last few breaths. His soul, I think, had already started its journey upwards to Heaven and to my girls. How I longed to say to him to tell them that I loved them. And then the body itself gave up. The final emptying of the container that had once held the soul of Eric gave up its task and all was quiet.

The way that day passed was controlled and impressive. The undertakers, who had been so good to us when the girls died, called and completed their business. The district nurse calmly answered all of Mary's questions. The family arrived and took her away for the Christmas period.

I wished that, when the twins died, it had been like that for them. But as the day closed, my concern was now for Steve. How would he cope with this new loss and unhappiness?

Steve:

Arrived home at about 10.00 am completely drained after the night's trauma. As we opened the door the telephone rang—it was D.C.I Gaskins ringing to explain the reasons for having to drop the murder charges.

I simply had to hand the 'phone to Vicky.

Vicky:

Steve has been so strong for me—but how much can a man take?

CHAPTER EIGHT

The Evidence and The Experts

early January 1992

Vicky:

The first day of this happy New Year dawned with a slight headache. There was just a little too much festive spirit at the party our friends invited us to. But it was lovely to be away from Cheltenham and to be with people who always made us welcome.

It's a sad time, of course, as it will soon be the first anniversary of the girls' deaths. People have told us that, once the first year is over, it all becomes easier. But I have not seen much sign of that yet. On top of everything else, my Mum is now poorly, just generally under the weather, and Steve's Mum is still in a state as you might expect. So, what with one thing and another, we are having to do a fair bit of running around.

We were briefly distracted from preparations for Eric's funeral with news from Dr Giraldi that the new Harper Clinic in Charlton Kings had organised a poetry competition among local schools—a nice, worthwhile way to carry on the twins' names which we appreciated. But the funeral on the 7th still dominated everything. Mary is very upset and so is Steve, as if he doesn't have enough to cope with. I seem to have found extra strength over the last few weeks and, although I am very tired, I feel that I shall manage at least.

We all met at the cemetery and went into the tiny chapel. Mary had asked for 'All things bright and beautiful', the same rousing hymn that Eric had chosen for the twins' Memorial Service. It was a very emotional time and I found it difficult to hold back the tears—for Eric and, of course, for Emma and Beckie. The Minister was a lady Methodist Minister who had called on Mary on several occasions to learn the background of Eric's life. She spoke well about him and Mary seemed comforted by her words.

173

After the Service, we walked round to the burial site. As I walked with Chris and Rose, the hearse passed by with one of its wheels squeaking. I smiled because Eric always used to call Emma and Beckie "the squeakies". But then, as we stood in silence around the grave, I could smile no more as I thought back over a year which had cost me the lives of three people. I only hoped that we should all be able to endure the year ahead.

When the burial was over, we went back to Mary's for a drink and some of the sandwiches I seemed to have been making endlessly that morning with Julia. It was sombre but we all remembered Eric in our different ways and sometimes we found comfort in our memories. I was glad to get home though and to be able to unwind. Both Steve and I had been strong for Mary's sake that day but now we gave in to the tension that was affecting us both.

late January 1992

Vicky:

Mum has been poorly for some time and now she is being taken into hospital.

I had been to see her every day and friends had been rallying round too. On the 17th, however, I arrived to find her very confused. It seemed that she had woken several times during the night and taken some of her antibiotics—but, because she'd been only half awake, she had also taken a sleeping tablet and goodness knows what else too. I 'phoned the doctor who diagnosed pneumonia and called an ambulance straight away.

In fact it was a great relief for me, knowing that she was now in safe hands. Caring for her myself as the anniversary of the twins' deaths approached would have been quite beyond my capabilities. We also had the Harper Clinic's poetry prize-giving to attend. Mum had been reading the various entries and she had also been invited to present the prizes. But thankfully, another friend and poet, Rosemary, agreed to stand in for her and to take me to the event itself. It was a lovely afternoon which the pensioners really enjoyed.

As the 23rd approached, life became more frenzied. Mary was not eating properly, Mum was still in hospital and Steve and I were trying to keep working. A number of friends supported me at this time by regularly visiting and encouraging me. But conversation always turned to events a year ago—

—at this particular time we were doing this with the girls. At that moment Emma said this. Do you remember that Beckie did that?

How much I longed to speak to them, to say they were not forgotten. Throughout the past year, their friends had remembered them on special days, with flowers and notes—they had visited us too which was nice. But now we could only put an *In Memoriam* notice in the newspaper and make our daily visit to the grave to make sure that everything was right.

On the Wednesday, 22nd January, we were surprised and delighted to find someone else had already been there and left some flowers. It was going to be quite crowded as I had brought with me two baskets from us and one from my Mum. I looked at the card—and found it was from Sian, a friend and chorister for many years. I always keep these cards for future reference.

On the 23rd, we received several other cards through the post. Cards from dear friends which made us cry but brought some comfort too. And on the 24th, we were obviously very unhappy after a stressful broken night.

At the grave, the flowers were spread out on the grass and I do so want to say thank you to those who remembered and paid their respects in this way—

—to Steve's mother, Mary. To June and Richard. To Charlotte, Stuart, Jo (weevil), Julia, Karen, Andrew and cousin Chris. To Mal and Pete, Ken and Trish, Nicky and the physios from work. To Leanne, Vicki, Justine, Steve's sister Julia, Marie and Sarah.

We spent some time in the quiet setting of the neat Garden of Remembrance at Christ Church, with the trees all around us. We read the cards and photographed the flowers. I don't know why we are keeping a record of these things because there is no-one left to pass them on to. But still it brings us some comfort to take back home.

Back at home, on this day of all days, there was ominous news waiting for us. Detective Chief Inspector Gaskins called to explain the report they had received from the pathologist, Dr Ian Hill in the Unit of Forensic Medicine at the London Hospital Medical College. Dr Hill had been consulted in order to provide support for the first forensic

175

report that no soot had been found in Beckie's windpipe. Now, it seemed, there had been something in her windpipe which he thought could be soot.

After much questioning and explaining, the police agreed that it would be simpler if we saw the reports from the scientists involved. To help us all try to understand what had been found, we would sit down and read through all the reports available. We were even told about the statements of the Fire Officers at the scene in order that we might gain the clearest picture of exactly what might have happened. And briefed upon the information gathered in interviews with those involved and witnesses. Later, the Home Office provided us with copies of these reports to keep.

Understanding as much as possible was the important thing for Steve and me. We had learned, for example, that it was policy to leave fires in barns to burn themselves out once any livestock and machinery had been rescued. But as the boys had left the scene without telling anyone that Emma and Beckie were still inside, the fire was allowed to continue burning and obliterating any traces of whatever had happened there. Among the questions we wished to be able to answer, therefore, was whether any of the boys knew about this policy beforehand.

Please bear with me as I try and lead you through the evidence that has been given us as far as I understand it.

the evidence and the experts

From Chambers Dictionary:

EVIDENCE—that which makes evident; the means of proving an unknown or disputed fact
EXPERT—taught by practice; having a thorough knowledge; someone who is skilled in any art or science; a scientific or professional witness
EXPERTISE—expert knowledge
EXPERIENCE—practical acquaintance with any matter, gained by trial; wisdom derived in the course of life; to have practical acquaintance with

Vicky:

I have no scientific training or expertise and, therefore, I must rely upon the experts to determine what caused the deaths of my children. I shall concentrate on what they said had happened to Beckie. You will see that it was impossible to deduce anything from what was found of Emma. You will also see why this new report from Dr Hill threw everything up in the air.

The first expert to be called to the scene of the fire was Dr Bogdan Hulewicz of the University of Wales College of Medicine (The Wales Institute of Forensic Medicine) who reported his *post mortem* examination like this...

Dr Bogdan Hulewicz:

At 2030 hours on Thursday 24th January 1991, I went at the request of Gloucestershire CID to Manor Farm, Tewkesbury Road, Uckington, Cheltenham. In "Bay 2" of a burnt out barn I saw human remains which were lying on partially burnt straw, the remains being located on the roadside part of the bay. The remains were in several separate pieces within which were identified bones, charred skin, muscle and intestines, part of a skull and a charred hand, a forearm with bangles around the wrist. I was informed by police officers that at approximately 0100 hours on Thursday 24th January 1991, a fire had been discovered in the barn which was full of bales of straw. When the fire had been brought under control a "JCB" mechanical digger was sent into the barn to remove smouldering straw, during this procedure and during raking of the straw, remains of a body were discovered. The remains were transferred on several metallic trays to the mortuary of Cheltenham General Hospital where I carried out a *post mortem* examination commencing at 2155 hours and finishing at 0035 hours in the presence of Detective Superintendent Hart, Detective Superintendent Shayle, DCI Gaskins, DS Brooks, DS Gibb, DC Jordan (Scenes of Crime) and J Coopey (Coroner's Officer).

Prior to the *post mortem* examination the remains were x-rayed by Miss Rimill (Radiographer).

The remains comprised:

1 The right hip bone (hemi-pelvis) with attached charred and cooked muscle and soft tissue. The upper part of the hip bone (iliac crest) was not fused to the major portion of this bone.
2 Two partly charred short segments of forearm bones with attached charred muscle.
3 Base and back of skull (foramen magnum and occipital bone) with a short segment of attached spinal cord, the first two bones of the neck (atlas and axis) charred muscle and skin and seven bones from the chest part of the back bone (thoracic vertebrae). The upper and lower surfaces of these vertebrae showed radial markings.
4 The lower bone from the chest part of the back bone (12th thoracic vertebra), five bones from the lower part of the back bone (lumbar vertebrae), sacrum, with attached charred muscle and cooked intestines, blood vessels, uterus (womb), fallopian tubes, both ovaries and bladder. A short segment of spinal cord (approximately 10 cm long) protruded from the exposed spinal canal. The cut surface of the uterus revealed no evidence of pregnancy or of an intra-uterine contraceptive device.
5 Five ribs with attached cooked muscle.
6 Upper part of right thigh bone (femur) including the head, neck and greater trochanter. The growing ends of the bone (epiphyses) were fused.
7 The upper half of the bone of the right upper arm (humerus). The growing end of the bone (epiphyses) was fused.
8 The upper third of the bone of the left upper arm (humerus) with attached charred muscle. The growing end of the bone (epiphyses) was fused.
9 Six ribs.
10 Three separate sets of seven metal bangles attached by metal clips.
11 The left hip bone (hemi-pelvis) with attached upper half of left thigh bone (femur). The upper part of the hip bone (iliac crest) was not fused to the major portion of this bone.
12 The right shoulder blade.
13 Seven ribs.

14 The left hand and lower forearm, the palm aspect of the hand was covered by charred skin. Charred bone and muscles exposed on the back of the hand. Two sets of seven bangles were present around the wrist.

15 Piece of charred skin approximately 22 cm in diameter with underlying cooked fat and muscle.

16 Four bones of the neck (cervical vertebrae) with attached soft tissues.

17 Left shoulder blade (scapula) and soft tissue, two thoracic vertebrae, lower half of the windpipe (trachea) and gullet (oesophagus), both lungs, segment of aorta, part of the liver, loops of small intestine, stomach, part of the right chamber (ventricle) of the heart, both kidneys and adrenals and spleen. There was no evidence of soot in the windpipe, both main bronchi or in the smaller airways.

During this *post mortem* examination samples of lung, muscle and clotted blood from the aorta were handed to DC Jordan (Scenes of Crime Officer).

The remains were transferred to the Wales Institute of Forensic Medicine at Cardiff Royal Infirmary for further examination...

At approximately 1315 hours on Monday 28th January 1991 I went to the mortuary of Cardiff Royal Infirmary where in the presence of DC Jordan (Scenes of Crimes Officer) and Paul Rogers (Fingerprint expert) I made a further examination of the original remains removed from "Bay 2" (Roadside) and also an examination of other remains which had been found subsequently. The latter comprised the following:

1 *Tray labelled specimen from "field site"*
   Prior to dissection this specimen was x-rayed. The specimen comprised charred muscle, the upper end of the right thigh bone (femur), the head (i.e. that part of the thigh bone which joins the hip bone to form the hip joint and greater trochanter were both missing). A short segment of the shaft of the left thigh bone (femur), two short segments of the left and right pubic bones, short loops of small intestine and a cooked uterus (womb), left fallopian tube and left ovary. The cut surface of the uterus showed no evidence of pregnancy or of an intra-uterine contraceptive device.

2 *Tray labelled "field site"*
There were approximately 75 separate pieces of burnt short bones (eg bones from hands/feet) and fragments of burnt long bones.

3 *Tray labelled "Bay 2"*
Approximately 70 separate pieces of burnt short bones and segments of burnt long bones. Head of upper arm bone which was partly calcine and two charred vertebrae.

4 *Bag labelled "Bay 2" (far side from road)*
Numerous fragments of burnt bones.

5 *Bag labelled "Bay 4"*
Four pieces of burnt bones.

6 *Bag labelled "Bay 4" (roadside)*
Two small charred bones.

7 *Bag labelled "Bay 2" (far side)*
Fragmented burnt molar tooth.

8 *Bag labelled "Bay 2"*
Approximately 20 small pieces of burnt bones.

9 *Tray labelled "Bay 2" (roadside)*
Charred muscle, skin, five segments of ribs and one bone of the neck (cervical vertebra).

I was also shown bags containing a belt buckle, hair clip and part of a burnt dress with an attached zipper...

Remains found in "Bay 2" on 24th January 1991/body No 1.

The remains belong to one body.

The presence of a uterus (womb) indicates a female.

The absence of fusion of the upper part of the hip bones (iliac crest) to the major portions of these bones and fusion of the upper growing end (epiphyses) of the upper arm bones (humerus) and thigh bones (femur) indicates an age of between 17-20 years.

With respect to the question "was the deceased dead or alive during the fire", the absence of soot in the airways only indicates that smoke was not inhaled. It does not necessarily indicate that the deceased was dead prior to the fire starting. Death may have occurred rapidly due to burning. Toxicological examination of the lungs and muscles for carbon monoxide may be of assistance.

It is not possible to determine whether there was any injury inflicted on the body prior to death. However, there is evidence of severe heat damage and of disruption of the body after death, the latter being entirely consistent with having been caused by a JCB digger.

Remains found in "field site" and elsewhere/body No 2.

The remains from the tray labelled specimen from "field site" belong to one body. The presence of a uterus (womb) indicates that it is a female. In the absence of the growing ends of the thigh bones and hip bones it is difficult to assess the age. However, the "rough" appearances of the articular surfaces of the two pubic bones (pubic symphysis) are in keeping with a young female. Due to the severe degree of heat damage it is not possible to determine whether the deceased was dead or alive prior to the fire starting, nor is it possible to determine whether injury was inflicted before death.

The bones from the other sites belong to both bodies.

In conclusion, the remains are of two young females showing severe heat damage and *post mortem* disruption. At the present moment the causes of death remain unascertained.

Vicky:

To us, the most important points in Dr Hulewicz's report concerned the JCB mechanical digger, which had been sent into the barn to remove smouldering straw, and the investigation of 'the remains' from Bay 2. The report tells us that 'the remains' had been discovered after the JCB had been sent into the barn.

It seems obvious, but still worth stating, that any contact between the JCB and the burnt remains of a human body would do great damage to an already fragile object. We automatically assume, therefore, that the incompleteness of 'the remains' and its dismembered state were actually the result of the work of the JCB. Dr Hulewicz even commented that:

> *"...there is evidence of severe heat damage and of disruption of the body after death, the latter being entirely consistent with having been caused by a JCB digger."*

Contrast this, however, with information from the fireman who first saw the 'remains' while raking straw, that the JCB did not go into that part of Bay 2 and that its work was confined to the back of the barn. Just as importantly, he says that great care was taken in identifying the objects he had found. People had been walking in that area but the disturbance, it seems, would have been unlikely to have caused the extent of damage done to Beckie's remains.

Whatever the truth of the raking and the walking, Steve and I see an immediate conflict between a *post mortem* report of damage consistent with disruption by a JCB and a fireman's belief that the JCB never went into the area where Beckie had been found. The JCB never went near Beckie. Something else must have caused her to be found in pieces.

The fact that Beckie was lying face down raises further questions. Why was Beckie lying face down? Why, if people had been walking over that area, did they not notice earlier what was left of her body? Why, if Beckie had been lying face down on partially burnt straw as Dr Hulewicz describes, was the front of her skull missing? How was it removed?

That other pieces were missing is important, too. All through the investigations, I have never understood the disappearance of Beckie's two braces. Let me explain why. Photographs of Beckie showed that her intestines removed from Bay 2 retained some of their colour—they weren't completely black and charred. This has to be consistent with "*...lying on partially burnt straw...*", in other words lying in a place where the fire had not been total. But why, if her intestines had only been partially burnt, weren't Beckie's two dental braces found in Bay 2 with the rest of her? Surely, skin and muscle would be destroyed before the metal attached to her teeth? After all, the bangles on her wrist all survived, so why not the braces in her mouth?

A tooth was found some distance from where both Emma and Beckie were located. We want to know how that tooth got from the mouth of one of the two girls to the place where it was found. Why, and how, had it been separated from the head to which it belonged?

The next important point to think about in Dr Hulewicz's report is the remark:

"With respect to the question 'Was the deceased dead or alive during the fire?', the absence of soot in the airways only indicates that smoke was not inhaled."

To us this means one of two things. Either Beckie was dead at the time of the fire. Or she was unable to inhale because of some blockage or covering of her mouth and nose—and presumably, therefore, well on the way to becoming dead. It could be argued that Beckie herself might have forced her face down into the straw to avoid the smoke. But I don't accept that unrestrained people would deliberately suffocate themselves if complete escape was an option—they would be screaming their heads off trying to get out and to raise the alarm. Anyone with the front of their skull missing, of course, would be incapable of blocking whatever remained of their airways. But fires don't remove the fronts of skulls, do they?

So much made dreadful sense in so many ways until Dr Hulewicz made the added observation that:

"[. . . the absence of soot in the airways . . .] does not necessarily indicate that Beckie was not breathing at the time of the fire. Death may have occurred rapidly due to burning."

But once again, I simply do not see a healthy 17 year old girl submitting quietly and totally to the agony of a fire. And I simply do not believe that the fire in that particular barn, however swiftly it spread, could have enveloped her so quickly that her life was extinguished before she could draw one single breath in an environment which tests proved was full of smoke and soot and carbon deposits. How could either of these possibilities—quiet submission or instantaneous loss of life through the threat of burning—have occurred when David Harper explains that he managed to stay behind in the barn without succumbing or being affected at all?

The Home Office forensic scientist, Dr John Fox, told us what the conditions must have been like based on official tests conducted at the Fire Services College, Moreton-in-Marsh, Gloucestershire:

"Two minutes from ignition the stack was burning intensely involving most of the surface. At four minutes, the stack was disintegrating and producing large volumes of smoke. At this stage

*[four minutes], it was not possible to remain within the building
structure for any length of time because of the intense heat and
choking smoke."*

In other words, you could survive briefly in the barn before dying or
making an escape but not for very long. Instant death through rapid
burning would have been unlikely in that particular barn fire. Yet again,
therefore, Steve and I want to know why Beckie didn't use those few
precious moments to get out to safety? Why, as the boys assert, no
sound was heard? Quite obviously, she did not block her own airways
for several minutes in the course of which something removed the front
of her skull. So what had already happened to Beckie's actual physical
condition, or what constraints had been made upon her actual physical
circumstances, to prevent her from making an attempt to get out as soon
as the fire started?

Dr Fox had more to say on the effect of carbon monoxide on people
exposed to it:

*"The smoke produced by burning hay and straw consists of the
major combustion products, water and carbon dioxide. Some
carbon monoxide will be present as a result of incomplete
combustion. In an open fire situation, I would expect this
concentration to be small and such concentration would not have
an immediate effect on a person breathing such smoke. Low
concentrations of carbon monoxide must be inhaled continually
over a long period to have any effect on the person involved."*

The extra information that the three boys made desperate attempts to
put out the fire—staying behind in the barn, jumping up and down,
throwing bales around and even urinating together on the flames in
front of them—might then be supportable.

Steve:

I find it impossible to accept that the three of them were urinating on the
flames together all at the same time. As Chadd, the prosecution QC, was
later to say in his address to the Court, this was a case of *"one for all and
all for one"*—the only possible explanation for the ease with which
three youths faced 25 feet flames, and urinated simultaneously shortly
after having sex.

Vicky:

This act of deliberate exposure and original fire-fighting effort does not, to my mind, quite tie in with the boys' failure to raise the alarm at the telephone box a few yards away. And it still does not explain why Beckie could not use the same period of time to make her escape. We found it impossible, therefore, to believe some of the things being said to us—especially in view of Dr Fox's final remarks:

"The smoke would contain soot particles. A person breathing such smoke would inhale those particles. The particles would normally enter the airways together with inhaled air . . .

"I would also expect the clothing of a person who attempted to extinguish an established hay or straw fire to show evidence of this attempt in the form of soot or smut particles and heat or burning damage."

The truth is that the three youths, who turned up at the police station nearly two days after the fire, were evidently none the worse for their experience. They had also, by their own admission, washed the clothes they had been wearing at the time. Was soot so damaging? And why did Beckie's leather jacket, which had been recovered from Winter's house having been worn by Smith and Winter, show no sign of heat marks at all? Why was there no evidence of scorching or burning on David Harper's jeans? Why was no evidence of burning or of hay or straw found on his boots? Why were Winter's trainers found in good condition with only some mud entrapped in the soles? Why was no burning or scorching found on any of the clothing worn by the three boys except for a melted thread end on the jeans belonging to Winter?

In fact it was only the right shoe of Wisdom Smith which was smeared black and carbonised with vegetable debris.

Confronted with such personal cleanliness, Steve and I could only keep asking why two of the five people at the scene of a barn fire perished while the three others walked away with no effects of smoke inhalation and neither burn nor scorch marks on their clothes. Dr Hulewicz didn't help us much in finding an answer:

"The absence of soot in the windpipe and airways raises a number of possibilities as to the cause of death. If death occurred before

the onset of fire, then it could have been due to natural or unnatural causes. The most likely causes of death in a young person are a heart defect ... or spontaneous brain haemorrhage... Unnatural causes include pressure on the neck, stabbing, blunt trauma etc. Due to extensive heat destruction of the body, it is impossible from the autopsy examination to determine whether any of the above caused death. If death occurred after the onset of the fire, then again a number of possibilities exist: death could have occurred as a consequence of burning (i.e. due to effects of heat or flame), carbon monoxide and/or other noxious gas poisoning, or due to natural causes. In the latter case, it is well recognised that in the presence of severe heart disease, acute mental and/or physical stress can induce heart stoppage and death. In my opinion, it would not have been possible for the soot to have been completely washed away by water from the Fire Brigade. In conclusion, the autopsy examination has failed to determine whether or not the deceased was dead or alive prior to the onset of the fire and has also failed to determine a cause of death."

On one point only did Dr Hulewicz say something definite by way of expert opinion. This was on seeing a video of the fire tests at Moreton-in-Marsh also observed by Dr Fox. Dr Hulewicz said:

"...If a person died as a consequence of smoke inhalation in a fire as shown on the video, then I would expect to find soot in the airways. Microscopic examination of Rebecca Harper's airways and lungs showed no evidence of soot."

On this had been based the charges of Murder.

With the investigations completed, we had been allowed to have the remains of Emma and Beckie back. We had cremated them and interned them in Christ Church Memorial Gardens. And, in so doing, we had unknowingly destroyed any evidence that was left. We could now only rely upon what the experts had to say.

I have never seen so many expert opinions or wild distractions in the months that followed. But at least Dr Hill's preliminary thoughts gave some support to Dr Hulewicz and reinforced our own conclusions:

"[...my experience of burning grass or straw ...] is that it gives off very acrid smoke which hurts the eyes and makes one choke. Therefore, it is hard to see why the girls did not respond...

"It is not inevitable that people who are alive in fires will actually have soot particles in the airways, but when they are there, then it indicates that they took at least one breath...

"People can die from the effects of intense heat. This can occur very quickly indeed. But I would not be happy at giving this cause here because, despite the tests and the speed of onset and spread of the fire, there would seem to have been enough time for smoke to have spread across to where the girls were. This strongly suggests to me that there is a good chance that they were not able to help themselves and indeed that they may have been dead before their bodies were consumed by the fire."

Dr Hill then asked for an opportunity of examining certain specimens before giving a detailed report. These 'specimens' proved to be slides taken from Beckie's remains (without our knowledge incidentally). You will understand our enormous shock, therefore, when Dr Hill announced, in a report dated 14th January 1992, that he had found a particle of what might have been soot!

Working from slides—whereas Dr Hulewicz had worked from the actual pieces that were left of Beckie, pieces that were now cremated and interred in Christ Church Gardens, Cheltenham—Dr Hill has found something consistent with soot.

Dr Hill:

Histological (Histology—the study of the minute structure of the tissues of organisms) examination of sections of the lungs and the airways, said to have come from the above named, whose remains were found in the burnt out shell of a barn at Manor Farm, Uckington, near Cheltenham, revealed the following:—

Airways
There is marked vascular (vessels containing fluid, blood, etc.) congestion. Some sections show deposits of black material, lying on or near the surface, within the lumen (cavity of an organ). The appearances of this

187

material are consistent with those of soot. There is also some blood lying on the luminal surface.

LUNGS

These show marked congestion, pulmonary oedema and heat artefact. (Pulmonary oedema—waterlogging of the lung tissue).

Opinion: The histological appearances indicate that this young lady was alive when the barn was ablaze. Whilst the amount of soot present is small, it can only have got there by inhalation. Contamination is unlikely. Support for this is to be found in the fact that there is vascular congestion in the airways. The appearances in the lungs, whilst they are not pathognemonic (characteristic) of fire deaths, are nevertheless consistent with such an aetiology (cause or origin).

These microscopic appearances do not indicate the cause of death in themselves. The differential diagnosis must still contain, injury predisposing to incapacitation and to possible inhalation of blood, inhalation of fire fumes and also being overcome by heat. In my opinion, it is impossible to resolve this question. Had there been some toxicological evidence, then this would have gone some way towards resolving the outstanding questions, but we do not have that. It is possible that she could have been unconscious before the fire was started, due either to injury or to an intoxicant. This, or covering her face, could have reduced the soot intake into the airways. It is also possible that she could have been subjected to intense heat, which would have killed her rapidly.

The only categoric conclusion which can be drawn from the available evidence is that she was alive in the fire.

Vicky:

Now you will understand how shocked we were by Dr Hill's expert opinion. Because no-one could explain why Beckie had not walked away from the fire as the three boys had done, all the horrors of not knowing what had happened flooded my mind once more. And if we couldn't account for Beckie's death, what did this mean about Emma's fate?

The newspapers were full of the news that the Murder charges had been dropped. The trial of Harper, Smith and Winter would now be heard on Manslaughter, Arson and Perverting the Course of Justice—

and determined by whether or not a jury feels that the three boys were responsible for the fire and for the deaths. No mention will be made of how and why the girls died which we find very hard to take. It is of paramount importance to us to know the details of our daughters' deaths.

I feel I want to hire my own expert, to give a third opinion at the trial. But I quite see the police worry that, if the first two experts so completely disagree, it's all going to look rather foolish in Court. It makes me wonder how many so-called miscarriages of justice are actually caused by differences of forensic opinion. How can two experts say exactly opposite things? What does it say about their expertise? Perhaps an expert only gains expertise through experience? How many forensic scientists have experience of identical twin girls—aged 17 years and fit and healthy—dying in the vicinity of a fire?

I feel dreadfully let down and embarrassed in some way that I cannot explain. We received some cards from people expressing their anger and outrage. And then, on Saturday, 25th January 1992, we received an anonymous 'phone call—

—people had been seen in the Arcade, drunk, cheering and shouting *"They've got away with murder!"*

Monday, 3rd February 1992

Vicky:

After several false starts, the trees will at last be planted today in Hatherley Park in memory of the twins. But even at this late stage, things were going wrong. About two hours before the planting, I received a telephone call to say that the trees had not arrived—would it be alright if they planted something else so that the small ceremony could go ahead? They would plant the two willows later.

I was very disappointed but gave my agreement. At least it was a nice day and the sun was shining.

Among the people who will be there are two friends of the twins. I wonder how they are feeling? It seems such a sad occasion for them but important, we felt, that the trees should be planted by young people. In this way we would be able to see new life in the trees and to say a lasting thank you to the two girls for the friendship they had given Emma and Beckie.

Rachael will plant Beckie's tree. It was Rachael who always used to

189

The trees planted in commemoration of Emma's and Beckie's lives in 1992.

wait so patiently for Beckie each morning, who came to see me on that dreadful Friday last year to find out if Beckie was alright, and who wrote beautifully describing her feelings when Beckie died. And Alison will plant the tree for Emma. Alison, the long-standing friend from school-days who was always there for Emma.

Things are delayed at Hatherley Park and, while we are standing around waiting, I suggest to Steve's Mum that perhaps a bench could be erected in front of the trees in memory of Eric. Everyone likes the idea and we talk to the man from the park who agrees to contact us later.

The sun stays out and the squirrels make an appearance. A robin flutters around us. We are told that the spade has been used by the Queen.

The ceremony begins with much giggling. The *Echo* photographer asks the girls to keep digging the dirt over and over again until she is satisfied with her picture. And we stand there keeping the smiles on our faces, our backs aching, while everyone else takes their photographs.

And then, as we quietly chat when it's all over, the sadness comes over me as it always does. It has been a lovely morning but the fact is that we are here because the girls are dead. Steve sees my sadness and remarks that, in a hundred years, when we are all long since gone, the trees will still be here giving pleasure to people—the girls' memories will hope-fully live on and thrive in the roots and branches of the two trees.

We left the park and, as if in sympathy, the dark clouds covered the sun. The squirrels ran to hide and the robin flew away.

Rachael Batchelor, who planted Beckie's tree:

When Beckie Harper died in a barn fire I couldn't believe it, it was just like a dream that one day I would awaken from and find Beckie here still with me.

Beckie and I knew nothing of one another before we came to College but from day one we hit it off straight away, we didn't need anyone else because it was impossible for us to lose one another. Neither of us relied on anyone else in class because we knew we'd be friends for life no matter what happened. My feelings for Beckie as a friend were very strong even though we had only a short friendship before she passed away. She was a true, trustworthy, honest friend.

I was so upset at the thought of her gone and never coming back. I miss her strolling into class late, giggling without any cares in the world. Beckie was an easy to get on with person. She would do anything for anyone and she was well liked and loved by everyone around her. I was so upset that she had died in such a traumatic way and when I think of it, I feel frightened.

Beckie is now resting in peace and her parents and the people around her parents are the ones that are suffering now.

I will treasure all my memories of her. She will never be forgotten. I remember the times we went back to her house for lunch and sat watching the television. People take it for granted but I will treasure all the happy times we spent together. Sometimes now when I am upset or depressed about something, I wish I could ring her up and talk to her about it and reach out to her for help. But when I do get like that I think back to the memories and that brings back smiles but at the same time tears.

Before something like this happens you think it can't happen to me or to anyone I know but people are mistaken, it can happen to anyone. It is so distressing but at the same time you've got to think of the treasured moments you spent together because nothing you do will bring them back. Beckie was a loved and treasured friend to me and she will be in my thoughts and prayers for as long as I live.

Vicky's Victim Support volunteer:

On our earlier visit to the Tewkesbury Magistrates Court, we had found the Court officials and staff most sympathetic. They were keen to help Vicky and Stephen with facilities in case they needed to retire from the Court if the Committal Proceedings became too emotional or upsetting. They also made alternative access doors available to us.

In the event, whilst the arrangements at the Court went well, the case only lasted one full day because, during January, the Crown Prosecution Service had decided that the evidence no longer supported a charge of Murder. At the Court, therefore, the charge of Murder was withdrawn and a charge of Manslaughter was committed to the Crown Court. This was on the basis of written statements. No witnesses were called.

This was a big blow to Vicky and Stephen whose expectations had been built up since June 1991 when the charge of Murder had first been brought.

In preparation for the Crown Court case, my fellow Victim Support volunteer and I began to make similar arrangements (with the assistance of the then newly formed Bristol Witness Service) to those made at Tewkesbury Magistrates Court. These covered special facilities including a separate room and separate exit if required, for the use of Vicky and Steve and their families during the lengthy proceedings.

Vicky:

My Dad and Pat are here. So are our two Victim Support volunteers, mine and my Mum's. Mum wanted to come but she is still unwell and it would be silly for her to turn out on a cold day like this. Fiona Barton is here from the Mail on Sunday and has brought a photographer with her. And our two police friends, Barbara and Sarah are here of course, too.

As we enter the Court we have to go past the family of one of the boys. I feel very nervous but say "Excuse me" as politely as I can. Apparently, there has been some trouble in the car-park but no-one will tell us quite what.

Next, the three youths come into Court. The Magistrates are told that Harper has already agreed to be tried by jury at the Crown Court at a date yet to be set. And that the other two, Smith and Winter, intend to prove at this hearing that there is no case to answer against them.

Curran, the prosecution barrister, speaks first. And as he begins, I am reminded of the stupidity of our not being allowed to talk to him beforehand. He is getting things confused. And why does he have to say that Steve is not the biological father of the twins? What's the relevance of that when our two teenagers perished and three youths walked away unharmed? He says I didn't see the girls on the night they died—but I did. It was only a brief visit but they did come in to see me before going out.

For Christ's sake, talk about the girls will you?

At last he's beginning to cast doubt on the three youths' stories. He's saying that two of them would have to pass Beckie on the way out of the barn. But he just hasn't asked why they left Emma on top of the bales. Or why they could stand beside Harper when he was with Beckie and still insist that they had not seen her. Curran is not asking the right questions. He is missing out the important things. He is going to blow it—

—God, how I wish we could speak for ourselves!

The defence barrister, Steen, has begun to talk. He says it's mine and Steve's fault that the girls are dead. That we should have been stricter and less tolerant. He insults us further by saying that, if Emma and Beckie had got out of the barn and the three youths had perished, there would have been no charges brought against the girls. I am getting angrier—

—I am furious.

We adjourn for lunch and in our room are sandwiches, cake, fruit and a bunch of flowers. They have done us well and everyone is being so kind. But all I can think about is the Magistrates' decision.

We learn that, in the car park, someone has exposed himself to the *Mail on Sunday* photographer and that the police have been called. Wouldn't you have thought that people would be on their best behaviour at a time like this?

On the way back into Court, my Victim Support volunteer points out a woman who has been taking notes throughout the day and who is watching us very carefully. Pat goes to ask who she is—but at that moment the boys, including Harper, file past us.

What can I do? What do I feel at being so close to them? I know I have to retain my dignity and not let my emotions get the better of me. But by now the strain is showing on everyone's faces. I pray it will be quick.

It is!

The Magistrates have decided that the two youths, Winter and Smith, do have a case to answer and that they must stand trial with Harper for the Manslaughter of Beckie and Emma. They will also face charges of Arson and perverting the Course of Justice.

Thank God! Thank God.

Friday, 22nd May 1992

Vicky's Victim Support volunteer:

The case again went into a sort of limbo with either myself or my fellow volunteer 'phoning the Crown Prosection Service once a month to see if any date had been set for the Crown Court trial.

At last a date was set for a pre-trial hearing in May. This is a fairly technical hearing in which the Judge and the prosecuting and defence lawyers determine the amount of evidence, the number of witnesses to be called and therefore the likely length of the case.

I was on holiday and therefore unable to to be present at this meeting which took place in Bristol, where the Crown Court case was expected to be held. Vicky and Stephen attended, as did my co-volunteer who was able to tell Vicky's mother and me what happened.

It was decided that the Crown Court case in Bristol would take place on 26th October where it was expected to last two weeks.

Vicky:

Barabara picked us up at 8.30 this morning. Detective Chief Inspector Gaskins is taking my Mum's Victim Support volunteer and also Rita Crane and Leslie Jens from the Crown Prosecution Service.

Feeling very nervous. We are not quite sure what's going to happen. Outside the court building, there are some press cameramen—but they are not bothering us. Inside the building, I find myself looking at David Harper and his parents. There's no sign of the other two.

We try and keep away from them. It's not comfortable and we go to a café to pass the time. Back in the court building, we talk to friends who have come to support us and we try to understand who the various press people are. It seems they are all independent. Nothing much seems to be happening. There are barristers around wearing wigs. The courtroom isn't as grand or intimidating as I had thought it might be.

At about 10.45, the boys were called and a new Judge came in. But I have to say that what followed was completely lost on me. I couldn't hear a word that was being said apart from when our QC, Mr Chadd, spoke. All I managed to grasp was that the three boys are each going to plead Not Guilty to Manslaughter and Arson—even though David Harper has admitted lighting the fire...

The charge of Perverting the Course of Justice has been dropped so that, should the jury be unsure of their verdict, they would not have the opportunity of finding them guilty on just that one charge. I understand the principle behind this decision but I find it very, very difficult to accept, especially as the boys did nothing to alert the authorities and waited 36 hours before contacting a solicitor.

The one thing which does give me some reassurance is that the Judge has agreed that he and the jury should be taken to the barn to see the scene of the fire. This is very important to Steve and me—they will then be able to understand just how close the barn is to houses and the various escape routes that Emma and Beckie might have used. David Harper and Wisdom Smith have worked on that farm and on stacking the barn. They know the layout, too.

Next the defence lawyer asked that the youths' reporting conditions be lifted. It was too much trouble for them to have to sign on at the police station once a week. I was shocked—especially at learning that David Harper would be allowed to go away on holiday by himself and without his parents who had guaranteed bail. Still, that's the law for you.

As I walked out of the courtroom, I heard a lawyer say in a loud, clear voice: "Well at least we got rid of that perverting the course of justice nonsense." Yes, that's the law for you.

Very upset indeed, I turned to go to the loo with Barbara Harrison, at which point I noticed David Harper's father going over to talk to Steve. I stopped and drew Steve away immediately. As we left, feeling very ill and shaky, people were grinning at us.

When Barbara dropped us off at home, she promised to ask Mr Gaskins the questions we wanted answered. They both came back to see us that afternoon. One of the questions we wished to ask concerned the

Sections of a letter to David Harper's parents, written at the time but never sent:

You asked Steve at the Court the other day how we are coping. The simple answer is that we are not. From my own point of view, I am alive today because I cannot rest until I know what happened. I cannot understand how you can ask such a question. Your son stands accused on two charges of Manslaughter, one for Emma and one for Beckie, plus a charge of Arson. Five people went into that barn, only three came out and the only ones who know the truth are your son and his friends. You ask if there is anything you can do? You could ask your son to tell us the truth...

...How can I talk to you? If circumstances had been different, Steve and I would have been the first to help. If David and the other two had called the Fire Brigade or made any attempt to save the girls we would have understood maybe. But they ran away, miles away, and did not even report it for 36 hours...

...In the short space of time I knew David, he always seemed to me to be cold and callous. Many a time when Emma's money had run out he would leave her to walk home the three miles or so from Bishop's Cleeve. Sometimes her father collected her, other times he was out and she either got a taxi which we paid for or she walked. He never brought either of the girls home on time and, when reprimanded for this by me, never again came to the front door but hid in the back lane waiting for the girls. On New Year's Eve I had to ask him to leave my house. I know that the twins were not perfect by any means but I can assure you that they would never have behaved as your son has...

...If I were you when the hearing is finished, I would swiftly take him out of the building. I would not stand there cuddling him in front of the childless couple whose lives are ruined. If I were you, I would not send messages through the police saying how sorry you are. I would not attempt to talk to us. I would keep my distance...

...Do you know what it is like to try to imagine how Emma and Beckie died? The imagination is a terrible thing and both Steve and I torture ourselves endlessly trying to find out. I believe that whatever happened, the girls suffered and must have been terrified...

...You ask how we are coping? The answer is we are not.

inquest: "When the inquest into Emma's and Beckie's deaths is re-opened, will we able to put the questions we want to hear answered?" But Mr Gaskins replied that he did not think the inquest would ever be reopened. Unless the cause of death was somehow brought out in court, the verdict would remain "Unascertainable".

Went to bed that night, feeling that the one step forward had cost us half a dozen back.

September 1992

Vicky:

Looking back over the last 17 months, I can see so many mistakes made in the panic and torment of those early months. Mistakes that can never be rectified. But if I put them down in writing, perhaps they may help someone else to avoid making the same errors in the future.

First, I should have had enough faith in my own children to realise, when they did not return home the next day, that something was seriously wrong. Emma, who was not working at the time, need not have rushed home but Beckie was at Tech and had to hand in her exam papers the next day. I should have know that she would not have given up her own future for a party. Of course, we know now that that there was no party.

And next, I should have rung the police much earlier than I did. But if parents rang the police everytime a 17 year old stayed out all night, it would become ridiculous, wouldn't it? It chokes me now, however, to think that I was eating and drinking at home, quite unaware of the horrors that lay ahead, while they were dying or already dead. Quite unaware that their charred 'remains' lay undiscovered in the smouldering ashes of some barn.

It is those 'remains' that bring to mind my deepest regret. Given the same situation again, I would insist on seeing at least the bags that contained what was left. We should have asked to go to Cardiff with the undertaker to collect Emma and Beckie—but we didn't think at the time that it would be practical or possible.

I remember reading about a woman whose daughter had been blown up by an IRA bomb. Her son identifed what little there was left and the Mother never had a chance to say goodbye. Two years later she committed suicide and I can quite understand why. This may sound morbid to

The trees in memory of Emma and Beckie, in 1994, 2 years after their planting.

those who have not experienced what we are going through. But you have to understand—there would not have been much of Emma to touch but at least I could have held through the bag the parts that remained of Beckie's arm and hand.

And why was I in such a hurry to get their remains buried? Having had my eyes opened about the ways of Forensic Science—and you have yet to hear the full story—I would have insisted on a second or even a third opinion on the cause of my daughters' deaths. I continue to believe that more could have been found and I still have questions I want to ask.

I regret not going to the Court the first time David Harper, Wisdom Smith and Daniel Winter ever appeared. I realise now that, perhaps, if the Magistrates had had some visible reminder of Emma and Beckie sitting there in the courtroom in front of them, bail would not have been given so lightly. But at the time, so shortly after the first dreadful shock of the twins' deaths, the three boys seemed unimportant and not really a part of what had happened. I suppose the brain can only take so much and that news of sudden, violent death is quite enough to absorb.

As it was, I allowed the three boys time—time even to wash their clothes.

I wish I had asked for Victim Support much earlier than I did.

I wish that there was more support for fathers in these sorts of cases.

I regret that I went to the dentist on 23rd January.

I regret that I am no longer moved when I hear of older people dying and I regret the bitterness I feel when I hear parents moaning about their children.

I regret that I did not take every opportunity to praise the efforts and achievements of my children. Instead I found fault with them.

I regret that I did not photograph every day of their brief lives—and that I was so blind to the qualities that others saw in them.

I regret that I did not tell Emma and Beckie how proud they made me.

I regret that I preferred to watch Coronation Street when I could have listened to their accounts of the day that had passed.

I deeply regret being a snob and for saying that some of their boyfriends were not good enough for them. My God, some of those other boyfriends would not have left Emma and Beckie in a blazing barn without raising the alarm.

I regret that my jealousy of Emma's fondness for Chris and his family blinded me to their kindness to her. And that rather than feeling proud that she was liked, feeling rather threatened.

I wish I had found the money for them to go to America to see their friends before it was too late.

And I regret the wasted years when family squabbles prevented them from meeting my Father until they were eleven years old—and that they did not meet his second wife, by then dead, who would have loved them dearly.

I regret so many things that sometimes it is hard to live with myself. All I can say is that, if you have a child—however old or however near or far away—go now and cuddle them. Tell them that you love them. They'll probably be highly embarrassed and say: "Oh, Mum" but you might wake up tomorrow to find that they are gone.

Forever.

CHAPTER NINE
Acts of The Apostles

Vicky:

If, like us, you are just normal people, your knowledge of the law is probably fairly limited. We always had faith in the system but, over the last 20 months, we have come to realise that our faith was misplaced. We have watched closely cases on television and read about them in the papers. And we have tried to make sense of the sentencing of offenders and to understand the way Judges interpret the law.

As far as I can see, it all very much depends on how the defendant pleads at the outset—and on the personal feelings of the Judge. It also depends on the mitigating circumstances put forward by the defence and on the behaviour of the defendant since the offence complained of. No account of previous behaviour is admissible. It is only after the jury has reached its verdict that it is then told whether or not the defendant has committed the same crime before. But I don't think this makes sense. Think of rape cases.

I was lent a copy of a law book called Archbold's so that I might try to understand the way the system worked. This is what I have learned. Bear with me because it is complicated.

The first thing to grasp is that, as far as the law is concerned, crimes against the establishment are more heavily punished than crimes against the person. That may explain why the maximum sentences for the two sorts of charges against the three youths, Manslaughter and Arson, are the same. To me, Manslaughter is more serious than Arson which my Chambers dictionary defines as "*the crime of feloniously setting fire to houses, haystacks or similar property*", although they each attract life sentences.

But it still sounds simple, doesn't it? If found guilty, they get life sentences. However, this is English Law and, to understand what might happen in the Crown Court at the end of the month, I had to go back to the initial pleas and start from there.

At the pre-trial review, the youths each pleaded Not Guilty to the charges and thereby gained 6 months freedom. Had they pleaded Guilty, they would have been remanded in custody and probably given a reduced sentence for being helpful and saving everyone lots of time and trouble. (After 20 months of undiminished pain and anguish and no explanation for the cause of our daughters' deaths, I don't feel that Steve and I have been 'saved' any trouble. But that's a matter of no concern to English Law.)

If the Judge decides that the initial pleas were tactical—in other words, made to extend the time of freedom—he may reject the defence plea for a reduction in sentence should the jury deliver a verdict of Guilty. (That sounds reasonable.)

If one of the three pleads Guilty, his sentencing will then be deferred until the trial of the two pleading Not Guilty is over. In that case, the two who pleaded Not Guilty will, if convicted, probably receive a longer sentence than the one who pleaded Guilty. (It's a bit risky pleading Guilty, therefore, because the other two might be found Not Guilty.)

If found Guilty, anyone under the age of 21 (in other words Winter and Smith) must be remanded before sentencing to allow the Court time to obtain social reports. This is because alternative punishments must be considered before a sentence of imprisonment is imposed. As Harper is now 21, this would not apply to him although reports might be required as this would presumably be a first offence. The social reports would be provided by a Probation Officer who would take into account the defendants' behaviour before and after the offence, their family backgrounds, their mental states and any references. (As they have been free for some time, we expect such reports to go against us in the event of Guilty verdicts. But to my mind, it won't matter what any social reports say that the youths are like now. It's what they were like on the night the twins died that matters.)

In Harper's case, the Judge need not call for social reports if he thinks the case is serious enough. (Will Emma's and Beckie's unexplained deaths be thought serious enough by a system which attaches more importance to crimes against the establishment?) The Judge can also defer sentencing for 6 months while the behaviour of an offender is studied—and if the offender is a good boy he needn't go to prison.

Once sentences have been passed, and it's up to the Judge to decide whether the sentences should run consecutively or concurrently, prisoners can expect to serve only a portion of their sentences. A prisoner serving life can be released at any time 'on licence'. He would then be on licence for the rest of his life and, provided he behaves himself, free to remain in society without society knowing he has taken a life. (Makes you wonder who is living next door to you, doesn't it?) On a sentence of, say, 4 years a prisoner can expect to apply for a licence after 16 months and to be free after a further 2 months.

The weight of evidence against a convicted person will affect the sentence. But, on hearing a Guilty plea, the Judge is only presented with a summary of the facts, not the whole gory detail. When two or more men are convicted for the same crimes, sentences should be the same unless there are relevant differences—for example, the amount of responsibility, the amount of danger to the public, the age of the defendant.

Arson sometimes carries high sentences because of the tendency to repeat the crime. Life is usually only given in Manslaughter cases if the defendant is a danger to the public, has mental problems or has a history of Arson. Drinking plays a part in sentencing too—and we knew that the boys had been drinking that night in January 1991.

Having read further, I formed the conclusion that things ought to be clear cut. The prosecution would have to prove a thing called *actus reus*, which means 'guilty act'. If a person accidentally starts a fire and thereafter, intending to destroy or damage property belonging to another, or being reckless as to whether any property would be damaged, fails to extinguish the fire or prevent damage to the property by that fire—then the guilty act of Arson is established.

I could understand that. I could also understand that Harper, Winter and Smith failed to do anything except get miles away from the scene and without raising the alarm at either the nearby farmhouse or the equally close telephone box. Doesn't that suggest a guilty act? And what does it say about guilty intent? Two of the youths had even worked on the farm stacking the barn with bales of hay and straw. They knew its layout and surely also, therefore, the dangers of lighting a match in such a space.

But on looking at the various cases or 'precedents', I began to realise that it was all very confusing, that rules do not seem to have been followed. All I can say is that the jury has to be convinced that what the accused did amounted to an offence, either because he actually intended to damage property or because he was reckless whether it might be damaged. Only if they are satisfied on that point, can they go on to consider whether the accused also actually intended to endanger someone's life—or was reckless whether a human life might be endangered.

In the end, having looked again at the evidence and the various accounts and the failure to report immediately what had happened, Steve and I came to the conclusion that David Harper would plead Guilty to Arson and perhaps also to Manslaughter. We think he will be given a suspended sentence.

We believe that Wisdom Smith and Daniel Winter will ask for the case against them to be dismissed.

Monday, 26th October 1992

Vicky:

After 22 months, the day has finally come. Up early to be ready for Barbara and Sarah to pick us up. On the way, they remind us that we must not attempt to speak to Chadd, the prosecution counsel. It seems it would not look good if he was seen to be friendly with us—

—words may not have failed me at the time but they did during the next eight days.

Vicky's Victim Support volunteer:

The Crown Court case was even more distressing than expected. We had been prepared for details that would come out and insinuations that might be made. On at least one occasion, Vicky had to leave the Court room when emotion overcame her. But it was some of the media coverage, combined with the gradual whittling away of the prosecution case, that were particularly painful.

Daily Express, 28th October 1992:

3 'KILLED BARN ORGY TWINS'
GIRLS SCREAMED AS BOYS FLED BLAZE
IT STARTED WITH GROUP SEX AT MIDNIGHT AND
ENDED IN TRAGEDY . . .

> *The Times, 4th November 1992:*
>
> TWO ACQUITTED OF KILLING GIRLS WHO DIED
> IN BARN FIRE
> by Robin Young
> Two men accused of the manslaughter of teenage twin girls who
> died in a barn fire were acquitted yesterday on the direction of the
> judge... Mr Justice Auld ruled that that there was no case for
> Wisdom Smith or Daniel Winter to answer...
> ...the judge said that Mr Harper was the only defendant who
> might have been guilty of recklessness. *"There is no evidence of
> Smith or Winter lighting a tuft of hay or encouraging or aiding
> Harper to do so,"* the judge said. When Mr Harper lit the first tuft,
> Mr Smith told him *"in the clearest terms"* not to be stupid and to
> put it out.
> The judge said that any reasonable jury who returned a not guilty
> verdict on the manslaughter charge would do the same on the
> arson charge. *"The arson charge does not add anything to the
> prosecution case against Harper, so you need only concentrate on
> the manslaughter charge..."*
> © Times Newspapers Limited, 1992.

Vicky:

I am shocked by the Judge's direction to the jury, to concentrate only on
the Manslaughter charge. Two lives were lost in circumstances which
have brought forth lies. What can be said about a legal system that
allows charges to be discarded in such a case?

But I have felt totally let down since the day the trial started—

—angry at having to walk through the hall where the boys and their
families were waiting. Disappointed that the Judge has been changed.
Intruded upon by the press and their cameras. Alarmed that things went
on in the Court room without our knowledge. Confused that three
youths accused of Manslaughter and Arson can walk around freely
while those accused of robbery in the next court room are under armed
guard. Distracted by the constant objections of the defence. Sad for the
young girl who is sitting in the jury and was to weep as the case
progressed. Frustrated at all the hanging around. Taken aback at the
cameramen waiting for us at home. Furious that the prosecution says

The barn at Uckington ablaze, 24 January 1991.

that the boys heard a scream while getting away across the field. Upset, bitterly upset, that the prosecution goes on and on about sex—and devastated by the way the press are sensationalising things. Angry that the prosecution explains that Steve is not the girls' natural father. Angrier at the things which are missed out. Insulted that people in the Court room are whispering about us. Distraught, depressed and destroyed.

A butterfly appears and hovers around us. It is brown and it flits from side to side, annoying the boys but pleasing us. I don't know what to think any more. Thump. The butterfly is dead, smashed to pulp like Emma's and Beckie's reputations, by a journalist's notebook. The man laughs.

Man's laughter, manslaughter. I am helpless, powerless to protect my children. I cannot even explain things to the prosecution counsel although the three youths can talk to the defence.

I catch a few words. It seems that they are all confused. There is a problem legally, something to do with a bloke called Caldwell in 1900 and someone who said that there must be an objective and a subjective test to Manslaughter and also for Arson—but also that, according to Newbury, none of it's right. They are going on about things that happened years ago. They bear no relevance to the case of the twins. There is no precedent for their case.

If you are ever in a similar position, with your children missing, be very careful about what you say in statements to the police. Our statements were made before we knew that the twins were dead. They were the first statements to be read out. We appeared to damn our own daughters, especially as the defence successfully used objections to filter out things unhelpful to their case.

The wrong words are being said. Again and Again. *"Emma was six feet above the ground with two young men. Her dress was undone and her pants were off."* When Emma went out that night, she was not wearing a dress that unbuttoned down the front as was later implied. She had a top and skirt on and was wearing a belt around her waist. The belt buckle helped us identify her. Why are they saying these things? They are not true. How can this be allowed to happen?

We go to view the barn. The Judge and jury are there when we arrive, the press are being kept out until we go. But the youths and their families are there inside already. I can leave my flowers when the jury go, but not before. I can hear someone laughing, but I am not allowed to express my outrage. I can see a juryman nearly falling out of the barn at the place where Beckie supposedly died—but I am prevented from asking why Beckie did not fall out to safety with such apparent ease, too.

In all my life I have never felt such pain. Not even the question put in court "Having just made love to Beckie, how could you take no notice of her once you saw smoke?" appears to have any impact upon anyone but me.

Wednesday, 4th November 1992

*Mr Justice Auld, summing up in R v. David John Harper
in the Bristol Crown Court:*

Members of the jury, the prosecution case is one of manslaughter by recklessness. That is, that this defendant, David Harper, caused the deaths of Rebecca and Emma Harper by a reckless act in setting fire to the barn. In summary, the prosecution maintain that for Harper to light tufts of hay in a barn of hay and straw was so obviously dangerous and full of risk to those in it that he must have appreciated the risks when he did it, regardless of what he did, on his account, to extinguish the lit tufts before putting them down on the hay floor of the level of the barn at which he was.

The defence case, on the other hand, is that although it was a reckless act, and though it did cause the deaths of the two girls, Harper mistakenly thought at the time that his act was not reckless and, therefore, that he has committed no crime. Put in other words, the defence case is that he did not think at the time that his act in lighting and then extinguishing a tuft, or tufts, of hay created a risk of fire and consequent injury by burning to anyone in the barn.

The short question for you is this: are you sure that Harper did realise the risks when he lit the tufts and dealt with them as he did?...

...Put out of your minds, difficult though it may be, the natural horror that you may feel at the tragedy of this case, the needless loss of two young lives and the inevitable sympathy that you must feel for those poor girls and their grieving family.

Put out of your minds also the behaviour of Harper after the fire had flared up out of control unless—unless—you consider that it may assist you in determining Harper's state of mind at the time when he lit the tuft, or tufts, of hay. The fact that he might have dealt more efficiently with the fire, when the flames broke out and he and the other two were throwing bales down and trying to stamp out the fire, is really by the way so far as this charge is concerned. The fact that he might have made more strenuous efforts to get those girls out of the fire and that he ran off leaving them behind not knowing whether or not they were perishing in the fire may be the subject of criticism or condemnation, but those acts are not in themselves the offences with which he is charged here. Concentrate throughout on his state of mind at the time when he lit the tufts of hay up in the barn with those others in the barn with him...

...It is for you to decide what evidence you accept, what evidence you reject or of which you are unsure. It is for you to decide what you make of the evidence, and what inferences you feel you can properly draw as to the state of this man's mind in the light of that evidence. If I appear to have a view of the evidence or of the inferences to be drawn from it with which you do not agree, reject my view. If I mention or emphasise evidence that you regard as unimportant, disregard that evidence. If I do not mention evidence which you regard as important follow your own view, take it into account.

You must decide this case only on the evidence that you have heard, not on speculation about what other evidence there might have been; there will be no more. In the case of each witness, and that includes the defendant, consider carefully whether he or she has been telling you the truth, and whether he or she has been inaccurate in the account given to you.

In this case, as in every other criminal trial in this country, the prosecution must prove the defendant's guilt on each of the charges of manslaughter that he faces. He does not have to prove his innocence. Before you can convict him of either charge you must be sure of his guilt. That is the same thing as being satisfied beyond reasonable doubt of his guilt.

As you will remember from the indictment, the two counts of man-slaughter in it are in the same terms but each relates to a different girl. The particulars of the offence that you see under that heading in your copy of the indictment simply recites that this defendant killed the girl in question. Normally, when there is more than one count in an in-dictment, the Judge directs the jury that it should consider the case against and for the defendant on each count separately, and that is technically so in this case. They are separate charges and you must enter separate verdicts on them. But you may think in the particular circum-stances of this case that if you find the defendant guilty on one count then it would be difficult for you not to find him guilty on the other count of manslaughter. Similarly, if you found him not guilty on one count of manslaughter it would be difficult not to find him not guilty on the other. For practical purposes, you may consider the two charges stand or fall together...

...First, you must be sure that [...Harper...] did an act, namely, lighting a tuft, or tufts, of hay in the barn, which created a serious risk of causing fire and thus of physically harming by burning, not necessarily killing, one or both of the girls with him in the barn. In short, that he did an act which created such serious risks.

Secondly, you must be sure that both of those risks would have been obvious to any reasonably prudent person. The prosecution case is that they were so obviously dangerous, so obviously stupid, that what the defendant did, and the risks flowing from it, would have been obvious to any reasonably prudent person. But that is not enough, because you must be satisfied, thirdly, that Harper, when he did it, either thought of and recognised the possibility of both of those risks but nonetheless went on to do it or did not think of the possibility of both of those risks.

The prosecution case here is that it is the first of those two alternatives which apply. The prosecution case is that he did think of and he did recognise the possibility of the risk of fire and consequent physical injury by burning from it but nonetheless went on to do it, not once but twice, by lighting the tuft or tufts of hay. The defence case is that dangerous, stupid or reckless though it may appear now, he did not think that at the time given the steps he took to extinguish the tufts of hay before putting them down on the hay floor of the barn on which he was.

Fourthly, you must be sure, and this is not in dispute, that his act in lighting a tuft, or tufts, of hay in fact caused the fire which in turn caused the death of each girl . . .

Vicky:

We dispute that the fire caused Emma's and Beckie's deaths.

Mr Justice Auld's summing up continues:

. . . So the critical question for you there, members of the jury, is . . . whether you are sure that he thought of and recognised the possibility of both of those risks but nonetheless went on to do the act.

On that critical question, whether he thought of and recognised the risks and nonetheless went on to do the act, . . . Harper has told you that on each occasion when he lit a tuft of hay he did not believe that there was a risk of setting the barn alight because he thought that it was such a small flame and that by extinguishing the tuft with his hands there were no such risks. If you think that that was, or may have been, his state of mind, however mistaken, you should acquit him on both charges of manslaughter. But if you are sure that, having thought about it at the time, he recognised that despite his precaution there was still a risk of setting the barn alight and of causing injury by burning to one or more of those in it, you should convict him.

As counsel have reminded you in their closing addresses, Harper had been drinking on that night. He has not suggested in his evidence that he was affected by the drink he had taken. Even if he was affected by drink, to whatever extent, so as to be unaware of the risks or their extent, that self-induced state is no defence if those risks would have been obvious to him if he had been sober. I say that by way of warning only, because, as counsel have both indicated to you, drink does not play a part in this case in the questions that you have to decide.

Let me now turn to the evidence. In January 1991 Emma and Rebecca Harper were aged 17. They lived with their family at Tivoli in Cheltenham. Of the two, Emma seems to have been more outgoing and independent. Both had at one time, at different times, been the girlfriend of the defendant, Emma more recently. Harper was then aged 19 or 20. He was a local boy, he lived in Uckington. He had worked on the farm where this barn was for one or two summers assisting the farmer in his hay-making. His work involved the carting of bales of hay and straw to this very barn and stacking them there. He was ... familiar with the hazards of hay.

Both girls were at home on the evening of Wednesday, 23rd January 1991. At about 8.00 or 8.30 pm, Harper telephoned their home and spoke to Emma. He invited both of the girls out that night, and arranged with Emma to send a taxi to pick them up. The taxi called for the girls at about 9.30 pm. From what they told their step-father, Mr Stephen Harper, before they left he expected them both to return later that night, also by a taxi organised by the defendant, Harper.

The clothing that the girls wore when they went out is not now of importance in this case. The taxi took them to the Staddle Stones bar and restaurant in Woodmancote, near Cheltenham where the young men met them. The defendant, Harper, and Smith and Winter. There the five of them sat and drank and talked until about 11.45 pm, maybe a little later.

[MR], a joint proprietor of the bar, saw them there that evening. They all appeared to be happy and enjoying themselves. She told you that, as she saw it, the three defendants had had quite a bit to drink and were in good spirits but not drunk or disorderly. She had no impression as to what the girls had drunk but did not suggest that they were in any way the worse for drink.

Vicky:

But we know that [MR] thought the boys had had enough to drink and that she gave instructions that the defendants were not to be served any more. Indeed, they were indeed later refused. They even tried to get someone else to obtain drinks for them but that was nipped in the bud too. We have also learned that there was an incident outside the pub when David Harper allegedly beat someone up.

Mr Justice Auld's summing up continues:

You also heard evidence from [MH] and [DW], who were working in the bar and restaurant that night. [MH], who was working mainly in the bar, told you that so far as she could remember each of the young men drank in the course of the evening two pints of bitter, a Jack Daniels, which is a rye whiskey, and two glasses of Tequila. Not very different from what the defendant told you that he had to drink. As to the two girls, she told you that each of them had a pint of lager which lasted them all evening.

Steve:

I was most surprised to hear that Emma and Beckie allegedly ordered pints of lager. Neither of them liked lager and I do not believe this would have been their first choice of drinks.

During the evening, while the boys were drinking a mixture of alcohol, the girls apparently drank less than a pint of lager each. I still find it very odd that two girls, having been invited out to a party, would be content with a pint of a drink they did not like. I began to wonder whether someone had put something in Emma's and Beckie's drinks.

Mr Justice Auld's summing up continues:

[DW], who was working mainly in the restaurant that night, told you that she saw Emma sitting between Smith and Winter, and being affectionate to both of them. She heard her remarking words to the effect that she was going to go off with both of them and have a good time.

[MH] remembers clearing up the tables at which they were sitting shortly before they left, and seeing a packet of Benson & Hedges cigarettes on the table. She knows that it had cigarettes in it because she picked up the packet for a moment while she was wiping the table. As you know from an admission made by counsel in the course of the case, Harper admits that there were Benson & Hedges cigarettes there. [MH] saw no matches on the table with the cigarettes, but she did see some on the bar which she did not connect with the defendants or the two girls.

At about 11.20 pm, [DT], a friend of the young men, joined them in the bar of the Staddle Stones for about five minutes. He remembers that they were still drinking and that some of them were smoking, and that Harper had Benson & Hedges cigarettes and, he says, some matches. He did not see any of the others with matches.

Some time after that one of the young men made a telephone call for a taxi to take them all to Uckington. The intention, however it was put or discussed between the five of them, clearly was that they were not going to go straight home that night. They were going to go to the barn in Uckington, which Harper knew well, and there, certainly two of the young men, were going to enjoy themselves with the girls, and they with them, in the barn.

[AH], a retained fireman who was working that night as a taxi driver, received their call and accepted the job. He told you that he drove to the Staddle Stones public house, arriving there at about 11.55 pm. Now, the times become important. Within a couple of minutes of his arrival the five got into his taxi and he drove them to Uckington. That was a journey of about four and a half miles, and took them about seven to eight minutes. So, on his evidence, they got to Uckington, and certainly close to the barn, within a few minutes after midnight.

[AH] told you that they were all perfectly well-behaved during their journey with him, and that he saw no signs that any of them had had too much to drink. Harper sat in the front with him and the two of them had some discussion about [AH's] job as a fireman. There was some kissing and cuddling going on between the other four in the back. There was a no smoking sign in the taxi and none of them smoked during the short ride. At Uckington, Harper paid the fare and they all got out. They all went to the barn.

[JS], the tenant farmer of Manor Farm, where the barn was situated, has given evidence to you that on that night the four westerly bays, that is to say the four nearer to you in the model of this 8-bay Dutch barn, were stacked with hay and straw approximately as shown on the model that has been produced in evidence for you. Working from the west end of the barn, the end nearer to you, he told you that bay 1 was completely stacked to eaves level, bay 2 was stacked with hay up to eaves level on its southern half, and that is the half nearer to Manor Farm, but was irregularly stepped down to the ground in its northern half as a result of the recent removal of bales of hay for feeding livestock. Bay 3 was stacked with straw right up to the roof space in its southern half, up into the pitch of the roof, and to eaves level in its northern half. Bay 4 was rather like bay 2 in reverse, stacked to the eaves level on the north side but stepped down to the ground, reaching the ground roughly in the middle of the barn on the other side. Unlike the position as you saw it on your view of the barn, the four easterly bays were empty save for some farm machinery which was parked in them.

If that approximate layout was as [JS] has described it, and is approximately shown on the model, anyone at any level in or close to bay 2 had two ways of climbing down from the hay or the straw to the ground, namely by the stepping in bay 2 or by crossing from bay 2 to the north side of bay 3 to bay 4, as you did on your view. There were other more extreme ways of getting out if someone knew the layout and could see at that time of night, which is most unlikely. How obvious and practicable the stepping on bay 2 or bay 4 would have been depended, of course, on the nature of the stepping in the 2 bays and how readily their existence and layout could be seen in the dark. You may think that these two young girls, unfamiliar with the layout of the stacking up in, or closeness to, the darkness of the roof space and with fire breaking out below and rapidly spreading towards them, would have found it difficult to find their way out in time before the flames engulfed them.

As I have indicated, the precise layout of the stepping in bay 2 is uncertain. [JS], when asked about this by counsel, told you that the stepping probably did not run across the entire width of the bay as you looked at it from the north side of the barn. He said that there was a sort of a platform of bales about half way up to eaves level which would be about 12 feet high. He said also that there may have been an initial step from the ground or a wall of about two to three bales in height which would have made it more difficult to start the climb. Harper's evidence to you was that bay 2 did not look like the layout of the stepping on the model. He said that the steps going up to the first level, the 12 foot level, which he also mentioned as half way up, were set back into the bay by about six feet. He also said that the steps were on the left and not on the right as you looked at it.

Steve:

How could Harper, without the aid of any light at that stage, have noticed the full detail of the barn layout? If he really could see that well, should he need to light anything at all?

Mr Justice Auld's summing up continues:

Before I turn to his account, which is the only evidence that you have of what happened when the five of them got into the barn let me run on for a little while with the evidence of those around who saw something of the barn just before and just after the outbreak of the fire. At about 12.33 am [DV], who lives in the Moat House a short distance to the south-east of Manor Farm, took his dogs out for a walk and stopped to have a smoke on the bridge over the moat just inside his front gate. I know that you will remember it, you have all stood there yourselves on the view. Whilst there he saw no sign of a fire, but heard a car on the main road through Uckington and voices as if in general conversation coming from the direction of Manor Farm.

He returned to his house and went up to his bedroom at about five minutes past one to go to bed. Just before getting into bed he looked out of his bedroom window, which was facing towards Manor Farm and saw that [. . . Manor Farm's . . .] barn was on fire. He described the fire at that stage as minimal, but you will remember that he was looking at the barn from the opposite side on which the fire had broken out and there were at least three bales of solidly packed hay and straw which must have obscured his vision of the rapidly developing fire on the other side. He agreed with the description that he had given in his witness statement shortly after the fire that when he looked out of his window a number of bays were then alight and blazing well.

He said that the fire was at the eastern end of the stacked part of the barn on the north, that is on the far side of the barn from him, and already at the top. He said that the south side, that is, the side facing his home, was not then on fire. He also said that the roof had not gone at that stage. [DV's] wife telephoned the fire brigade and then [JS]. In the meantime, [DV] rushed out to the fire, making his way to the north, the road side of the barn, through the eastern end of it where the machinery had been parked. He was the first person there. He told you that the blaze increased—as he put it—incredibly quickly as he approached the barn, and that in the two minutes or so between first seeing the fire and reaching it the barn, as he put it, went up.

Just a little before that, between 12.45 am and 1.00 am, ... a taxi driver employed by A to B Private Hire of Cheltenham, drove past the barn at Uckington, taking a fare from Cheltenham to Tewkesbury. He saw no sign of fire as he drove through Uckington. Having dropped his fare in Tewkesbury, he returned along the same route. As he came off the motorway to the west of Uckington between 1.00 am and 1.10 am he saw the fire ahead of him. He said there were about fifteen minutes between his passing the barn on the outward trip and seeing no sign of the fire and his first sighting of the fire on his return trip.

[The taxi driver] stopped in Uckington to look at the fire, and to report it on his radio telephone to his controller. He told you that at that time the whole of the side of the barn facing the road from about half way up was engulfed in flames and that there was an obvious blackness below. It was raging, as he put it, up to the roof of the barn—

Steve:

I don't think I would have cared to stand in front of such a blaze with my trouser zip undone.

Mr Justice Auld's summing up continues:

[The taxi driver] saw no-one around. The person on duty in [... the taxi ...] control room who received his message immediately made a 999 telephone call to the Gloucester fire brigade, reporting the fire. The call was logged by the fire brigade at 1.11 am.

At about that time too, [AT], who lives in the corner house at No 1, The Green, Uckington, was awakened by what he thought was heavy rain on his bedroom window. He went to the window, which faces west and towards the direction of the barn. He saw it ablaze. Really raging, as he put it, and with the roof gone. Within moments he took the photograph which you have as photographs 5 and 6 in your bundle. He

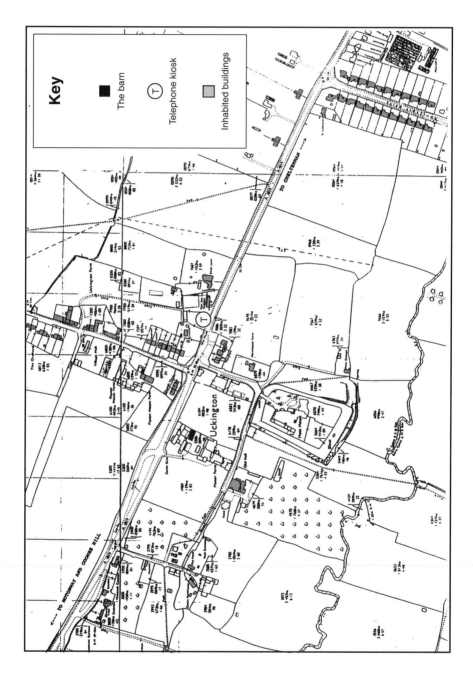

Detailed map of the village of Uckington.
(*By kind permission of the Gloucestershire Police Force*)

saw neighbours standing about who had been similarly alerted to the fire, but no-one close to it. He did, however, see three youths walking together towards Cheltenham on the opposite side of the main road from his house and almost level with his house. From the lights of on-coming vehicles they seemed to be wearing jeans and trainers.

Nobody knows who they were. The evidence from Mr Harper is that there were not three of them together at that point after the fire, the other two had run on up the road going north from the main road, and he had followed them, joining up with them later.

Steve:

How did Harper know where they had gone? Why could two of them run off? Because Emma and Beckie were dead and destroyed that night, you will understand why I am asking questions about the people who were left.

Mr Justice Auld's summing up continues:

Two fire appliances arrived at the scene at about 1.19 am. In charge of them was a sub-officer, [JU]. He told you that as he approached the scene from the Cheltenham direction he was able to see the glow of the fire from about a mile away. He said that the appearance of the fire on his arrival at the scene was as shown in [AT's] photographs. He estimated that it must have begun, that is to say, broken out, within the previous 25 minutes. All that he and his colleagues could do—and they were shortly joined by a third appliance—was to let the fire take its course and to protect the area immediately surrounding the burning barn by playing jets of water on and around the outside of it. The fire eventually burnt itself out at about half past three that morning.

Steve:

We believe it is Fire Service policy to allow barn fires to burn themselves out once livestock and machinery have been removed. Did the three boys know that? Did they hear it from the fireman who took them to the barn in his taxi?

Mr Justice Auld's summing up continues:

As I have indicated, members of the jury, it looks, does it not, as if the group of five arrived at the barn at about five minutes past midnight, and it looks from the summary of evidence that I have just given to you that the fire broke out about 55 minutes later at about 1.00 am—one cannot be precise. No doubt, it had been smouldering for some time before the break-out of the fire at about 1.00 am.

What happened during that time? Well, as I have already said, the only evidence you have of that comes from the defendant, Mr Harper. This is what he told you.

He said that he and the other two younger men went up into the barn by the stepping in bay 2, leaving the two girls on the ground at the base of it. He said they got to what he described as the first level, about half way up, 12 foot high, possibly higher. He said that the three of them were exploring. They were looking for places where each of the girls could be taken. He said it was very dark in the barn, and you may think the higher they climbed the darker it got as the roof crowded in on what light there may have been. They settled upon the first level as a suitable place at least for one of the girls, and whilst Smith remained on that first level, Harper thinks, he and Winter went down to the ground to help the girls up into the barn.

He remembers that it was very steep, the stepping in bay 2, and it was not easy for them and the girls to climb. It was during the course of bringing the girls up the stepped area in bay 2 that he told you that he first saw a match being struck. He says that he did not light that match, and he does not know which of the others lit it. The short glare from the match was enough to enable him to see a little of the first level where they were all congregated. He told you that he had no cigarettes or matches with him at that time. He said that he wanted to have a better look at the first level, and asked if he could use the matches that he had seen being struck. He spoke in the direction of where the light had been. He reached out, and from somebody's hand in the dark he received a matchbox.

By this time all five of them were on the first level. He took one of the matches and did not just light it. On his own account, he picked up a clump, or a tuft, of hay off a bale and lit it. He said that he did that to see the first level and where it led to. He said that the tuft, or clump, was about six to eight inches long, and that he folded it over. He illustrated, as I am doing now, what he did with it in order to make a more efficient use of it as a small torch. Having lit it and having used the light from it in that way, he told you that he then put it out with his hands clasping together around the folded hay, putting out the burning by removing the air from the hay. He said in that way he put it out.

Steve:

I have tried time and again to reconcile this explanation with the report by the Fire Service during reconstruction tests:

> "*In the very early stage of the fire, within seconds of ignition, it is possible to beat out the flames or to stamp on the flaming straw on the ground. However, the person doing so may suffer burns to hands and exposed areas of the body. Some damage to clothing will certainly occur to the shoes and the bottom of the trousers, unless protected by knee length boots. Shirt or jacket cuffs will also suffer damage. It is interesting to note that my fire-fighting tunic which is made of Nomex, a fire-proofed material, which I was wearing for the fire tests, has small spot burns on the sleeves. This was caused when I beat out the flames during the ignition tests.*"

I cannot believe that burning hay could be extinguished in the way the Court was told without some injury, or that the following description of throwing out blazing bales could have left the boys' clothes unmarked.

Mr Justice Auld's summing up continues:

[Harper] put the time for which he held that small clump alight at about three seconds. He told you that when he lit it and held it in that way, Smith, who was still nearby, told him not to be stupid and to put the hay out. He put the extinguished clump of hay, as he thought, down on the hay floor on which he was standing. The light had been enough to enable him to see a suitable spot for him and Rebecca, and he took her along that first level, about ten feet along to the right hand side of it, where he settled with her. According to him, the other three carrried on up to the back area of the barn to a second level which he put as about three or four bales further up.

So, they are somewhere about fifteen to eighteen feet above ground level and he is about twelve feet to fifteen feet. It appears, too, from a description that he later gave that they were in a sort of alcove, like a hollow where bales had been pulled out. Once he settled down with Rebecca he decided that he would light a second tuft of hay, despite Smith's warning to him earlier on. He did not give you a very precise reason for doing that. He said: "*I vaguely remember it was to assist Rebecca in some way.*" He told you that he did this before she took some of her underwear off. So, it was before they began to have sexual intercourse.

He told you that he did exactly the same with that tuft of hay as he had done with the first. He said that it had remained alight for about three to four seconds. He said that he put it out with his hands by clenching them around the tuft as he had the first time, and he put it down on the floor of hay on his left, as he had the first time, believing it to be extinguished. He put the time between the lighting of those two tufts of hay at about five minutes. First, when they were all congregated on the first level; second, after the other three had gone up a level and he was about to have sexual intercourse with Rebecca on the first level.

He spoke of an incident of Smith coming down to the first level while he was with Rebecca there and interrupting him—some joke—and then Smith going back up again to the upper level. After Smith had gone back up he and Rebecca resumed making love, he said, for about three or four minutes, and it was towards the end of that period that he became aware of smoke or smouldering. His eyes began to water. He could smell smoke, he could smell burning. It is common ground from the way in which the defence have put their case that one of those tufts which he thought he had extinguished, maybe both, and certainly one, had smouldered somewhere beneath them, probably in the crevices between the bales and was gradually smouldering towards ignition.

He told you that he panicked when he smelt the smoke. He said that he was terrified. He said that the first thing he did was call Smith over. He shouted at him, "*I can smell smoke, get down here quick.*" So his first reaction at the sign of fire was to call for help to put it out. Smith and Winter came down. He, Harper, jumped up. He said that Smith found the smoke, it was coming from the inner side of a bale right on the edge of that first level near where he had been lying with Rebecca. Smith was the one that got down and found it.

As they looked they saw a small round glow at the bottom of a bale. Smith pulled out a bale, threw it out on to the ground, and no doubt the release of that bale and the influx of air that it produced accelerated the glowing down below. According to Harper, Smith put his foot down into the smouldering area, trying to stamp it out, and as he did so that is when it burst into flames, as Smith pulled his foot out. You will remember the scientific evidence of some carbonised deposits being found on certainly the right boot that Smith had been wearing, and possibly some on the left as well.

Well, with that, all three of them began, in a frenzied way, to start to throw down the bales contaminated by fire at the first level, to throw them out of the barn, to get the fire out of the barn. In the doing of that there was more oxygen to the place where the fire was causing it to spread, oxygen rushing by the bales as they tumbled down the side of the barn, causing smouldering to ignite on them too and to spread to the side of the barn as they fell.

So, the three men, according to Harper, found themselves on the first level confronting not only fire on that level where it had all started but the beginnings of a fire from down below where unintentionally they had spread it by throwing down the lit bales. According to Harper, he was in sheer panic. No doubt the other two were as well.

Steve:

What condition were Emma and Beckie in, I wonder? I can't believe they were cool, calm and collected—but even so there should have been no reason for them not to get out.

Mr Justice Auld's summing up continues:

Now, in all this there is no mention of the girls. According to Harper, his mind and his concentration were entirely on the fire and how to deal with it. Rebecca must have been near at hand but he was not conscious of her. Emma was a level up and not within his sight. He told you that Winter and Smith rushed down to the ground to try and get the fire under control whilst he, Harper, remained at first level still throwing bales down and patting at the developing flames there with his hands. He realised that it was getting out of control despite his efforts up there and their efforts on the ground.

He said that he jumped down to try to help them in what was by then the more serious part of the fire, and that as he did so he shouted to the girls to get out. He was not conscious at the time whether or not Rebecca was still there. He was still concentrating only on the fire. The other two must have gone pretty quickly because he said that by the time he got down to the ground they had gone. Later in his evidence he said that he saw them running off. He said he tried to do something about the fire on the ground on his own, but only for a short time because he realised that it was hopeless. So he too, once more shouting for the girls to get out, took to his heels and ran.

He told you that the flames by then had reached the top of the barn, and he kept going until he caught up with the other two after two to three minutes. He said that his state of mind as he left was still one of panic and fear, and that he simply did not know whether the girls had got out or not.

You know what happened after that, and I need not take a lot of time over it. The three young men made their way to the house of [JH] in Stoke Orchard, a village a short distance to the north of Uckington. [JH] lived there with his daughter [T] and some dogs. They all knew [T] and her father. According to her evidence she had, in the past, gone out with David Harper and Daniel Winter and she had been at school with Smith.

Parked in [... JH's ...] front drive was a Spitfire sports car which belonged to [T's] boyfriend, [DP], and which was under repair. That night [T] had gone out with her boyfriend and some other friends and her father was alone in the house with his dogs. He had gone to bed about midnight. On their arrival at [JH's] house the three young men appeared to have sat and waited in the sports car, and they waited there some time because it was not until between 2.00 am and 2.30 am that [T] and her boyfriend, [DP], arrived back at her home in a car driven by a young man called [NW].

[DP] got out of the car to say good-night to [T] at her front door while [NW], who was going to drive him home, remained in the car. As [T] and [DP] were saying their good-nights at the front door the three young men left the sports car in which they had been sitting, and approached them. According to [T] they were in a dreadful state, and obviously

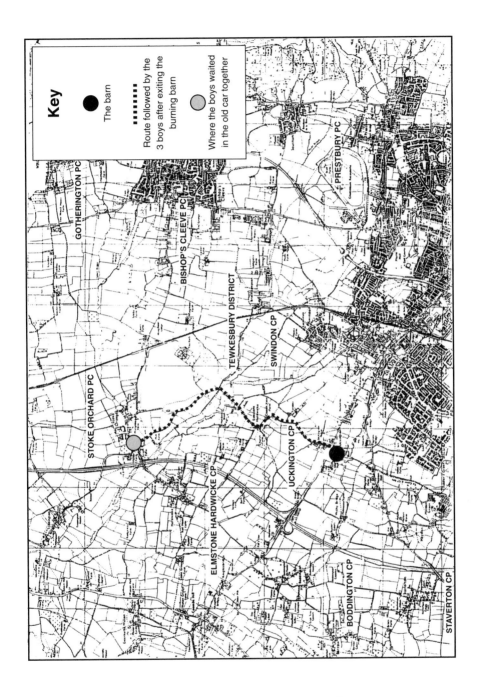

General map of Uckington and the surrounding area.
(*By kind permission of the Gloucestershire Police Force*)

frightened. [DP] described them as terrified, panic-stricken and in a state of shock.

Harper was the first to speak. He asked for help. [DP] asked them what they were doing there, and in his car too, and one of them said that they had been waiting in the car for some time, waiting for someone to come home. One of them said, *"We've set a barn on fire"*, or *"We've burnt a barn down"*. The immediate help that the three young men clearly wanted was a lift away from the area and [DP] got his waiting friend, [NW], to give them a lift to Bishop's Cleeve where Smith lived. When they had all got into [NW's] car and were en route he and [DP] noticed that they gave off a strong smell of smoke, and [DP] saw that they looked dishevelled.

According to [DP], one of the young men remarked that they could not believe how fast the barn had gone up, and one of them said that they had run across the fields to get to [T's] house. According to [NW], Harper and Smith said that they had been in a barn which had caught fire and that they had been unable to put the fire out. None of them said anything about the girls. According to Harper, he still did not know whether the girls had got out of that fire. [NW] drove them to Bishops Cleeve, dropping off Harper and Winter shortly before reaching Smith's house where they got out ...

... Harper told you that he stayed the night with Winter at Smith's home in that village. The next morning, still not knowing whether the two girls had survived the fire, Harper and Winter went swimming. Harper told you that he did that partly to remove the smell of smoke from his body, and partly to take his mind off what had happened.

After that he made enquiries through Winter and his brother of the girls' family to see if the girls had returned home. You will remember the account given by [Vicky] of telephone calls and visits to the house, and Harper himself spoke of having arranged those because he was concerned to know what had happened to the girls. By the evening of that Thursday, when Harper knew from those inquiries that the girls still had not returned, he told you that he was shocked. He said that it was then it began to go through his mind that maybe they had been caught in the fire. The following morning he and the other two young men consulted a solicitor and, with him, went to the police station. That Friday morning, too, Mrs Harper telephoned the police to report that her daughters were missing. As you know, there is no dispute that they perished in that fire, and I need say no more about that.

At the police station Harper and the other two young men were each interviewed separately a number of times by the police in the presence of a solicitor. The interviews were tape recorded and the tape recordings have been transcribed. By agreement between the prosecution and the defence summaries and edited versions of those very long transcripts have been given to you. I must give you a warning about those transcripts. It is a warning that I would have given to you if all three young men were still in the dock. It is all the more important now that Harper is there alone.

This is the warning: statements made by Smith and Winter in the course of their interviews about Harper's part in this matter are not evidence against Harper. He was not there to hear or contradict what was said, and neither of those young men has given any evidence confirming or challenging what they told the police. You have heard the evidence about their interviews only because it was relevant at the time for the case that they had to face. It had nothing to do with the case against Harper. So, disregard what you can remember of it when you now consider the case against him.

You may have noticed that the summaries of the interviews of Winter and Smith have been removed from your bundle of exhibits. The position is different with Harper's own police interviews. What he told the police, and how it marries up with what he told you in his evidence to you, is clearly relevant and important to you in your determination of what happened and of his guilt or innocence of the charges. In the early interviews, as you will recollect, he told the lying story that he had agreed with Smith and Winter about lighting a cigarette in the barn and stubbing it out with his shoe. That was a lying story which he has admitted to you was concocted largely at his instigation to protect him. He said nothing in that lying story about having lit tufts of hay while in the barn.

Well, although he undoubtedly lied to the police at that stage, and for the reason he has given, you must still consider whether those lies have any help for you in the determination of the issue which you have to decide. The mere fact that a defendant tells a lie is not in itself evidence of guilt. He may lie for a number of reasons. He may lie, for example, to conceal conduct of his of which he is ashamed but which falls, or which he believes falls, short of the offence charged. For example, here the fact that he set fire to tufts of hay which in hindsight only struck him as reckless. He may lie for example, out of panic or confusion. If you think

225

that there is, or may be, some such innocent explanation for those early lies then you should take no notice of them. But if you are sure that he did not lie for some innocent reason of that sort, then those lies can support the prosecution case.

Let us look now, members of the jury, at some of the passages in the transcript which you have of his interviews. It is in the fourth interview that he began to give the account which he has given to you. An account of lighting one tuft of hay which he took up from the bales at a time when all five of them were together and still finding their way about the first level to which they had all gone, of Smith telling him not to be stupid and to put it out, and of him then going on to light a second tuft of hay when he was on that level and alone with Rebecca.

Go to page 43, where he began to give that account. About three quarters of the way down the page, after some pointed questioning by the officer, he said: "*All right, then, I'll tell you. Sod it.*" He went on: "*All this thing about the fag, that's a load of crap. It was the matches that did it. I said about the fags, that was the only thing we could think of. I don't know. And what it was, I lit some hay to see what we were doing and put it out. This is when I was with Beckie. Just lit some hay, put it out, to see what we were doing like.*" The officer asked: "*What, like a handful, a torch?*" and he replied, "No. *Well, just a little bundle to see what we were doing and then I put it out and then … No, I can't even think now.*" "*Take your time,*" said the officer. He went on, "*I couldn't see what I was doing with Beckie before we had sex, so I lit this little bundle of straw, put it back out, and then I smelt the smoke, and it was coming up. And all that's true.*"

Move on to page 47, members of the jury. In the middle of an answer at the top of the page he said: "*The fire started where I was, where I lit that little thing. That's where the fire started.*" A little further down the page, just above midway, the officer asking him: "*You were striking matches, lighting straw, patting it out.*" He replied: "*That was in the beginning, to see what we were doing.*"

Turn now to the top of page 49. He said, at the answer at the top of the page, in response to the question of the officer about matches, that they were using it purely as a candle for a few seconds: "*Yeah, we tried it to start with, and then I lit this thing on the floor, only a little light. That, just to see what we was doing, and then put it out. Obviously, it didn't go out properly but someone did pass me the matches. I remember that bit*".

In cross-examination [... on this point ...], he told you that the clump of hay that he lit was not on the floor when he lit it, but that he had picked it up from the floor to light it, and that was what he meant when he gave that answer.

Turn on to page 57, members of the jury. About quarter of the way down the page he is dealing with the first occasion when he lit the tuft of hay, and he gives this answer. "*I think I put it out. It was a couple of seconds, you know. I just started to light them. That was it. What I did was put it out with my hand. That was it. It was that small. And then me and Emma and Beckie, and all of them, we just had sex, and that was it.*"

Further down the page, about two thirds of the way down, the officer asked him this question: "*You were doing a lot of striking of matches, lighting straw and patting it out. Well, several times.*" He answered: "*I'd say twice.*" The officer asked him: "*And it culminates in actually, physically—*" Then he interrupted the question by this answer: "*That, including different places.*" He went on, on page 58, to repeat that he had lit a clump of hay twice.

Move on now, members of the jury, to page 73 of the transcript of the interview. There is an answer in the middle of the page, when he again was talking about the lighting of the first tuft of hay. He said: "*Yeah, we all were sort of in a bunch, first together, when we all got up there, and then we sort of split up, you know, but when we were all up there in a bunch together that's when I lit a bit of hay to see, you know what, just to see, to get some light, and then I banged out, but it wasn't when we were going down.*"

Then the next answer at the bottom of the page. He said this in response to the officer's question, "*So whereabouts did you light it, on the edge?*" His answer: "*Just on the corner. Just a little piece to see where we were, and then put it back out. But that was all right, and then that, I did that, twice on the same bale, and that was all right. And then we split up.*"

There again, members of the jury, he appeared to be suggesting to the officer that it was not so much the taking up the piece of hay and lighting it in his hand, but lighting it whilst it was actually on the level on which he was, on the bale—on the corner of the bale. He was asked about that answer in cross-examination by Mr Hamilton. He told you that he was confused when he gave that answer. He told you that he had not lit a corner of a bale, and he had not intended to suggest that in this answer.

227

Turn over the page, please, to page 74. In the middle of the page the officer asked him this question: "*So you split up and then you do a bit more lighting where you are?*" His answer, "*Yeah*". The officer then put to him a question he had put before. "*You were lighting bits and patting out and lighting bits and patting it out?*" His answer: "*No, I did that, it was three times. I'm sure of it because the first when we got up there, as I said, we were all there, and now someone was striking matches before me because that's why I said 'Pass us the matches'. I had matches on me.*"

Mr Chadd asked him about that answer, in particular about his reference to three times. In answer to Mr Chadd's question, Harper told you that he was not prepared to stand by that statement. He said that he was confused at the time when he made it to the police officers.

Finally, members of the jury, turn to pages 78 and 79. He said, in an answer at the top of the page, in response to a question by the officer that it was all pointing to him: "*Because it was my fault, that's why. It was my fault. I was stupid enough to light the flipping hay to see. They didn't light the hay to see. I did.*" Then he remarked, half way down the page, towards the end of the answer: "*I was stupid enough to light lit bits of hay and put them out.*" Then his next answer, about three quarters of the way down the page in response to the question by the officer. "*You lit it at the top and you lit different things when you and Beckie were alone*" : "*No, I didn't. When me and Beckie were alone, right, you say I'm lighting different things, all I did was light it once, just a little pile of hay once.*"

Then his final answer on page 79 in response to the question, "*The bale of hay that Wisdom Smith picked up and tossed over the side was actually one of the first bales that you lit*": "*No, no, it wasn't. It wasn't one of the first bales I lit, because one of the first bales I lit was on that step up to the ledge from my level to the second level. The one that I lit, that obviously the fire was caused by, was where I was sat with Beckie. They weren't sat over there by there, so obviously he's mixed up about everything, so I am. But I know that that was the one that started the fire, and I was the one who lit that little bit.*" So, he is referring there to the second lighting of hay by him.

Mr Elfer asked him questions about that answer. Harper said that he had not meant by the answer to indicate that he had actually set fire to bales, but to clumps of hay taken by him from the bales. So there you have the account that he ultimately gave the officers of how he came to light the fire which eventually caused the deaths of these two young girls...

Vicky:

People reading this book must understand that Steve and I cannot accept that the fire caused Emma's and Beckie's deaths. We are appalled that the crucial question of how they died can have been allowed to slip from the concentration of the Court, only to be replaced by distractions.

We will never stop wanting to know how Emma and Beckie died. We will find out.

Mr Justice Auld's summing up continues:

...and you will, as I have already indicated to you, put it together with his evidence to you largely of a piece, largely consistent, with his evidence to you, although different in some respects, particularly as to whether he lit hay on the bales or took hay up from the bales to light them and whether it was two or three times.

In respect of those apparent inconsistencies he has indicated that he had not intended, when he was talking to the officers, to suggest that he had lit bales, and that it was twice that he had lit a tuft of hay as he said in his evidence to you.

Members of the jury, I should warn you about Harper's acceptance in interview that he had been reckless, and his acceptance in evidence to you that he had been reckless. First, that is his assessment of the matter after it had occurred. You are concerned with his state of mind at the time he set fire to those clumps of hay. Second, it is not his later assessment on the value judgement of reckless or no as a label to his conduct which counts, it is your assessment of that which matters. As I have told you you can only approach that exercise by considering what was, or what must have been, his realisation of the risks he was taking at the time he lit and extinguished those tufts of hay in this hay and straw stacked barn and put down at least one incompletely extinguished tuft on the hay floor on which he was inside the barn.

The prosecution case is that as a matter of common sense Harper must have known at the time what serious risks he was taking. He agreed in cross-examination by Mr Hamilton that he had known the hazards of hay. He told you that it was a risk of which Smith had given him a sharp reminder when he, Harper, lit the first tuft of hay—"*Don't be fucking stupid, put it out.*" And yet he went on to light a second. The prosecution maintain in the light of such circumstances and evidence Harper is lying to you when he says that he did not appreciate at the time the serious risks he was taking. His case, on the other hand, is that, whatever his later realisation of the risks, at the time he did not regard what he was doing as creating a serious risk of fire and injury by burning.

At the end of his evidence to you he agreed that what he had done was a dangerous and reckless thing to do, but he continued in this way—and this is my summary of the evidence he gave in answer to a number of questions put to him by Mr Hubbard: "*I extinguished the hay the first time because Smith told me to, and the second time because I no longer needed it. When I lit the tuft of hay the first time I did not believe that there was a risk of setting the barn alight. I thought I had it under control. I was trying to be clever, I suppose. I thought I had it under control because it was such a small flame, there was no way it could catch a barn on fire. When I lit the second tuft I was in the same state of mind.*"

That, members of the jury, concludes my review of the evidence in this case on both sides. Let me just remind you that Harper is aged 21; he is a cabinet maker; he lives at home with his parents in Uckington not far from the barn. Apart from one traffic conviction he is a person of good character. Give weight to that good character in two ways. First, as with any person of good character, it supports his credibility as to whether you can believe him. Second, the fact that he has that good character up to now means that he is less likely than otherwise might be the case knowingly to take risks with other people's safety in the way alleged.

One other matter to which I must return. At the outset of my summing-up I urged you to put aside natural feelings of sympathy, and to concentrate on the evidence in the case and the questions in the case about which I have directed you. You may have seen some publicity in the course of the case and since the start of my summing-up. You may have heard some. Put that out of your mind, and cling to the evidence in the case and the questions that I have put to you about the evidence in the course of the summing-up . . .

The Clerk:

Members of the jury, will the foreman please stand. Will the foreman please answer this question either yes or no. Has the jury reached a verdict upon which they are all agreed in relation to counts 1 and 2 in the indictment?

The Foreman of the Jury:

No.

Mr Justice Auld:

Members of the jury, I mentioned to you towards the end of my summing-up the possibility of a majority verdict. It did not arise at that time but you have now been considering your verdicts for some time in this case and the time has come when I can direct you that I can accept a majority verdict from you in relation to either count in the indictment. That is to say, a verdict with which at least ten of you agree.

What I will direct you now to do is to retire once more and urge you to continue to try to reach a unanimous verdict on each of the two counts that you are considering, but if you cannot I can accept a majority verdict as I have indicated, one with which at least ten of you agree. Will you retire now, please.

The Clerk:

My Lord, three hours and fity-seven minutes have lapsed since the jury first retired to consider their verdicts.

Members of the jury, will your foreman please stand? Mr Foreman, please answer this question yes or no. Has the jury reached verdicts upon which at least ten of their number have agreed?

The Foreman of the Jury:

Yes.

The Sun, 5th November 1995:

A Mum whose identical twin dughters died in a barn blaze wept yesterday as a youth accused of their killings walked free from court.

Heartbroken Vicky Harper said: "*We waited 22 months for justice and are appalled at the verdict.*"

Minutes earlier, carpenter David Harper, 21—who is no relation—was cleared of manslaughter by jurors at Bristol Crown Court.

He had admitted telling police "*a pack of lies*" about the fire which started after he and two pals took Emma and Rebecca Harper, 17, for a midnight sex session in the barn at Uckington, Gloucs.

The prosecution claimed the defendant, from Uckington, lit bundles of hay to see in the dark, then fled with his pals when the blaze broke out, leaving the twins to die.

Both of his friends were cleared this week.

Yesterday, twins' Mum Vicky said: "*The circumstances of our girls' deaths are still unclear. We won't rest until we know what happened that night.*"

Vicky's Victim Support volunteer:

The whole experience was a traumatic one and my feelings tended to be a reflection—albeit pale in comparision—of those felt by Vicky herself. I have found myself extremely depressed and distressed at times, very worried and frustrated at others. But I have also found much to admire in both Vicky and Stephen's reactions to the tragedy and its legal outcome—and in the way in which they carried on with life afterwards.

The whole case had been a series of let-downs for them when they had reasonably expected someone to be found responsible. They had expected an account of the twins' deaths. But instead a charge of Murder in June 1991 was reduced to one of Manslaughter and Arson in February 1992. And next the case against two of the defendants was thrown out by the Judge at the Crown Court and the jury was instructed to find them Not Guilty. And finally there was the verdict that David Harper was Not Guilty on any count.

From the ending of the case—ironically and cruelly the day before the 5th November, Guy Fawkes night, with all its bonfires—the support I could offer Vicky would no longer be of a practical nature. It would need to be emotional support, to try to help Vicky cope with this ebbing away of any hope of someone being found responsible for the loss of her two daughters in such a horrible way.

Vicky:

Throughout these last few days, Steve and I were helped—and recognised that we were being helped—by family, friends and police. But not even gifts and flowers left on the doorstep at home after each day in Court could ease the dreadful shocks we were experiencing there.

Steve:

I found it disgusting that the people involved in Emma's and Beckie's deaths were allowed to be physically so close to us. I have conditioned myself no longer to hate them because that is self-destructive—but at home that night, after the Crown Court verdict, I suffered a violent explosion of grief and anger that was totally overwhelming.

After nearly two years of supporting Vicky, my turn to lose all sense and self-control had arrived.

Vicky:

Neither of us can face the truth yet. Soon we go to bed. I take my tablets and hope for peace.

It is dark.

I can hear a strange noise. It is coming from Emma's room where Steve is sleeping tonight in the hope that we may rest. It is a noise like an animal. A great roar and an intake of air so deep.

I get up and there is Steve trying to crawl up the wall. He is so distressed that he cannot breathe and is clutching his chest. Oh God, am I going to lose him as well?

I pick him up from all fours and bring him to bed. I try to ease the sobs and comfort him. I make some tea and hold him while he gains control over his panic. We sit up for most of the night. Nothing I can do or say will help him. He has finally succumbed to his grief and to the verdict of the jury.

No, don't think. Don't let that particular disease into your mind.

We have been sentenced to misery for life. Auto-pilot is on.

CHAPTER TEN

The Agony and The Ecstasy

Vicky:

Christmas is coming and we have lots of visitors. Friends from the past including friends of the twins. Christmas Carols at the Harper Clinic with the pensioners enjoying their sherry and the raffle and the food. We, too, gain some pleasure from their enjoyment.

Back home one evening, while preparing the tea, I put my oven gloves on to check the sausages under the grill. Unknown to me, however, the gloves have caught fire. They are warm and I put them against my chest—and of course my jumper, which is nylon and polyester, catches light too and begins to melt.

Steve was there in a second putting out the fire in the oven gloves while I battle with the jumper before quickly pulling it over my head. The blouse underneath saved me from major burns but a small hole had allowed a tiny area of my chest to burn. My fingers and thumb were black and sore and again it was only Steve's help and quick thinking that saved me from getting blisters.

This was a terrifying experience under any circumstances but I could only think of the girls and what they might have suffered. And I cried for them. It also brought home to me how unlikely it was that someone repeatedly putting out flaming tufts of hay could escape without so much as a singe. But that is what the jury believed.

Sunday, 20th December 1992

Vicky:

A year ago tomorrow Steve's father, Eric, died. We visited Mary again, taking round her present and having a coffee with her—just to make sure she was alright. Then up to the cemetery to put some flowers on

235

Eric's grave. Shopping at Sainsbury's. Visits from friends. And finally getting ready for Carols by Candlelight at Christ Church.

I still had a pain in my chest but I wanted to go the Service. We got there at 10 past 6 and went quickly to the twins to check their flowers. The church was packed and we had to sit upstairs. It's a lovely church and everything has a kind of smoky haze—

—I think it is this haze that makes me quite sure that I can see Emma and Beckie standing in the choir. I can certainly hear them singing the old, well-loved carols they used to practise at home. Yes. I feel their presence very strongly...

It was a peaceful feeling and we came home with a sensation of love in our hearts. When we reached home, there was a message on the ansaphone from the next forensic scientist to be involved in the case, Professor Gresham. He wanted us to ring him back to discuss what he had found.

Pills or no pills, I drank a glass of sherry to fortify me, smoked a cigarette and dialled the number. Steve was listening to the conversation.

Professor Gresham had been sent five slides by Dr Ian Hill at our instigation. It was Dr Hill, remember, who had thrown the *post mortem* report up in the air by declaring that he had found something which could be soot—and therefore that Beckie must have been alive when the fire started.

Professor Gresham told us that he had found evidence of Pulmonary Oedema or water-logging of the lungs. I believe it is also called Dematitis. Then saying that he did not think the particles found by Dr Hill were important, he went on to explain the three causes of Pulmonary Oedema—heart failure, which has to be unlikely in a 17 year old girl, an overdose of drugs or a blow to the head.

When I asked him if he could do any more tests for drugs, he said that he would have been able to carry out the tests if the large sections of Beckie's lung had not been lost—

—lost! I reeled. This was the first we had heard of evidence being lost. Professor Gresham told us that Mr Gaskins' letter to him had said that large lung samples "had gone missing" from Cardiff Royal Infirmary.

Well! We had always been a bit suspicious about what had become of the two uterus that had been recovered from Uckington—and we had certainly not known at first that this part of Emma had been available for testing. But now lung samples? And yet, according to the forensic reports, they had not been able to test for DNA or the presence of drugs in the girls' remains.

The two statements just did not match up. But it was even worse that we had not been given all that was left of Emma and Beckie to cremate and inter. How dare they destroy or lose pieces of our children without doing more tests or without telling us.

It infuriated me to think that in such a case, where every piece of evidence was crucial, people had apparently not been more careful. I took great care, therefore, to make sure I really understood what Professor Gresham had said about the particles Dr Hill had reported that he had found. With Steve listening, I asked again. Professor Gresham replied that, in his opinion, the particles were not soot at all but pigment caused by the use of Formalin to preserve the specimens!

And so it seemed that, if Dr Hill, who was once a student of Professor Gresham's, would allow him to retest those slides for Formalin, the Murder charges could be shown to have been wrongly dropped. I cannot really describe how I feel. Shocked, I think, but pleased that we may be near the truth at last. God bless Professor Gresham who quickly put his conclusions in writing.

January 1993

Dear Mrs Harper,

I have examined the sections of lung labelled Rebecca Harper.

They show heat coagulation of the tissue and coagulated oedema fluid in the alveoli. Pigment is present often in or on alveolar walls. I suspect that this is formalin pigment (i.e. an artefact) and not soot. Most of the recognisable bronchioles do not contain pigment.

I agree with Dr Hulewicz that there is no clear evidence of soot inhalation in these sections of lung.

The sections provide evidence of acute pulmonary oedema which may be due to a variety of causes such as asphyxia, acute heart failure, head injury and drug intoxication.

The lung sections do not provide evidence that Rebecca was alive when engulfed in smoke.

Yours sincerely,

G A Gresham
TD MD ScD FRCPath

Vicky:

Professor Gresham also wrote to the Coroner in Cheltenham in terms which surely meant that the Crown Prosecution Service would have no option but to reopen the case and restore the original charges. If they didn't, the consequence would be that not even the Coroner could use forensic evidence to contradict the Court's unthinking acceptance that Emma and Beckie were killed by fire. And that was an explanation which we now knew we were right never to accept.

> *Dear Mr Maddrell [the Coroner]*
>
> *Re Rebecca Harper (deceased)*
>
> *As you know I have reviewed the slides of Rebecca's lungs which came to me from Dr Hill at the Royal London Hospital.*
>
> *In my view they do not provide any evidence that Rebecca breathed smoke into her lungs and that she must have died before being exposed to the fire.*
>
> *The lungs showed evidence of oedema for which there are many causes. Sadly, the body was so badly burned that we shall never know the precise cause of death. Frankly, I don't know how one can go on from here, short of any circumstantial evidence that may subsequently arise. I gather that the accused were acquitted which does leave the matter open for any future developments should they arise.*
>
> *I am sorry that I cannot be more definite. I understand that nothing else remains from Rebecca that might be examined.*
>
> *Yours sincerely,*
>
> *Austin Gresham*

Vicky:

It is now essential that we get some untreated blocks of samples to Professor Gresham who had only seen the slides provided by Dr Hill. With blocks, he can prove once and for all that Dr Hill was mistaken in his findings and that the particles of 'soot' were no more than formalin pigment.

Once again we set out to track down the samples and get them to Gresham. And we inform the Crown Prosecution Service, the Coroner and the police of what he has told us. But the Crown Prosecution Service is not terribly interested, preferring to save money and put their trust in Dr Hill's report. It worries me greatly that so many convictions are gained, or cases lost, on the basis of scientific evidence. Clearly it isn't all that it ought to be. We now have two people who say that Beckie did not inhale smoke but I cannot see that anyone cares about it. The weeks are passing and I am getting crosser.

It seems almost impossible to get the blocks to Gresham. The Crown Prosecution Service are holding things up saying that they cannot comment until they have spoken to Hill. Eventually, we get the samples to Gresham and he tests them again. He was right the first time:

Dear Mrs Harper,

I have received and examined further sections of lung and bronchus from Rebecca Harper. Pigment was present and this was removed by treatment with saturated alcohic picric acid for 15 minutes. A little carbon pigment in para-bronchial lymphatics remained. This is a usual feature in adult lungs and does not indicate inhalation of smoke in a fire.

Burned vegetable material was a surface contaminant in the section of bronchus. This was not affected by picric acid.

In conclusion, most of the pigment in the lung section was formalin pigment. The alveoli contained coagulated oedema fluid and strands of mucous indicating forceful inhalation. There is no evidence that Rebecca Harper died from a fire.

Pulmonary oedema has several causes one of which is hypoxia. The cause of such hypoxia is not evident.

Yours sincerely

G A Gresham
TD MD ScD FRCPath

We sent this latest report off to the Crown Prosecution Service expecting that at least an Inquiry would be launched into the case. The presence of burned vegetable material was easily explained because poor Beckie's head was missing so exposing her windpipe. So how could the system not be asking the sort of questions which the Coroner was prevented from putting?

I continue to write endless letters to everyone I can think of—but time is running out and they must be sick of hearing from me.

Lady Thatcher continues to be a source of great comfort and the police still come round and listen. But realistically, while Hill's report still stands, I cannot do very much. The Coroner cannot re-open the case—indeed, he's limited in what he can do by the Court findings. Strange isn't it? It's his job to find the cause of death. Talk about the law perverting its own course of justice.

HM Coroner for the Cheltenham District of Gloucestershire (writing to Vicky and Steve):

Since the end of the trial I have been considering the question of the twins' inquests, which were opened formally on 30th January 1991.

Where criminal charges of a serious nature are brought as a result of a death, the Coroner is required to adjourn the inquest until after the criminal proceedings have finished. The Coroner then may resume the inquest *"if in his opinion there is sufficient cause to do so"* (Coroner's Act 1988, Sec. 16(3)) but, if he does, *"the findings must not be inconsistent with the outcome of the relevant criminal proceedings"* (Sec. 16(7)(a)).

Vicky:

And then later in the year, eight months later, the Crown Prosecution Service replied that they would not be re-opening the case at all. To our utter disbelief, they didn't think there was any new evidence. And so we went constantly back to the drawing board. I wanted to tell the girls not to worry—we would continue to fight on their behalfs.

The press got hold of the story and once again we were to become the centre of attention. We would not say too much, however, because we wanted to have more tests done and we did not want to reveal Professor Gresham's name until we were ready.

One of the TV men suggested a press conference when we had all the facts. I asked Professor Gresham if he would be willing to participate in such a conference and he agreed, bless him. Some newspapers tried to force us to reveal his name but we were not going to bullied into saying anything which might jeopardise our position.

Vicky:

Media madness was no new thing. It actually started just after the twins' deaths but, since the trial, it has been even worse. Sometimes I wonder seriously about the sanity of the press. First, we saw the unscrupulous newspapers pretending, just after their deaths, to be friends of the twins. Reporters going from door to door, trying to dredge up some scandal about Emma and Beckie—telling our neighbours in a most distressing way that the girls were dead.

But for all that, our local newspaper, *The Gloucestershire Echo*, has been mainly very kind and sympathetic. We have even learned over the last three years to turn the interest of the media to our own advantage. I have also learned to say exactly what I want in a very short space of time. This is important to remember: when you do a TV interview, it lasts about three minutes of which only seconds will actually be broadcast. So you have to get the point over quickly.

Central Television has also been very considerate and helpful in all our dealings with them. *Sky TV* were mindful, too, of our distressed state. But, alas, some of the newspapers and magazines have not been so kind.

For us, the *Daily Express* headline during the trial was the worst. We were given a chance to redress the balance when appearing on *Central Weekend Live* and, unfortunately for Alan Frame, the newspaper's Executive Editor, I had been so intensely annoyed that I was ready for him . . .

Central Weekend Live:

[A *verbatim* account of a debate hosted by Nicky Campbell (NC) with Alan Frame (AF), Executive Editor of the *Daily Express*, Laurie Manifold (LM), ex *Sunday People*, Vicky Harper (VH), Stephen Harper (SH) and others]

NC   . . . Government plans to outlaw intrusive press behaviour. So, is the government right to get tough with tabloids and the rest of the media? What about the freedoms of ordinary people? That's the other side of the coin.

Vicky and Stephen Harper are in the studio tonight—thanks

241

for coming in. Your daughters, two daughters, died in a barn fire after they went there with three young men, who were later acquitted of the charge of manslaughter. Now, as if your grief wasn't enough, it was made worse by the way it was reported in the press. How was it reported in the press?

VH   Well, it is very interesting what the gentleman on the end says (Laurie Manifold)... But when your daughters and wives die, they get slandered in the newspapers because the dead have no defence.

Not only have we lost our daughters, we went to trial expecting the press to be interested in the three boys who were accused of killing them, not in the alleged sexual activities of our twin daughters. And the *Daily Express* on the Wednesday of the trial—'Three Killed Barn Sex Orgy Twins'.

No one had mentioned the word orgy. Do you know what orgy means? Do your journalists know what it means? It means naked worship of the Devil and drunken revelry. We only have the three boys' word that the twins agreed to go to the barn in the first place. They're dead, they have no defence. They certainly wouldn't have taken part in a sexual orgy whatsoever.

AF   Can I come in here? I would like to apologise for the headline. It should never have been written and I, personally, am sorry it was written.

VH   [background] No it shouldn't.

NC   Will you be apologising in print?

AF   I would like to, I think we have certainly apologised by letter.

VH   No, no you haven't. Oh no you haven't. We've had no apology.

AF   I will take this opportunity now of apologising for that headline.

VH   But don't you think it's a bit late? These members of the audience, who did not know our twin daughters, have read about them in the papers and, as far as they have read, they were sexually promiscuous 17 year old twins. They were not. They were decent, kind, loving, ordinary girls who were invited to a party that night that never existed. It's too late. I'm glad that you're apologising but I'm afraid it's too late now. The damage has been done.

Princess Diana has power and money to take people like you to Court. We have nothing.

SH   Not only that but we can't take people to Court for people who are dead.

VH   For slandering the dead. The dead have no defence.

AF   Can I also say though, that the proceedings in Court, when the boys were in Court accused of those dreadful incidents, they were reported accurately. The headline may have been inaccurate but, sexual activity did come out in Court and we were merely—

VH   The alleged sexual activity.

AF   Quite so, I accept that but, nevertheless this was given in evidence in Court and it was reported by the newspapers. Unfortunately, this is most unpleasant for those who are intimately involved in these cases. It's bad enough, as you obviously know, having lost your children, but then to see the thing reported in the newspapers, no matter what headline—we've discussed that already, but seeing it brought up again is clearly very distasteful, very hurtful.

VH   The twins weren't actually the ones on trial at the end of the day.

NC   It is noble of you to apologise but, perhaps it would be nice if there was to be an apology in print. A lot of people remember the case—it's tarnished in people's minds.

VH   Yes, yes...

Vicky:

Appearances on *Good Morning* and *This Morning* also gave us the chance to put our points forward. When *Press Watch* was launched by Clive Soley MP, I was appearing on *Good Morning* and then we went up to London for lunch with him. In the afternoon, I did an interview with Angela Rippon which again allowed me to give vent to my feelings.

Even now, we occasionally get asked to participate in TV shows and Radio Broadcasts. Steve was interviewed by Frank Bough and recently a national radio station did an article on the invasion of the press following the 'Diana gymnasium' scandal.

Me magazine, which printed an article on us in January 1993, was not too bad although they got some of the facts wrong. But *Woman* magazine, however, disgraced itself. The editor was away at the time of publication and the headlines, in what was supposed to be a sensitive article about defending the dead, speak for themselves: "*Our daughters weren't tarts!*" The article also dealt with another family's grief in a similar tragedy to our own and they were appalled at the article, too. We both rang the editor to complain. And we did each receive an apology and a bouquet of flowers—but, of course, once the article is printed the damage is done.

The press have a long way to go before they can be trusted with self-regulation. This year, *The News of the World* 'phoned me to ask if we were going to start a civil action against the boys. I told them we were not. The following weekend, the headline was "*Parents to sue death blaze trio*"—exactly the opposite of what I had said, resulting in a storm of publicity and a very nasty letter to me. Eventually, the Press Complaints Commission ruled in my favour and a minute apology was printed. The matter was dealt with compassionately but, when you consider that the newspaper editor was a member of the Commission, you have to wonder if it's that objective. The 'ombudsman' who followed things up? Yes, he appeared to work for *The News of the World* too.

Autumn 1993

Vicky:

My Mum has received a much deserved award from the Arts Council. This was in recognition of her writing and poetry contributions over the years. She also makes tapes for the blind and gives talks all over Gloucestershire. I was very pleased for her.

The local newspaper was given a list of the prize winners and promised to be at the presentation with a photographer. But they did not appear, perhaps because something else cropped up. It was a nice presentation, however, which was given by the late Sir Charles Irving, our local MP and a long time friend of Mum's.

When *The Echo* did do an interview with Mum, they obviously suddenly realised who she was. And once again the press produced sensational and most hurtful headlines: "*Poetry trophy for blaze horror gran.*" This provoked another wave of media interest—from *Hello* magazine and from the TV and radio people. It may have been nice for Mum but I felt they weren't interested in her award at all. They just wanted to hear her speak about Emma and Beckie. It caused some upset between us and in the end I asked her not to give any more interviews. The Arts Council complained and eventually an article was written about all the deserving people who had won awards.

Even today, we are still in contact with several daily newspapers who are awaiting further developments. But now, of course, we can speak to them on our terms and when we are ready. Some newspapers have treated us decently and we thank them for it.

A year ago tomorrow the trial started and yet we are no nearer understanding exactly what happened. Looking back at the newspaper reports of those awful eight days, I am so incensed by the way the press misrepresented things that I find it difficult to control my rage—and believe me, it is rage.

Only one thing was accurately printed and that was part of a statement made by Steve and me, read out for us by a family friend, Peter Quigley. It says that Steve and I were each facing a life sentence while those who had walked away from the barn were free of any such burden or responsibility. I want to expand on that remark. If you have not suffered a tragedy, it is truthfully impossible to imagine what it feels like. All the standard phrases used at the time by well-meaning people are worthless and totally wrong. Soon, it will be three years since Emma and Beckie died—but life gets worse not better.

Particularly at this time, it is harder to bear their loss than at any other. Perhaps it is because things are so quiet for me at the moment? I feel 'surplus to requirements'. Steve has a lot to do which means that he has to work every day of the week including weekends. And because he's in the house, I find myself creeping around in an effort not to disturb him. I am unable to sit down—I daren't weep because he'd get upset. He will say to me: "*And what are your plans for today?*"—but how can I tell him: "*Just to reach the end of it*"

So I am left with hours to fill, pretending to be busy so that Steve does not feel obliged to sit and drink yet another unwanted cup of coffee with me. Once upon a time, my hours were filled with working and generally organising a family of four. But now I am hard pressed to find anything to fill my days. I cannot do endless washing, it's hard enough to find just one load a week. I have no-one to organise. No children to chivvy along to work or to college. Only one bed to change, not three.

Meals have become the highlights of the day for me because I can guarantee to waste a couple of hours planning and preparing them. But the trouble is, I am getting earlier and earlier in their preparation.

I would genuinely like to find something to do but I am afraid of being in contact with people for fear of passing on the plague I carry. I would have liked to have invited some Spanish students to stay in the summer but how can I ask young people to live in a house full of despair and photographs of dead children? I am even scared of buying things for people in case my bad luck goes to them.

Ridiculous self-pity, you say. Well maybe. I have tried to think what I might have been doing if Emma and Beckie had just left home to pursue their own lives, but it is just impossible to imagine. Even if they had moved away, I would have been able to visit them and their loved ones. Maybe even grandchildren. But there is simply nothing there anymore.

People say time heals but it doesn't. It just gets more frustrating trying to recapture the times I had with them. Silly questions come to mind. Did they have baths together when they were little? Was it Emma or was it Beckie who didn't like faggots for tea? Not being sure of the answers is like being disloyal to them. But at the time, these things were quite unimportant because I had the rest of my life to be with them and revel in more important things.

Perhaps if I knew the detail of how they had died—and if someone had borne responsibility for it—it would all be easier to accept. But as time goes by and as we steadily uncover more evidence and continuing refusal to act upon it, nothing gets easier.

October 1993

Vicky:

Today in the paper, I read a report of a man who has been found Guilty of Manslaughter *and* Arson. But the Judge in our case said that a person could not be tried for both crimes. Is there a law or just guidelines open to interpretation by individual Judges? Here I go again, over the same path, the same questions. How? Why?

In our case no-one was even charged with the destruction of hay and straw and yet I often read now of people being jailed for exactly those offences. Small wonder that each waking moment is filled for me with torment.

I cannot think or concentrate and, as Norma said to me last Wednesday, I am now in a mess. I know I am a mess and I would give the world to be out of it—but that in itself brings problems. I need to make a Will, to ensure that Steve gets what little I have, and he needs to make a Will in case we die together in an accident. But he is reluctant to talk about such things and we would then both have to decide where our estates went if we did both die at the same time.

I would like to leave my money to some worthwhile cause in the twins' names. This would ensure they weren't forgotten and would help those less fortunate than myself. But even this raises difficulties. I cannot really afford to set up trust funds and so on—and I don't even have the capacity to think about it. I tried to tell Norma and Steve how I was feeling. I do not want to live, I wanted to tell them. If I have to live while fighting for the truth, then I do not want to live in Cheltenham. I hate the place and everything in it.

So, while Steve has a job and a house and a car and all the things needed for a fairly full life, I have nothing. It's not a recipe for happiness. When this is finally over, I will not continue to live in Cheltenham. If I live anywhere, it must be somewhere that the boys have never been and where no-one has ever heard of them.

I cannot bear the constant clamouring of people each offering their own bit of gossip. To know that David Harper is a singer with a band is all very well but it doesn't help me. To know that Wisdom Smith is going to be a father doesn't help me. These are just more smacks in the face. Do the parents of these boys ever spare a thought for us now? Do they have any idea of the torment we are condemned to? I would have thought probably not.

Weekends are the worst—especially when friends unthinkingly wave good-bye with "*Have a nice weekend, won't you!*" Sundays, which always used to be so busy with church services and lunch and preparation for Monday, are particularly hard. Steve now cooks lunch on Saturdays and Sundays so I have lost that job too.

I am a wreck, I know it and I am powerless to do anything about it. To talk of killing myself only causes upset to those who love me and ordinary people shy away from such taboo subjects.

I think that Steve thinks that I only feel this way occasionally. But it is a constant thought in my mind.

I have worked out the music I want to be listening to when I die. And in which room I will do it.

It is something which preoccupies me. To be at peace and with my girls is my idea of Heaven. Life is Hell. Anyway, enough waffling and self-pity—it's 11 o'clock. Is that too early for lunch I wonder?

Vicky's Victim Support volunteer:

I continued to see Vicky after the case every month for about four to five months. It is always difficult for Victim Support volunteers to know when to start withdrawing. I did not want to withdraw entirely, yet I did not want to continue to visit on a routine and regular basis unless I was helping—and I was increasingly doubtful as to whether I was doing this.

On advice from professional counsellors, I suggested to Vicky that rather than have a regular appointment, it might be best if she called on me when she felt the need. She agreed but this did not really work as she did not call upon me for some nine months.

Not knowing whether she genuinely did not need help, or did not like to ask for it, I hesitated to impose myself again or to encourage any feeling of dependency (not that Vicky seems or has ever seemed to me the dependent type).

In the event, a chance meeting with Vicky led to the resumption of our periodic meetings which have continued to this day.

Vicky:

After nights of sweating, tossing and turning, I realise I have become addicted to my sleeping pills. I have tried everything to get off them—even two different sorts of homeopathic tablets, one of which gave me dreadful nightmares. I thought I had experienced all the worst sort of dreams but this new breed brings me hellish images. The second lot of tablets send me off into a bodily sleep, my limbs paralysed except for the occasional terrible spasm of activity.

Part of my mental agony is that I am surrounded by other parents' horror. The trial of the two boys accused of killing little James Bulger. The release of the man accused of killing Nikki Allen. Do people realise just what sort of legacy the families of victims of violent death are left with? Do they understand the agonising that we go through over and over again?

Separating fact from speculation is not easy when Emma's tooth has been found out in the field and Beckie's head disconnected from her body. Naturally the boys were questioned for some time at the beginning in an attempt to answer just the straightforward questions. However, finding out exactly what happened must have been made more difficult because of the false account about a cigarette that was told at the very beginning. And even after that first statement, their accounts varied several times while, in the end, Harper refuted everything.

Does that mean that he was accusing the others of lying, in order to protect his own position? But if all three were at first in agreement about what they would say and then Harper refutes everything—that must mean also that he, Harper, could be lying. The Judge said he lied but then he merely dismissed the Arson charges against all of them and decided to concentrate on Manslaughter.

And then the defence put forward pleas that Smith and Winter had no case to answer for Manslaughter and the Judge directed the jury to bring in verdicts of Not Guilty against them. But there was a sworn statement by Harper that one or other of the boys had lit pieces or bales of hay or straw—and yet this statement was inadmissible because all three were at the outset co-defendants. Constantly turning these things over in my mind, cross-checking the statements and reports released to us by the Home Office, I came to the conclusion that the reluctance or inability of the Court and judical system to use any of the evidence beggared all belief.

During their original questioning, all three boys denied hearing any noises coming from Emma or Beckie. They were quite clear about it. But when the charges were increased to Murder, Winter suddenly remembered hearing a scream—and when asked whether he thought this was important, he replied that it was indeed important because it proved that one of the girls was alive. When asked why such an important point had only just come to mind, he admitted that he had only just thought of it. What does that tell you?

At the trial, much was made of this scream and naturally it registered in people's minds that one of the girls was alive. I do not believe that there was a scream and we now even have proof that Beckie was dead before the fire. And we know, too, that the Court was allowed to assume that the JCB digger caused the break-up of Beckie's few remains when there has to be considerable doubt on the matter.

Sub Officer Stephen Knight:

I found the 'remains' of Beckie about 14 hours after the first call out. At that stage, mid-afternoon of the 24th January, the team was damping down the fire working along the back of the barn from Bay 4 towards Bay 1. We hadn't yet reached Bay 2.

I found Beckie near the front of Bay 2 when all the action, particularly the work of the JCB, was at the back of the barn. As soon as I found her, I impounded the whole area and can categorically state that the JCB was not allowed near the place where Beckie was lying.

Although nearly 14 hours had passed since the call out, it is unlikely that the JCB went near Beckie during that time. Firefighters had certainly walked across that part of Bay 2 but I think it unlikely that the JCB had been there.

Vicky:

Do you know that we have even spoken to members of the legal profession who have told us that, in their view, the prosecution barrister closed the case in his opening speech. And you wonder why I am hooked on sleeping pills?

Although I still cannot accept it, it seems to be too late now for this comedy of errors to be changed. To me, it was a fiasco in which the Crown Prosecution Service discarded charges, in case the jury was confused, only to end up with the Judge being confused by the mess that was left for the Court to consider. About a third of the evidence came to Court and that was distorted by the media or by legal jargon.

God help the innocent in the hands of a system like this. And God help them if they were already dead before the fire began.

Vicky:

We now know that lots of tests had not been carried out that could have been—tests for carbon monoxide poisoning and the tests to establish toxicological evidence that Dr Hill mentioned in his report. When first in contact with Professor Gresham, I had been reading an article about the National Poisons Unit at Guy's Hospital and re-reading the scientific evidence given. It stated that, had these toxicological tests been carried out, a clearer idea of the causes of death would have been available.

I had to get my dictionary out because I had not heard of the word 'toxicology' before. It means the science of poisons. So putting two and two together, I had 'phoned the National Poisons Unit where some nameless individual told me that no tests were possible at all. But then Professor Gresham had put me in touch with Dr Toseland, who was to provide the link with the drug Ecstasy. Dr Toseland was the best in the field, he had said. There was not much hope, I was also warned, but I did try Dr Toseland and explained the problems in the way that Professor Gresham told me to.

Dr Toseland was very helpful. He wasn't optimistic but he did agree to look at some paraffin blocks of samples. There is a difficulty with these blocks because the human 'remains' which are stored in them are injected with several drugs first—which makes it difficult to extract certain chemicals later. Dr Toesland knew of a way to test for drugs but, because of the nature of the experiment, the sample under test was always destroyed. Nothing is straightforward, is it? Still, we had to try to get some of the precious paraffin blocks to him.

By now, and ever since the trial ended, I was wary of everyone. I couldn't trust the system and I thought that the best solution would be for us to collect the blocks from Cardiff and deliver them personally. However, I was not too sure about the ownership of them and contacted Mr Coopey at the Coroner's Office first. He was as always very kind and helpful and agreed to talk to the scientist in charge, Dr Leadbetter. In the end, he agreed to send the blocks direct to Dr Toseland but postal strikes and holidays intervened and it was some time before they arrived—and some time before results were known.

These delays seemed to happen to us all the time. I know that Dr

Toseland had his own job to do in addition to lecturing, appearing in Court and so on. And as you might expect, his professional skill was very much in demand. Patience, therefore, was a particular skill that we had to try to develop however difficult and stressful the experience.

As the weeks passed, the tension took its toll upon my health. With the strain of appearing cheerful at work, I found myself growing bitter inside—which I had been warned against. I found myself wanting to be cruel to people. Especially to the families of those who had walked away from the barn. On many an occasion, I wanted to 'phone them to explain how I was feeling. But I never did.

At long last, after what seemed a lifetime, Dr Toesland wrote to us on the 20th November 1993:

Dear Mrs Harper,

This is to confirm the telephone conversation that we had last week, concerning the analysis of the sample of preserved lung tissue that I had received from Dr Leadbetter.

I analysed the sample for as wide a range of compounds as possible and I found the tissue sample to contain compounds, Methylene-dioxy Methylamphetamine and Methylene-dioxy Amphetamine. The first compound is more commonly known as 'Ecstasy' and the second is its principal metabolite. A metabolite is simply a breakdown product of the drug 'Ecstasy' that is produced in the body.

I have identified the drugs by 3 separate analytical systems, including the process of Gas Chromatography-Mass Spectometry. The analytical details are in my possession and they can be made available to anyone that you wish. I consider that the analytical details are your property and I will treat them as such.

Yours sincerely,

P A Toseland

BSc PhD FRCPath

Steve was over the moon. It seemed to confirm everything he had thought. During their evening out, the twins had been bought a pint of lager each, of which about half a pint of each glass was drunk. Steve insists that this is out of character—not drinking half a pint but drinking lager. Emma might occasionally have asked for it but Beckie wouldn't have touched it. Given a chance, she would have gone for something more exotic.

On their own admission and from the evidence of the barmaid, the boys consumed a large amount of alcohol in the pub—Jack Daniels, Tequila Slammers, beer and some other drink. Surely during this time, and with cash so freely available, the girls would have asked for some other drink? It didn't sound right to us at all. Was something dropped into pints of lager which would have been noticeable in a smaller glass?

I was not quite sure what I felt, especially as we now had to wait for independent confirmation. There were two people Dr Toseland could think of who were capable of performing the delicate task of Mass Spectometry—but again, the odds were against us. One of them refused to help.

Eventually, he enlisted the help of a young woman who he knew was excellent. But she, too, was very busy and so the waiting started all over again.

Holidays and work intervened. Dr Toseland heard nothing from his colleague and then went off to the Gulf on a lecture tour. On his return, I rang him straight away, to learn that the young woman scientist had telephoned in his absence. But it seemed that she had not left a message.

Sunday has now become the day before the day I telephone Dr Toseland to see if there any test results. When I know, I shall have something to occupy my mind working out what to do with the information. I am very wary of exposing the revelation to the press—just imagine the headlines: "Sex Orgy Barn Blaze Twins were Drug Addicts!"

—God, how frustrating this all was! I pushed Dr Toseland as hard as I dared. Every day. And then I found myself one Tuesday, 'phoning on several occasions when he promised in turn to try the other scientist yet again.

I called back at the time we had arranged but Toseland wasn't there. I was nearly in tears trying to get ready to go to work myself and felt quite awful. Finally, the 'phone rang and Steve answered. He called up to say that it was Dr Toseland and, with bra on but very little else, I flew downstairs to hear what he had to say.

"Are you sitting down?" I said that I was although I was actually close to falling over. Dr Toseland continued: "Yes, we have the confirmation!"

Vicky with her daughters Emma (*left*) and Beckie, aged 11.
(*By kind permission of Rick Henderson*)

I cannot tell you what I said to him. Just accept, please, that I was so relieved as he went on to explain in more detail what his colleague had found. It didn't mean a lot but evidently it was good news.

Working that afternoon was very difficult indeed. After all, what did this confirmation that Beckie (and presumably Emma) had taken Ecstasy prove? And who would listen to us? But for Steve and me, at least the waiting was over and we could press ahead. I wasn't sure how to press ahead because I had written to just about everyone—but at least I knew we were moving forward.

Michael Howard, the new Home Secretary, was featured strongly in the media and he seemed to want change in the legal system. Having tried his predecessor, John Patten, I wrote to the Home Office again. I told him everything in this book—and yet I heard nothing. I 'phoned up the Home Office to ask if my letter had arrived and was told that only recorded delivery could confirm that they had received the letter. So I wrote yet again using recorded delivery.

I still heard nothing and next I wrote to John Major saying that I wasn't very happy about being ignored. At least I received a reply from a secretary explaining that the matter was being looked into and that the Home Secretary was being sent my letter. That makes three copies that Mr Howard received.

And then, in the local newspaper, I read that our friend and former MP, (the late) Sir Charles Irving, was to soon to have a private meeting with Michael Howard. I sent another copy of my letter off to Sir Charles and asked him to pass it on at the meeting. And of course, he responded at once and we are most grateful to his memory. He also suggested that we contact our new MP, Nigel Jones, who had more access to Government Departments as well as the right to ask questions in the House. This I did with yet another copy of my letter. Poor Mr Howard has now received five copies—he won't forget us in a hurry.

After some delays, Sir Charles received a reply. Things were moving. Investigations will be made into all the questions I have raised. At last!

I suppose that, as time had passed, we had subsided further into shock and despair leaving the police to investigate what seemed relevant to them. The possibility of drugs had never been pursued and we allowed our early suspicions to lapse—with hindsight, however, we should have insisted that tests for drugs were carried out on the pieces of Emma and Beckie and on the boys themselves. But once again we relied upon the experts. It was a mistake. Why won't they rely upon the instincts of parents and families?

Vicky:

Although things might have been moving at last, we did not pursue a civil action against the boys. In December 1992, our application for Legal Aid had been turned down on the grounds that Harper, probably the only one we could sue successfully, was unemployed. He would therefore be unable to satisfy any judgement made against him. But this was of little interest to us. It wasn't the forecast damages, only £3,500 for each girl, which were important to us. It was that we wanted someone to be held responsible for what had happened, someone to be held responsible for what no-one would explain.

We tried again for Legal Aid this year, in October, and were granted it *"on legal merits"*. They obviously felt that by then Harper did have a case to answer. I was told that, if I co-operated with the Department of Social Security about my financial status (which I did), the certificate would be forwarded. It was difficult filling in the forms because Steve had only been self-employed for about six months and could therefore not provide a forecast of earnings. We remained hopeful, however, because of the legal merits of our case.

But then, without having been asked any questions at all, we received a letter to say that Legal Aid had been refused because I had disposable income of £7,300 a year. There was no appeal, we were told, although I could apply for a breakdown of their calculations.

However, there was no reply to my immediate letter back requesting such a breakdown. And still no reply to my second letter four weeks later. So I wrote again and telephoned on several occasions until the system sent me a short form which must have taken no more than two minutes to complete. Apparently, they take your mortgage into account but allow you no money to eat or live on.

It was now the 14th of December and time was running out if we were to start an action before the third anniversary of Emma's and Beckie's deaths. We arranged an urgent meeting with our solicitor to bring him up to date and to discuss what a civil action would accomplish if the Home Secretary reopened the case. The point was that, by commencing a civil action, we would in effect be admitting that the girls were alive at the time of the fire—which we are quite certain they weren't.

What were we to do? Were we to pay for such an action which went against our every instinct? Were we to pay for a barrister in such *"a very, very complex case"*? We were told that we could even end up having to pay Harper's costs in the event that we lost the case—which was quite unacceptable to us. Steve would have gone to jail rather than do such a thing.

The discussion continued but the risks we eventually rejected. We felt that another door had slammed in our faces. There weren't too many avenues left open to us. Were any that remained ever going to deliver results?

In fact, the answer was 'No'. And I have now come to the conclusion that the Home Secretary avoided the issues we had raised rather than reopen the case and enable the Cheltenham Coroner to declare that the Crown Court was wrong to accept without challenge that a barn fire killed my girls. His letter below had not kept abreast of developments from Professor Gresham and Dr Toseland. It also contained a denial of any mislabelling of the parts of Beckie taken for forensic examination—a denial which he partly retracted eight months later in August 1994. And it admitted that, as a result of procedural error, samples were destroyed when the police had requested their retention.

Thursday, 23rd December 1993

The Rt Hon Michael Howard MP,
in a letter to the (late) Sir Charles Irving:

I promised to write to you about the forensic science issues, within my responsibilities, surrounding the tragic deaths of Emma and Beckie Harper. I have now received advice from the Chairman of the Home Office Policy Advisory Board for Forensic Pathology and the Director General of the Forensic Science Service on the points raised by Mrs Harper.

It may be helpful if I first explain that, although the Home Office certifies pathologists on the advice of a panel of leading practitioners, the individuals so certified are independent practitioners and are not employed by the Home Office but by police forces and coroners. We have, however, made enquiries of Dr Hill and informal contact has been made with Dr Gresham. Dr Hulewicz has since moved to Australia. I understand that Dr Hill would be happy to meet Mrs Harper if she would find this helpful.

I fully appreciate Mrs Harper's concern that differing opinions could be expressed by the pathologists, particularly when the issue of whether Beckie had inhaled smoke would appear to be so crucial. It is often difficult, particularly for a lay person, to accept that an expert may not be able to supply an unequivocal answer to every question, or indeed, that there may be different interpretations of the same scientific findings. In this case, I am advised that it is most unlikely that the matter could be unequivocally resolved because that material available for examination was limited and not of sufficiently good condition to allow the experts to be more precise.

I am advised that Dr Hulewicz's conclusion that the autopsy "*failed to determine whether or not the deceased was dead or alive prior to the outset of the fire*" is almost certainly the most realistic conclusion which can be drawn on present information; but I understand that Mrs Harper has retained Professor Gresham to look further at whether there was any evidence that Beckie had inhaled smoke.

Mrs Harper expresses concern that samples were destroyed or mislabelled, and that paraffin blocks containing sections of Beckie's lung were retained without her knowledge. As regards the retention of samples of tissue, a distinction needs to be drawn between parts of the body itself, which will obviously be buried or cremated as soon as possible, and samples which are of necessity removed at autopsy and preserved for specific tests. Such samples may be destroyed, or may be retained for a longer period. I understand that it was these samples in paraffin blocks which were located at the Wales Institute of Forensic Medicine earlier this year. There is no evidence that any of these samples or any of the body parts had been mislabelled by either the pathologists or the scientists involved.

Vicky:

I felt sick after reading this part of the letter. Be it a sample of tissue or an actual part of a body, these pieces were once living, breathing human beings—my daughters, Emma and Beckie—and I would have hoped that as such they would have been treated with the respect they deserved.

The Home Secretary (continuing):

The Forensic Science Service (FSS) involvement began when a scientist based at the Chepstow laboratory attended the scene on the morning of 25 January. A summary of the work they undertook is enclosed.

As you will see, the work undertaken was extensive and thorough and covered many different aspects of the case. The poor quality of the samples as the result of the fire was a fundamental problem in the analysis of whether carbon monoxide was present in the lungs, and in the DNA analysis...

Vicky:

Later investigation showed that, in the opinion of the scientist concerned (an expert in forensic science from Aldermaston specialising in deaths by fire), although it was now impossible for him to test for Carbon Monoxide because of the age of the specimens, it should have been possible to test at the time of the Post Mortem and Autopsy.

The Home Secretary (continuing):

I should also perhaps note that the police did not request drug analysis at any stage, and it was not therefore carried out. It is a matter for the police what lines of investigation should be pursued.

As regards the destruction of the samples, it is usual practice for the FSS and other public sector laboratories to destroy biological samples after a period of time for health and safety reasons unless there is a specific request for retention. This follows completion of the relevant tests or analyses, completion of a witness statement and an opportunity for a defence examination to take place. A statement was made by the FSS on 18 February 1991 concerning attempts at carbon monoxide determination. Attached to it was the standard letter to the police advising that the samples would be destroyed unless retention was requested.

The police did in fact request a retention in a letter dated 12 April 1991 asking that DNA work be conducted. The letter was forwarded to the DNA team who were unfortunately aware that the retention request should be copied to colleagues in other teams and some samples were subsequently destroyed. The FSS Director General is taking steps to ensure that it does not happen again. Samples submitted for DNA testing were retained as a result of the letter and remain at the laboratory in Chepstow...

New Year's Eve, 1993

Vicky:

Another year is over.

What have I achieved, I wonder?

I am weary of fighting. I am tired of waiting and I am sick to death of it all.

As far as this book is concerned I have finished. I would like to think that one day it will be published. And that, when I am gone, the twins' names will live on through these pages and in the memories of those who knew and loved them. And perhaps also endure in the thoughts of those who have learned about Emma and Beckie through reading this, our tragedy.

Wish us luck.

Epilogue

Martin Kay:

When I first read Vicky's story, I was appalled by the human tragedy she described. I felt it was a story which should be told, if only to try to create some calm in which she and Steve might be able to start the grieving process. Others will know better than I what five years without grieving might begin to mean. I can only speculate that five years in such circumstances must have depressed Vicky particularly to some sort of sub-human level of existence. She has not been living as you and I know it. Her outward composure successfully masks something truthfully hellish and I do not know where it will take her.

I have now spent some fifteen months intimately involved with Vicky's thoughts—often on the receiving end of her impatience that the book should be finished, published, done with. She has not liked uneven attention but our relationship has survived!

During these months, my concerns have begun to shift away from her human tragedy—although I have never once forgotten the few dreadful details available to us. Indeed, it is impossible to write and talk about Emma and Beckie without shuddering and without finding myself in the early hours of the morning, sitting at my word processor with one of Vicky's chapters, as my own tears start to fall.

My concerns have shifted away from the human tragedy towards the institutional affront. For me, this is now not so much a story which should be told: it is a story which should not be kept quiet. It is unacceptable to me that the weight of evidence and the reasonable expectations of victims and their families can have such little impact upon the way in which two violent, unexplained deaths have been 'written off'.

As a publisher of the words and ideas of young people, it has been almost a matter of obligation to help Emma and Beckie tell us through their mother that events in the early hours of 24th January 1991 could not have been as they were accepted.

Alison Flowers, Editor:

The first time I met Vicky I remember her as confident and articulate—but very wary of me. In the first half hour of our meeting she must have asked me at least three times was I really who I said I was or was I a girlfriend of one of the three lads who went to the barn with Emma and Beckie. Over the last 15 months I have met almost on a weekly basis with Vicky and Steve and I have been privy to their intimate thoughts and feelings about their daughters and what the whole family has had to endure.

Being only 18 months older than the twins the full horror of their fate naturally shook me to my core. But on working with Vicky and Steve my understanding of what happened and its widest implications have deepened to a level I could never have imagined. I feel as if in some small way I have gone through similar sensations of anger, intense grief and total disbelief that Vicky and Steve must have felt. I should think, and hope, that readers of this book will undergo this process too.

Despite the nature of this book working with Vicky and Steve has been enjoyable. So much so that sometimes I have come away from their house, where the twins grew up, suddenly feeling guilty, remembering what has brought me into contact with the family. Guilty in the knowledge that once I have left their home I go back into my own life—happy and lucky to be alive. For Vicky and Steve can never escape. But I so admire their courage and strength for their continued battle simply to understand how their children died and to find some way of existing peacefully themselves.

WDC Barbara Harrison:

For the first time in Gloucestershire and at the instigation of DCI Gaskins, two officers—myself and Sarah—were allocated the task of 'family liaison' officers. Sarah and I did all the enquiries involving Vicky and Stephen so that they would not have a succession of strange faces to put up with.

I hope we served them well. I have learned so much from being involved with them. They have pointed out areas where they felt our service could be maintained or improved in the future.

Sarah and I are no longer stationed in Cheltenham but we keep in touch. Sarah's sense of humour helped us along, with laughter breaks among all the so serious enquiries and the Court case.

We are still in contact with Vicky and Steve and intend this to continue. They are incredible people. I admire their strength.

WDC Sarah Morris:

I hadn't known the twins but, by hearing about them, by looking at photographs and by seeing drawings they had done, I felt I got to know them.

I can say now that Vicky and Stephen were, and still are, a wonderful couple to have dealings with. I am just sad that we met in such tragic circumstances. I felt that they complimented each other so well and that their love and obvious affection towards each other pulled them through their days of grieving.

As time moved on, words became easier to find and our grieving and concerned faces showed signs of change. Laughter came into being and I felt that Barbara and I had touched the hearts of this couple—just as they had touched ours.

Over the years, there have been numerous funny times between the four of us. We've discussed Vicky's choice in curtain material, the number of cigarettes she smokes, and a particular red and white 'snow-flake' sweater. With regards to Stephen, we've noticed his dry sense of humour, his love of a 'tipple' and the fact that he is one for playing the odd practical joke. He was the one who suggested that Barbara and I should have Drawer Linings as a Christmas present! What he meant by referring to women's knickers I will never know!

Detective Chief Inspector Gaskins:

The longer I got to know Vicky and Stephen, the more I admired their strength and support for one another. Our openness and honesty with one another laid the foundations of trust that remain to this day.

There is nothing that any of us can do to bring Emma and Beckie back, but they will never be forgotten. God bless them.

Vicky:

I am starting to write this epilogue today for two reasons. First, I have nothing else to do. And, second, because I want to start the New Year knowing that there is very little else I can do on the book.

I have by necessity had to re-read the manuscript I finished two years ago. It has been very hard and has brought back many deeply buried memories. Until Martin Kay contacted me, only three other people had read the manuscript of the book and they were all in London. It was like having given birth to a baby and then allowing someone to look after it for a while.

When Martin first began to edit the book, I felt as if that baby had been kidnapped and was being taken away from me for ever. However, we are nearly finished. I have found it difficult to let him cut bits out but I do realise that once I have said "I wish I was dead" fifty times it does become boring! I had not realised either that publishers have their own style and may use words that I would not even know the meaning of! However with his editor, Alison, acting as mediator, Martin and I have avoided coming to blows and our sensitive natures have both been protected. Alison, who is not much older than the twins would have been, has been an excellent go-between and could now probably get a job in the Diplomatic Corps.

My Mum rang this morning, very upset. She has lost those family Christmases we used to have and now spends the 25th December with one friend or relative, or another. This year she has not felt well enough to travel far and her good friends, John and Sheila, have come to the rescue again. I suppose some people think I am mean not to have her with us but I will never 'do' a Christmas again—it is too painful.

Steve and I spend the day quietly, going to the grave and the park. Went to the grave this morning. Flowers from Emma's friend, Alison. She remembers every year. It brightens up the day.

Our Christmas cards, done so kindly by Chris and Rose, have been a great success each year and it is certainly the only nice thing about Christmas for us. We have now used two by Beckie and two by Emma, a nice reminder of how talented they both were.

Vicky:

Well, another year. I wonder what this one will bring. At least the publication of this book, at long last. It has been like having a baby, a long hard labour but I hope it will be worth it at the end.

The situation now is much as it was five years ago. We still do not know how the girls met their deaths. We are still having tests done on the remains of Emma and Beckie that we have found scattered in laboratories around the country. Although we were horrified at the time to find that we had not had all the remains back, perhaps in hindsight it was fate. Since I finished this book two years ago yet another scientist has confirmed that in his opinion there was no soot in Beckie's airways. Three to one—but the Crown Prosecution Service insist that, as long as one scientist says there was something that could have been soot, they can do nothing. Is that really true?

The scientists working for us do so out of kindness and interest in a baffling case. We do not pay them so we must wait until they can spare the time to undertake the experiments. They are busy men, famous in their own fields. It is hard knowing that one man in particular could change our lives forever if he found new evidence during his tests. We can only wait and hope.

The three men in the case have never contacted us, never said they were sorry. Perhaps one day, when they have children of their own, they will break their pact of silence and tell us what happened that night. For our part, we will always remember that whatever happened in the barn on the night of the 23rd January 1991, three people got out and two did not. Why?

Over the last 5 years I have watched and listened in dismay to the disasters and tragedies that these years have brought. Since our daughters' deaths, it has become the norm for funerals to be televised, appeals made on television and flowers to be laid where people have died. I am glad we did not go down that road. It does no good. It is simply media madness. We have watched appeals from husbands sobbing for the public to come forward, begging for information to be given. And then the very people who have appealed are themselves charged with the killing, making a mockery of such television drama.

Counselling too has become the 'in thing'. No sooner has a tragedy occurred than the 'experts' rush in. People whose children have died only hours before appear on News Conferences. Perhaps *they* feel it will help other people to tell them about the people who have died—but *I* feel it cannot be good for their own grieving process. I could certainly not have appeared on TV the day we found Emma and Beckie had been died. I just wanted to curl up and die myself. I also feel that the enormity of the tragedy will hit them much later when other disasters have occurred and they and their lost relatives have been long forgotten by the media. That is when the pain really sets in. We have been lucky, people are still interested in Emma and Beckie's case. Perhaps because we retained so much information to ourselves and have tried not to sensationalise things in the press. God knows, the press have done that themselves.

The destruction of the girls' characters in Court and in the media was another thing I found hard to bear. The dead have no defence and we were not allowed to enter statements about their characters in the Court. Many times in the trial, I had to leave the room and each time some of the press said it was because of the sexual allegations about the girls.

It was not.

Once it was because we had just been shown the model of the barn. And I could not see how Beckie could have failed to get out—she was so close to the edge, so close to freedom and life. Another time, I cried because I could not believe that some facts about the case were being withheld from the jury.

Steve:

It seemed incredible to me that I had to be reminded in Court that I was not the twins natural father. Having brought the girls up since they were three I had naturally thought of them as my own daughters. Even close friends were amazed at the revelation.

Having kept my personal life private I felt particularly ill at ease that I had lost control of who knew what—and through no fault of my own.

Vicky:

The jury itself was an education. Recently a new trial was called for because a member of the jury had been asleep. One of ours fell asleep and the same man was very late back from lunch. He was not reprimanded. Perhaps he did not feel that the case was of interest to him?

What must also be remembered is that at the end of the trial a unanimous verdict was not reached. As the legal system has asked twelve people to come to a decision, how can it be right that when they do not all agree they are told to go away and talk, and keep talking, until enough of them have changed their minds to reach a majority decision. After all, if they have changed their minds in an effort to please the Judge and get home early, what is the point of a jury?

I would like to thank the people who have retained a true interest in our case. Some politicians and prominent people did respond to our letters and many forwarded our comments to the Royal Commission on Criminal Procedures, among them The Queen, John Major, Paddy Ashdown, Neil Kinnock, the Lord Chief Justice, the Director of Public Prosecutions.

Lady Thatcher has remained a constant comfort throughout and has very kindly agreed that extracts from her letters to me may appear in this book. Her staff have always been willing to help in any way they can. I am grateful to them, particularly to Mark Worthington who has never been too busy to listen to my questions and to answer them if he could.

Thank you also to the Chief Constable and Deputy Chief Constable for allowing the police involved in our case to express their emotions and thoughts and for allowing us to reproduce material relevant to the case. I know that, bearing in mind the West case and its subsequent flood of books, it must have been a difficult decision to make.

I have now served five years of my life sentence. In those five years, I have changed beyond recognition. To an outsider at a glance I probably appear much the same, older certainly but apart from that still the same old Vicky, cracking jokes and putting others at their ease. Deep inside however the scar is still raw. I have not had the chance yet to go away and lick my wounds in private as so much of the last five years has been spent as public property.

My lifestyle has changed of course. The food I buy now is for two people, expensive items that when Emma and Beckie were alive we would not have been able to afford. Strangely enough, I now look forward to going shopping. I feel quite safe in the supermarket and can browse and look for bargains. Pathetic how a trip to Tesco can brighten up one's day.

I would like to become a recluse and move away from Cheltenham. Somewhere where no-one knows me and there is no phone and no-one will come to the door. I cannot cry when I feel like it for fear of that knock on the door. And so I try, as ever, to make an appointment with myself. But the unexpected visitor still arrives or the telephone rings. And then the actress in me takes over.

Now the book is to be published Steve and I have to decide our future. It will mean many difficult decisions, forced upon us through no fault of our own. I cannot yet face selling the house where the twins spent so much of their lives. Realistically we cannot afford to stay here unless I go back to full time work. I cannot do that in Cheltenham. The thought of going for interviews scares me. The questions and conversations will once again come round to children. How do I tell a prospective employer about the twins? If he asks if I have children I cannot say no, that would be to deny them. But how can I explain that my children are dead. If he asks how they died, I cannot tell him. To go to work in a new environment would bring nightmares. If I worked with women who did not know my circumstances they would naturally talk about their children and grandchildren. What would I say?

I do not want to upset other people because of my misfortune. I would still like to move away but that would mean Steve getting a job elsewhere. He too is scared. Then where to go, where to try to start again? I only know that if I have to continue to live it must be on my terms and with some prospect of 'happiness' and a way of being a worthwhile human being. Steve, although sympathetic, does not feel as strongly as I do. Will we be able to survive yet another crisis?

Going out is hard. Recently I have seen one of the boys in the Bath Road in Cheltenham. It was the first time since the trial. This particular boy is well known in the area for his singing and I have found it hard to read about him in *The Gloucestershire Echo*. I was amazed at the strength of my feelings when I did see him. I'm afraid that I chased after his bike and shouted at him in the middle of the street—Steve told Martin that I went beserk.

I was ill for days after that and no longer go to Bath Road, an excursion I used to enjoy. Going out at night is worse. One of the boys may be there and I wouldn't know what to say. Noise and crowded places frighten me. I have got used to the quiet of my home now without the noise of two teenage girls. Time has not distanced the pain of missing them. But even time has done damage. For five years, I have had to compartmentalise my feelings. You cannot talk about your children's 'remains' and organs and really think of them as your daughters. I have now learnt to talk to the forensic scientists coldly about the remains and they have learnt that I can cope with discussing things no mother should ever have to discuss. Unfortunately, this distances Emma and Beckie, as my children, from me and sometimes I have to fight to bring them back.

I listen to the tapes of their Choir concerts and try to remember them as living human beings, simply Emma and Beckie. My Victim Support volunteer has been very helpful to me in this respect, allowing me to talk about them. Very often I have told her things that I hadn't realised I had thought of until I said them. I have learnt to discuss the legal process with people in a calm detached manner pointing out to them, when they get cross, the whys and the wherefores.

For Steve and me even watching TV can be a nightmare. Every programme brings a new idea or a new test and I immediately rush for a notepad so that I can follow up the questions. Debate programmes, science programmes and even *London's Burning* all fuel my imagination.

Whilst on holiday in Spain I saw on *Sky News* a report about a new scientific test that could possibly determine a cause of death in badly burnt remains. I could not wait to get home and follow that line of enquiry. I have learnt a great deal about the law and forensic work over the years but it has taken its toll.

Steve:

I find it particularly difficult that prior to the trial we were not allowed to comment on the girls' deaths because this would have been *sub judice.*

During the trial we were restricted by the fear of the trial being stopped. After the trial we were restricted because of the Not Guilty verdict. Five years on we were still being restricted by the laws of libel and, as a consequence, the general public only knew a fraction of the facts surrounding the girls' deaths.

These restrictions have been infuriating. But now we have the proof and the confidence to ask publicly the questions which were never raised.

I would hope that our letters to prominent people have contributed to the changes in the judicial system to try to redress the scales of justice, namely the Disclosure Act and the right to remain silent, both of which were changed after the Royal Commission Inquiry.

I believe the trial of the three youths was unfair. The Judge and jury did not have the full facts of the case. After the Murder charges were dropped all relevant evidence relating to those charges had to be withdrawn and, as a result, the full facts of what occurred on that fateful night were not heard by those who had to decide the verdict.

It was sheer lunacy that, only one day before the trial ended, we and the prosecution were presented with yet another alteration to Harper's defence when he "refuted" all earlier statements.

Like Vicky I feel the need to continue our investigation into what happened on Wednesday, 23rd January 1991.

Going out can be difficult. On the rare social occasions when we have been out in the evening I have sometimes seen people I knew from before. I have felt ashamed that they were looking at me and feeling that I should not be out after what has happened.

This obviously has a similar effect on work. But, having built up a respectable client base working for myself, new battles are to be fought with Vicky, who seems to expect a move to another area, not necessarily in this country. Over the last two years I have had to contemplate moves to Scotland, Ireland, Wales, France and Spain—depending on Vicky's particular mood.

Needless to say this causes friction between the two of us since I too do not particularly relish having to make new contacts or to be interviewed for new employment. While Vicky tends to limit these problems to Cheltenham, for me it seems a problem that is going to have to be carried far and wide. For this reason I am reluctant at present to throw away an income and the security of a roof over my head. This inability to plan a 'new' future is a direct result of the vulnerability I feel after such a cruel event. I dare say that once the book is published a compromise will have to be met. However, for now I prefer Emma's philosophy—'one day at a time'.

Vicky:

When I am alone and allowed to remember Emma and Beckie as they were, the shock is still enormous. Because I have been fighting to find the answers I have not been able to grieve. The realisation that I may never see them again is too much to bear even now. I do not think I can ever rest until I find the truth. Some people say it is time I left things alone but those people have not lost a child and do not have the questions reeling round in their minds that I do. Steve and I have grown together more since the twins' deaths but our life is not a normal one, it is simply adapted to survival. We lurch from one crisis to another and sometimes at the end of the day we have nothing left to give, certainly nothing for each other. I can only say that I do not want to go to my grave without knowing how and why Emma and Beckie went to theirs.

I hope that this book has answered some of the questions people have asked of us. We do not know all the answers and perhaps we never will. But I ask that, in the words of that young girl who bravely delivered her letter to me in January 1991:

> *... you think of them sometimes and give a little smile for Beckie and Emma's sake.*

Chronology of Events

1973

3 April   Emma and Rebecca Harper born, Cheltenham, Gloucestershire

1991

23 January   Emma and Beckie go out to a party, but do not return

25 January   News programmes report a barn fire at Uckington, near Cheltenham, and the discovery of human remains within the barn

     Vicky Harper reports her daughters as missing and the police visit the family home with the news that Beckie and Emma were most probably dead

     Three youths, David Harper, Wisdom Smith and Daniel Winter, contact the police regarding their presence at the barn on 23 January with Emma and Beckie

28 January   David Harper appears in Court charged with Manslaughter, Arson with intent to endanger life and, also with Winter and Smith, Attempting to Pervert the Course of Justice. All three are released on bail

11 February   Emma and Beckie's memorial service

13 February   Harper, Smith and Winter in Court—all 3 now charged with Manslaughter, Arson and Attempting to Pervert the Course of Justice. All three bailed

15 May   Emma and Beckie's funeral

     The inquest into Emma and Beckie's deaths closed—cause of death unascertainable

15 June   Harper, Smith and Winter appear in Court and the Manslaughter charge against them is increased to one of Murder. Bail is refused

20 June   Bail is refused once again

272

22 June	Vicky and Stephen's car is broken into
26 June	A final request for bail for Harper, Smith and Winter is granted at the High Court in Bristol
16 August	Vicky and Stephen's home is broken into and two silver crosses belonging to Emma and Beckie are stolen
19 September	Dr Bogdan Hulewizc, Home Office Pathologist, reports he can find no soot in Beckie's windpipe which would seem to indicate that she was not alive prior to the fire
30 September	'Baggy Pants' play centre is opened at Broadlands Nursery in memory of Emma
17 October	The Beckie Harper Memorial Plaque is awarded for the first time at Gloucestershire College of Arts & Technology
21 October	The Harper Clinic for the Elderly in Charlton Kings is opened in memory of Emma and Beckie
21 December	Eric Harper, Stephen's Father, dies from cancer The Murder charges against Harper, Smith and Winter are reduced to those of Manslaughter owing to a subsequent forensic report by Dr Hill, who reports finding what he believes to be soot

1992

3 February	Willow trees are planted in memory of Emma and Beckie in Hatherley Park, Cheltenham
17 February	The committal hearing for Harper, Smith and Winter takes place at Tewkesbury. All three are committed for trial on charges of Manslaughter, Arson and Perverting the Course of Justice
22 May	Pre-trial review: Harper, Smith and Winter plead not guilty to all charges against them
26 October	First day of the trial
3 November	Smith and Winter cleared of all charges
4 November	Harper cleared of all charges

| 20 December | Professor Gresham makes a further Forensic report on the remains of Beckie and Emma. He refutes the earlier report of Dr Hill—what Hill thought was soot, Gresham believes to be formalin pigment used to preserve specimens |

1993

| 20 November | Dr Toseland performs toxicological tests on the remains of Beckie and finds Ecstasy. This evidence is independently confirmed |
| 14 December | Vicky and Stephen decide against taking a civil action |